WHAT FOREVER MEANS
AFTER THE DEATH
OF A CHILD

The Series in Trauma and Loss

Consulting Editors

Charles R. Figley and Therese A. Rando

What Forever Means after the Death of a Child

Transcending the Trauma, Living with the Loss

Kay Talbot

Brunner-Routledge
New York & London

Published in 2002 by
Brunner-Routledge
29 West 35th Street
New York, NY 10001

Published in Great Britain by
Brunner-Routledge
11 New Fetter Lane
London EC4P 4EE

Brunner-Routledge is an imprint of the Taylor & Francis Group.
Copyright © 2002 Kay Talbot

Printed in the United States of America on acid-free paper.

10 9 8 7 6 5 4 3 2 1

Excerpt from THE PROPHET by Kahlil Gibran, copyright 1923 by Kahlil Gibran and renewed
1951 by Administrators C.T.A. of Kahlil Gibran Estate and Mary G. Gibran. Used by Permission
of Alfred A. Knopf, a division of Random House, Inc. Excerpts from *Grief: The Mourning After—
Dealing with Adult Bereavement* (2nd ed.), copyright 1999 by C. M. Sanders. Reprinted by
permission of John Wiley & Sons, Inc.

Library of Congress Cataloging-in-Publication Data
Talbot, Kay.
    What forever means after the death of a child / Kay Talbot.
      p. cm. — (The series in trauma and loss, ISSN 1090-9575)
    ISBN 1-583-91080-8
    Includes bibliographical references and index.
    1. Grief. 2. Bereavement—Psychological aspects. 3. Children—Death—Psychological
aspects. 4. Parent and child. 5. Loss (Psychology) I. Title. II. Series.

BF575.G7 .T35 2002
155.9′37—dc21

2001043966

BECAUSE OF

Leah Talbot
[August 16, 1973–July 9, 1982]
who came to bring love and joy to our world

AND

IN HONOR OF

all the children gone too soon, who teach us that love never dies,

THIS BOOK IS DEDICATED TO

all bereaved parents and those who support them.

Blessings for your continuing journey—I hold you in my heart.

—Kay Talbot, Vallejo, California

Contents

List of Tables

List of Figures

Series Editor's Foreword

"When do you recover from the death of a child?" It was a question, asked of me by a survivor of the New York City terrorist attack on the World Trade Center. He was a survivor. Call him Manuel. He worked for the Local 32B–J of the Service Employees International Union. There were 1,500 fellow union members in the WTC when it was hit. I was there as a volunteer with the Green Cross Projects (www.greencross.org).

Manuel, like many traumatized and bereaved survivors often looked past his own sadness and stress to others worse off. But he knew the answer to his own question. "I haven't," he said gently, as tears in his eyes welled up. "Sissy passed 12 years ago next month." His struggles to cope with the loss of so many people he had known for so long brought forward numbing feelings of losing his youngest daughter.

Yet it does not take an extraordinary, deadly event like the September 11 tragedy to awaken the pain connected with the loss of a child, no matter the years since that loss. Not understanding this hampers the effectiveness of mental health professionals working with the parents of children who have died. This is why Kay Talbot's book should become a timeless classic, to be cited by experts, students, and professors as a source of guidance in working with survivor parents like Manuel.

What Forever Means after the Death of a Child: Transcending the Trauma, Living with the Loss will become a classic because Dr. Talbot combines all of the vital elements of a vital resource for helping. She has assembled the lessons of science. The few good studies of parental survivorship are explained and applied in ways that provide concrete direction to helpers and to the parents themselves. She has also assembled the lessons of fellow specialists in this area. Her final chapter, "The Legacy of Loss," is an example of these lessons, starting with the "Mothers Now Childless" study and ending with a discussion of the clinician's role in helping.

Losing a child is one of the greatest fears of life and its biggest agony. Yet, over time the survivor parents accommodate but never fully recover. As Dr. Talbot notes, "healing evolves—it is not a destination."

This is the latest in the Brunner-Routledge Series in Trauma and Loss. As series co-editor with Dr. Therese A. Rando, a pioneer in thanotology and herself a parental survivor, we are proud to welcome this new addition. The series intends to publish innovations in understanding the interface between trauma and loss. For far too long those who attend to the grieving have not appreciated the extra burden of the traumatic circumstances of the death. They were not aware of how the trauma slowed the grief process. At the same time, for far too long those who attend to the traumatized have not appreciated the time required to accommodate to loss. This book and those in the series published before it are closing the gap of awareness and providing the tools and theories for helping and studying the traumatology of grieving.

My experiences as a member of the Green Cross Projects working with Local 32B–J blocks from "Ground Zero" reinforce my faith in God and working with the traumatized and the grieving. As the world braces for a new era of uncertainty and fear this book and the others in the series will, perhaps, reduce the pain, strengthen the resolve, and renew our love in life.

Charles R. Figley, Ph.D., Series Editor
Director, Florida State University Traumatology Institute, Tallahassee, Florida

Preface

It has been said that life is what happens to us while we're busy making other plans. This was true for me in 1982 when tragedy struck. I wasn't planning for trauma or loss of any kind, and especially not for the death of my beloved nine-year-old daughter Leah, my only child. Given any other set of circumstances, I never would have planned to write this book, to conduct this research, to become a therapist helping people understand and cope with their own life-changing experiences. Back then, at age 34, I hadn't done much thinking about either death or destiny. Since then, I have come to appreciate that while we feel helpless in the midst of tragedy, in its aftermath there are some choices we can make. I have chosen to share with you what I have learned both personally and professionally about surviving the death of a child. In reading this book, you are choosing to accompany me and the people I have learned from in exploring what possibilities lie beyond traumatic loss. My hope is that having read this book, you will then choose to pass along whatever you gain from it to others. In doing so you not only honor the lives of bereaved parents and their children, you participate in humanity's reach toward immortality in a very personal way. Those who are committed to helping others know only too well that "we can only comprehend the consciousness and behavior of others to the degree that we accept our own humanity" (LeShan, 1990, p. 156).

PURPOSE AND SCOPE OF THE BOOK

The goal of this book is to offer a deeper understanding of the lifelong, evolving bereavement process after a child dies. A child's death under any circumstances is traumatizing (Figley, Bride, & Mazza, 1997; Rando, 1994). In this book you will read about parents who demonstrate it is possible to transcend the trauma of a child's death and embrace life in new, meaningful ways while living with the ongoing loss. You will read about what helps and what hinders bereaved parents as they strive to understand their loss, adjust to and accommodate the pain, and move toward reinvesting in life, often in new ways.

The epistemological stance I take in my research is that human beings are able to transcend themselves (Schutz, 1966). We are able to assert ourselves in the world in which we find ourselves and forge considerable changes, sometimes abandoning our personal world and creating a new one (Wagner, 1983, pp. 16–17). Looking at the phenomenon of survival as experienced by bereaved parents requires looking at both their inside and their outside experiences. By *inside experiences* I mean those thoughts and feelings that arise in consciousness to a level of awareness and reflection. By *outside experiences* I mean the conscious behavior and decisions of parents as they relate to the significant others in their lives. The totality of these two kinds of experience, inside and outside, comprises an individual's life-world, the world of everyday life. "Whether I cooperate, fight, or manipulate, I live actively in the world of my daily life, and can and do influence and modify some things, some events, and some people. I am part of the dynamic of the world" (Wagner, 1983, pp. 108–109).

The search for meaning, the symbolic, spiritual, and existential modes of dealing with death, the lived experience of losing the role of parent—all of these are elements for exploration within the life-world of bereaved parents. The major distinction I describe in this book is between mourning process and outcomes (which may or may not be correlated to specific attributes or actions that are part of the grieving process) and the lived, consciously perceived experience of surviving the death of a child. It is the difference between "how" or "how well" and "what," between how and how well or how poorly a parent believes he or she has dealt with the condition of bereavement, and what that someone's view of their irrevocably changed world looks and feels like. My aim has not been to assess or diagnose these parents but to understand and describe how they experience their life-worlds. Their stories convey the *qualitative difference* between what it means for a parent to survive and reinvest in life after a child's death and what it means for a parent to remain physically alive but in a state of chronic mourning (Rando, 1986, 1993).

The main focus of this book is on issues that impact personal identity and reinvestment in life following the death of a child. My research questions prior suggestions that it is necessary to give up attachment to the deceased child in order to heal parental grief (Bowlby, 1980). Catherine Sanders's (1999) integrated model of movement through bereavement describes a "healing phase" that includes searching for meaning, relinquishing roles, and restructuring identity. My research suggests that the role of parent becomes an integral part of the self, and in order to survive the death of a child, it is necessary *not* to relinquish this construct. Rather, it is important to find meaningful ways to continue "nurturing" as a part of a new, more integrated identity, which acknowledges the child's death but also preserves the child's memory and honors the parent's past life.

This is crucial information and especially important for anyone who may be encouraging bereaved parents to detach from their child and "accept" the death in ways that are counterproductive to the healing process. Clinicians are encouraged, instead, to help bereaved parents (a) reframe their role as that of the child's biographer (Walter, 1996); (b) build a new relationship with their deceased child

(Rando, 1993); (c) integrate their child into their life in a different way than when the child was alive (Klass, 1996); and (d) find personally meaningful ways to reinvest in life that honor what has been learned from parenting their child and from surviving that child's death.

UNIQUENESS OF THE BOOK

This book grew from the first and, to date, only existing study of the death of an only child and thus the loss of the role of parent (Talbot, 1996, 1996–1997, 1997–1998, 1998–1999). The research participants were 80 mothers whose only child had died 5 or more years previously due to accident or illness. The book goes further to point out differences and similarities in the experiences of mothers and fathers and of parents with and without surviving children.

Both empirical and phenomenological research methods were used to answer key questions such as:

What does life as a bereaved parent look and feel like now?
What level of grief is still being experienced?
Does the parent attend a support group and/or discuss the grief with others?
How helpful are family and friends?
Has the parent experienced a spiritual crisis resulting from the child's death?
Has the child's death changed the parent's beliefs about how the world works?
Have there been other significant losses since the child died?
Has the parent made a conscious decision to survive the loss?
How has the parent's personal identity been changed by the child's death?
Has the parent found ways to build and maintain a new relationship with the deceased child?
Has the parent found personally meaningful ways to reinvest in life?
Does the parent reach out to help others?

These critical questions help us understand the "what," and to some extent the "how," of daily life years after the death of a child. The purpose of phenomenological research is to see the phenomenon being studied ("survival") in its own right, with its own meanings and structure, and not as an example of this or that theory. The editors of *Continuing Bonds: New Understandings of Grief* (Klass, Silverman, & Nickman, 1996) pointed out that "we need to bring into our professional dialogue the reality of how people experience and live their lives, rather than finding ways of verifying preconceived theories of how people should live" (p. xix). That is what this book does—it illuminates the life-worlds of bereaved parents, what their irrevocably changed lives can look and feel like. I do not intend to offer a new model, or to imply there is one best way of grieving this loss. Reading this book will, however, help you understand how the bereaved parents included here view their adaptation to life without their child and what has been helpful or hurtful to them.

OVERVIEW OF MAJOR TOPICS

Becoming a parent is a milestone event for those who have or adopt children. Learning how to parent is not a singular event, however; it is a process—one that parents expect will continue throughout their lives. Similarly, the death of a child is a milestone event; it marks a before and after in parents' lives. Parents who were learning how to parent their child must now learn what they never wanted to know how to do—how to be that child's bereaved parents. Chapter 1 describes how I began my study of surviving the death of a child and introduces what I have learned from my research and continued clinical work with bereaved parents. Chapter 2 is different in format from the other chapters. It describes the design and findings from the "mothers now childless" study. Readers not interested in this level of research detail will still benefit by understanding the design of the study as described at the beginning of chapter 2 before going on to chapter 3.

Bereaved parents *do not expect to ever "get over" or "recover"* from their child's death. Rather, as discussed in chapter 3, they expect to continue processing what the death of their child means to them for as long as they live. Those who are eventually able to reinvest in life see their bereavement as an evolutionary process, and many see themselves as becoming better people as they actively confront key issues and experiences. I am *not* saying here that there are "appropriate" ways to grieve that lead to survival and once they know these ways, parents have only to put their new knowledge into action in order to achieve a better outcome. What I am saying, building on my study of "Mothers Now Childless" (Talbot, 1996, 1996–1997, 1997–1998, 1998–1999), is that *there is a qualitative difference in the life-worlds of parents who come to feel they have survived this loss versus those who don't.* Such differences are discussed throughout the book.

Bereaved parents *struggle to make sense of their suffering and re-evaluate their worldview* in light of what has happened to them. Chapter 4 discusses the use of "logotherapy"—therapy through meaning (Frankl, 1955, 1963, 1969, 1975, 1978, 1997; Yalom, 1980) and meaning reconstruction techniques (Neimeyer, 1995, 1998).

A child's death sets in motion a multilayered continuum of experiences that evolve over a lifetime. As their bereavement evolves, parents search for *understanding* from others (discussed in chap. 5), for answers to their *spiritual questions* (discussed in chap. 6), and for *new meaning and purpose in life* (discussed in chap. 7).

The trauma that accompanies the death of a child often brings stress symptoms that require intervention before parents can proceed to process loss-related aspects (Rando, 1993). Parents can be incapacitated by unrelieved stress; they can find themselves fixated on certain aspects of their loss and unable to move beyond this point; some may grieve acutely until they die (Sanders, 1999). As discussed in chapter 8, most make a conscious *decision to survive,* to move forward in their bereavement, sometimes backward and then forward again, but gradually learning and adapting to a life without the physical presence of their child. It is a life that is meaningful in new and different ways because of their loss, even as it remains a life "made poorer" by the child's death (Klass, 1988).

Surviving and adapting to their new role of bereaved parent does not mean detaching from or forgetting their child. Rather, chapter 9 gives examples of the many ways parents find *to remember and honor* their child and their life as that child's parent. Many bereaved parents who re-invest in life do so by *reaching out to help others,* as discussed in chapter 10, either by volunteering or by making career changes to "helping" professions.

The death of a child directly impacts parents' identity, both how they see themselves and how others see them. Some parents experience *identity disintegration,* while others experience a less severe *identity crisis. Identity reconstruction* after the death of a child, as discussed in chapter 11, continues the bond with the child in new ways and for most requires validation from the parent's social group, relatives, and/or friends (Doka, 1993b; Klass, 1988, 1999).

Thus, the death of a child presents not only a severe challenge to survival but also the *potential for personal transformation.* Five or more years after the death of their only child, some women in the "mothers now childless" study felt they had changed in *negative* ways. Some felt they had changed in both *positive and negative* ways. Those who felt they had survived their loss and changed in *positive* ways had four transformative factors in common. These mothers had:

1 Resolved a spiritual crisis brought about by their child's death (discussed in chap. 6).
2 Made a conscious decision to survive (discussed in chap. 8).
3 Reached out to help others by volunteering or working in a helping profession (discussed in chap. 10).
4 Integrated what was learned from surviving the child's death into a new, more compassionate identity (discussed in chap. 11).

It is the content and context of bereaved parents' lives that get us closer to understanding what forever can mean after the death of their child. The experiences described here begin to answer a compelling question posed by Phyllis Silverman and Steven Nickman in *Continuing Bonds* (1996, p. 29): "In what way is the past incorporated into a new identity after a death?" The kinds of reinvestments made by many of the parents described in this book help answer that question. The material presented also supports prior research that has identified "altruism" and "commitment to social and political activism" as essential to the healing of psychological distress (cf. Higgins, 1994).

THE AUTHOR'S PERSPECTIVES

All researchers know that it is important to recognize, clarify, and as much as humanly possible set apart one's own biases. Those of us who do phenomenological research know this as "bracketing the researcher's experience." My challenge has been to integrate my "insider's perspective" as a bereaved mother, my clinical experience as a therapist, and a researcher's scholarship in order to comprehend the life-worlds of bereaved parents. Although I see my three roles as separate but interrelated, I am frequently viewed by others first and foremost as an "insider," one who has shared the experience, rather than as an "outsider," someone who has relevant expertise but no similar personal experience. Often I've been told: "I would never tell you this if you hadn't lost a child too." I would never have chosen this kind of "insider" status, yet I know it has helped me connect and share with other bereaved parents at very deep levels. I feel honored and entrusted to pass along their collective wisdom as accurately and honestly as I am capable of doing.

The research findings and conclusions presented here cannot be generalized to the entire population of bereaved parents. It is equally true, however, that what has been learned is potentially transferable to others in similar situations. As I interviewed bereaved mothers, living in different states around the country, I began to wish I could gather them together in the same room so that they could share and learn from each others' perspectives and experiences. I envisioned those who felt they were further along in surviving, sharing what had been helpful to them and demonstrating hope to the others who at that time were still struggling with acute trauma and grief. In a sense, what you will read here is a gathering together of collective wisdom. These parents show us that there is no one best way to survive this devastating loss. Rather, the lives described here demonstrate the multiple realities of parents who are changed forever by the death of their child, and how others help or hinder them in their evolving process of learning to live with this loss.

I try throughout this book to clearly delineate my voice and my reality. Thus I begin by introducing you in the Prologue to some of the details of my own loss. Throughout the remaining chapters I describe some of my experiences where it seems appropriate to explain how my perspectives may be similar to and/or different from other bereaved parents. Similarly, each reader brings a set of experiences and perspectives to the reading of this book. "We all see the world through the windows of our own eyes and interpret our perceptions in the light and darkness of our own experience" (Mindess, 1988, p. 173). The snapshots in time that any research and evaluation produces continue as an evolving work in progress. If this book adds a new level of understanding to your own experiences and clinical challenges, however different or similar they may be to the life-worlds of the bereaved parents presented here, then it will have been more than worthy of my efforts in writing it.

I welcome your comments, which can be mailed to me at this address:

Dr. Kay Talbot
180 Wildflower Avenue
Vallejo, CA 94591-8061
E-mail: kaytalbot@aol.com (please put "WFM" in the subject box)

Prologue

I became a bereaved parent on July 9, 1982, when my daughter Leah died unexpectedly after an unexplained brain seizure. During the night of July 7, while at a one-week summer camp for the blind and visually handicapped, Leah suffered a low-blood-sugar attack. She was found unconscious beside her bed in the early morning hours of July 8 and was rushed to the hospital. The emergency-room physician called me at my office and while I drove to the hospital he worked to stabilize her blood sugar level. When I arrived, she was crying frantically and fighting the nurses, and as I told her, "it's OK, mama's here," she collapsed exhausted into my arms. As Leah's blood sugar level returned to normal, the doctors did not understand why she remained semiconscious. Twice she moaned, "I want to go; I want to go," but did not respond when we asked her where she wanted to go. A spinal tap ruled out meningitis. That afternoon Leah was transferred by ambulance to the hospital where her pediatric endocrinologist practiced. There a brain scan showed no change from previous scans. Leah's father and I stayed with her throughout the night as she tossed and turned restlessly, occasionally moaning softly. Leah awoke the morning of July 9 lucid enough to answer her doctor's questions. Did she know where she was? "Yes, in the hospital." How old was she? "Eight and three-quarters." She complained of a headache. Her father and I argued briefly about the level of her bed, and Leah irritably told us, "Oh, just forget it." She was given some Tylenol and ate part of a Popsicle. By late morning on that fateful day, she was resting somewhat peacefully. Her doctor assured us he expected her to continue to improve, as she had after previous hypoglycemic episodes. I told her I loved her, was going home for a shower and change of clothes, and would be back soon.

A few hours later as I drove back to the hospital, I felt tired but relieved. I realized I hadn't eaten since the day before, so I stopped at a store long enough to pick up an ice cream bar. I expected Leah to be sitting up in bed to greet me when I arrived. Thus I was totally unprepared for what I saw when I entered her room. What I saw first were her feet, sticking out from under the covers, and they were blue! With disbelief, I called her name as I looked up and saw she had slumped down in the bed and was unconscious. I stumbled out of her room toward the nursing station just outside, too overwhelmed to speak. The look on my face alerted the young resident on duty, who dropped the phone he was speaking into and ran into her room. Before I could begin to speak, "code blue" rang out over the PA system. Within minutes a tracheotomy had been done and Leah was breathing with the help of a respirator. The resident came out long enough to tell me this and that he had called a surgeon to install a pacemaker in Leah's heart. I paced up and down the hallway just outside Leah's room as the doctors operated on her. I began to feel the physical effects of shock—dry mouth and chills. Someone brought me a cup of water. My mind fought the numbness as I took stock of all I had seen. The resident came out again, this time to telephone Leah's endocrinologist and brief her on Leah's condition. When he finished, he motioned me to come take the phone and talk with her. I remember telling her, "They're doing everything they can think of but I don't think it's going to be enough." She tried to reassure me that there was still hope, but already my mind was admitting the possibility that Leah was beyond medical help. My heart desperately hoped I was wrong. A nurse suggested I call someone to come be with me. I phoned my cousin at work, leaving a message that I needed her to come right away. Then I returned to my pacing outside of Leah's room.

It wasn't long before the surgeon and assistant emerged and walked off down the hall. I was encouraged when I overheard the assistant say, "You did a good job on her." The resident then came out and asked me to follow him to another room. I hoped those words "good job" would translate into good news. Instead, he quickly told me Leah was still alive but that she had suffered too much brain damage to ever recover. He added, "We can keep her on the respirator if you want, but Leah will never be Leah again—it's just a matter of time." I used every ounce of self-control I had left to tell him, "No, I won't do that to Leah. I want you to disconnect the machine." As he left to do so, I collapsed into a chair and allowed the tears to come. It was my first experience with the horror and indescribable pain of emotional anguish. My body responded with the kind of shrieking and wailing I had seen on television but never experienced personally until that moment.

Nothing in my 36 years of living prepared me for the trauma of a loss such as this. And I had had quite a few losses and challenges. My mother had given me up for adoption at birth, and although I was blessed with loving adoptive parents, I will always live with unanswered questions about my biological heritage. My childhood was further complicated by my adoptive mother's congenital heart condition—the reason she could not have her own children. Shortly after she and my father married, she became pregnant and had to have an abortion because neither she nor the baby would have survived. This was a "forever loss" my parents mourned deeply.

When I was four, my mother underwent open-heart surgery at the Mayo Clinic, while I remained in the care of my aunt. As I watched my parents drive off, no one had to tell me my mother might not be coming back. And the mother I had known did not come back. The mother who returned several months later was so thin, so ill, I barely recognized her. The structural repair of her heart was success-ful with the help of an experimental drug, but 3 days later she had to have lung surgery. She spent months recovering physically but lived the rest of her 78 years with deep emotional scars. She yearned for more children, and I yearned for sib-lings. When I was 10 my parents adopted a baby boy. Helping to care for my new brother became early training for later motherhood.

I married at age 18 and 7 years later, we decided to start a family. After a year of trying to conceive, we learned my husband was infertile and began the long, emotional wait to adopt a baby. The pain of not being able to bear my own chil-dren was a bittersweet irony. Adoption was, after all, the form of motherhood I knew the most about. I will never forget the overwhelming joy I felt as 2-week old Leah was laid in my arms by the county adoption agency's social worker. The joy, however, was accompanied in a few weeks by worry about her health.

Leah's birth had been a difficult delivery that required forceps rotation of her head. She had a low-blood-sugar attack a few hours after birth, and the adoption agency told us she had inherited hypoglycemia from her father. Within a month, we began to notice problems with Leah's vision. She often opened only one eye at a time and she didn't seem able to focus. At 3½ months she developed a cold and had what appeared to be another low-blood-sugar episode. Thus began a long series of doctor visits, tests, and infant stimulation therapy sessions. During Leah's first blood test when she was a month old, I was amazed at the intensity of my own pain as the needle pierced her skin. It felt like that needle was piercing my heart. I couldn't know then that there was much greater pain to come. I am grate-ful that I didn't know. I wonder if knowing would have robbed me of the joys that came from helping Leah develop her potential despite the limitations of precari-ous health. I hadn't expected to love being a mother this much, to find caring for this beautiful, unique child so fulfilling! I knew Leah's vision problems were serious and as yet unexplained. I just chose to set aside my fears and focus on what I could do to stimulate her growth. Each day brought new excitement as she continued to grow. She would wake in the mornings cooing and "talking" to her-self and her toys.

At 6 months of age, Leah had another frightening low-blood-sugar attack. She was referred to a pediatric neurologist for a week-long neurological workup at a hospital in Los Angeles. We were shocked when X-rays revealed she had suffered a skull fracture at or just after birth, which had since healed. An electro-encephalogram (EEG) showed a slight discrepancy on her left side, but no cause could be determined for her low vision. Leah was referred to an ophthalmologist to evaluate her vision. I held her on my lap in his darkened exam room, as he shone a bright light in Leah's eyes. They didn't move or respond at all. He con-cluded she was virtually blind and would never be able to see. He followed this prognosis with the question, "Have you considered not keeping her?" I was stunned and horrified. How could he think that our daughter was exchangeable? I grasped Leah even more tightly to me. It felt like he had punched me in the stomach. When I was able to get my breath, I responded, "No, we will just work with whatever eyesight she ends up with," and quickly left his office. He obviously had not believed me when I told him I knew Leah was not blind, that she had begun to reach out to grasp her toys.

With physical therapy, lots of play stimulation, and a high-protein diet, Leah's growth and development continued, but at a slower pace than for healthy children. Her father completed college and accepted a new job that required us to move to northern California. In 1975 I wrote to Leah's neurologist to request that her records be transferred, telling him that she had had another hypoglycemic episode and her vision was limited but "despite these minor problems, Leah is very much a normal, active two-year-old now and her charm and intelligence never cease to amaze us."

I was sure by this time that Leah's neurological damage would not result in her being mentally handicapped, and I was so grateful for this. Yet whenever we were around other children her age, I felt the painful reality of her visual handicap and compromised motor skills. Loud noises such as the lawn mower frightened her; she couldn't see what was making the noise. Playground equipment that was so enticing to other children challenged Leah's courage. I tried to envision in my mind what it must feel like to be at the top of a slide and not be able to see the bottom. There was little time to grieve for what Leah would miss out on in life. Our energy as parents was instead devoted to helping her use what vision she did have as efficiently as possible.

I was concerned about whether Leah would be able to attend regular school by the time she was old enough. I requested an evaluation from the Blind Babies Foundation in San Francisco and a vision counselor was assigned to visit us monthly. She helped get Leah referred for additional testing by a world-renowned pediatric ophthalmologist at the University of California-San Francisco. At age 3½ Leah underwent a 2-hour Visual Evoked Response test. This required her to lie very still with electrodes pasted on her scalp and her eyes held open by a metallic apparatus, leaving her unable to blink. Patterned images were flashed in front of her eyes for periods of 2 minutes at a time. The electrodes measured the electrical impulses from her retinas through the optic nerves to the areas of her brain that received visual information as the images were flashed in front of her. It was a test that had not been done on someone so young before. The technician met us with a straightjacket and was skeptical when I said no, Leah would be able to do the test without that. After explaining what was going to happen, I handed her a Kleenex for one hand, held her other hand, and sang to her for the next 2 hours. I sang every nursery rhyme I knew, several times. Everyone was amazed at how Leah was able to remain relaxed and cooperative for so long. When it was over, she was up bubbling with excitement about going home; I was exhausted! That test was followed by a computerized tomographic scan of her brain. It confirmed the neurological damage shown by previous EEGs ("mild to moderate enlargment of lateral ventricles; mild to moderate hydrocephalus"), which was thought to be the result of either lack of oxygen during delivery or convulsions due to low blood sugar shortly after birth. These tests allowed the ophthalmologist to finally diagnose the cause of Leah's impaired vision as congenital maldevelopment of the optic nerves. Her vision would not get worse, he believed, and her astigmatism could be corrected with glasses. He predicted she might eventually be able to read small print but doubted she'd ever be able to drive a car.

By the time Leah was 4½, her vision had improved to 20/100 with corrective lenses. She could watch television up close and recognize faces across a room, but she had poor peripheral vision and was considered legally blind.

As Leah grew and embraced life, I returned to college part-time, taking evening classes. Slowly I completed a degree in behavioral sciences at the University of California–Davis. During my final semester there Leah attended the university's preschool while I attended classes. She loved school and frequently amazed her teachers. One told me of how another child began crying one day because her mother had left. Leah went over and patted her and said, "I know, I feel sad sometimes when I miss my mama too, but she'll be back." Her teacher added that Leah loved to sing songs and would entertain groups of other children by singing to them.

At age 5 Leah had another low-blood-sugar attack, was hospitalized, and doctors had to do a "cut down" to insert an intravenous (IV) line in order to stabilize her blood-sugar level. Shortly afterward, another neurologist reviewed her brain scan results and concluded that additional seizures due to "mild to moderate hydrocephalus" were "possible but not anticipated." Additional testing by a pediatric endocrinologist confirmed that a lack of normal adrenal and pituitary function was responsible for Leah's slower than normal growth in height. She was accepted into an experimental growth hormone treatment program, which involved my giving her injections three times a week. Over the next few years, this treatment helped her grow and gave her more energy.

Although Leah was usually carefree and optimistic about life, she wasn't immune to angst. On one occasion when she was 4½ I recorded one of our discussions in her baby book:

> This morning Leah told me, "Mama, I'm unhappy about me." I asked her, "What are you unhappy about?" And she replied, "about my inside voice." "What about your inside voice?" "Well, it's ridiculous!" "How is it ridiculous, I asked?" "Well, because it's 'contraire,' and I don't like being 'contraire!'" [Since she was 2 this had been our word to describe disagreeable behavior.] We then had a short discussion about how to become happy and cheerful after you've been feeling "contraire."

Leah's doctors were always surprised when they compared the child before them to the files of test results. Despite her physical limitations, she just flourished. She loved school and her teachers described her as "very self-directed, with inner strength, and a precocious ability to empathize. She is extremely verbal and does not attempt to limit her motor activities." Leah's physical growth had improved over the past few years but still lagged behind other children her age. She was assigned an adaptive physical education teacher, who wrote us a lengthy letter after her death. In it she described how Leah dealt with her physical challenges:

Sometimes Leah was frustrated—walking the balance beam and stepping off in the middle, tossing the ball but missing the catch—but she'd eventually accomplish the skill. She never used her vision as an excuse for not being able to do something— she just worked longer and harder to accomplish the tasks. She was such an extraordinary girl. She always had such a good time, especially on the bowling alley field trip and the Special Olympics meets. (When we were at the Special Olympics this year your note in her lunch box brought such a bright smile to her face as she read it!). Leah had such a free spirit. I can picture her during free dance time as she twirled round and round. I turned rope as she chanted the lyrics. Just walking to and from the classroom, she'd hold my hand and relate the latest adventures of Huck Finn, how she'd made a tent in her dad's living room, roller-skating, and the trip to Disneyland. She had such a wonderful, positive outlook on life. She was always so eager to learn, looking forward to everything. I hope I've been able to convey to you what a unique, special child you have shared with others. I know she loved you and her father very much and had a beautiful life with you.

Besides music and dancing, Leah relished humor. When she was 5, we were driving to the zoo one day when her grandfather jokingly asked Leah if they had any "eggephants" there. Leah laughed and said, "No—elephants!" Then he asked if they had rhinosofrus. She laughed again, then thought for a minute and replied, "No, but they have catalopes! Ha-hah!"

Parenting a child with special needs can be wonderfully rewarding, and certainly this was true for me. It was also emotionally and physically exhausting. While Leah grew and made remarkable use of what vision and energy she did have, her father and I grew further apart. Ending our 15-year marriage was a difficult decision we struggled to make for some time. Ultimately, our divorce in 1980 was amicable, yet it meant heartbreak and many changes for each of us. Leah's father took a new job in a town 50 miles away. Leah and he missed each other terribly. She spent weekends and the summer months with him, relishing their special times together, and they talked on the phone and wrote each other. Leah loved her "Papa" dearly, and I don't think she could have had a better father. She was not hesitant to let us know she hated the divorce, but she seemed to adapt as well as any child ever can to divorce—it is another "forever loss." There were ups and downs in adapting to life as single parents. But I am grateful that we parted as and remain friends. I'm so grateful Leah did not live the last years of her short life in the crossfire of a war zone, as happens in many divorces. I believed and still do that the divorce was the best decision, given all the complexities of our disintegrated relationship.

While staying with her father during the summer of 1981, Leah had another low-blood-sugar attack and had to be hospitalized. She recovered quickly, however, and later flew by herself to visit her grandparents in southern California. She loved these visits. After one return flight home the stewardess who brought her off the plane told me, "This is just a delightful child. I wish I could take her home with me. And I mean that!"

By the end of third grade, Leah was reading above her grade level. She loved to make up stories and wanted to become a writer. After Leah's death as I was cleaning her room I found the table of contents she had compiled for a book she planned to write. She has helped me write this book instead. Leah also left behind a letter to her grandparents, written during her last week at summer camp, that was both heartbreaking and comforting:

> Grandma are you still taking that awful tasting medicine? Are you still drinking cranberry juice and water? If you are, are you used to it by now? Well, I hope your kidney stone gets better. I hope you and Grandpa are both feeling fine. I have a cough and I can't go swimming but that doesn't spoil my fun one bit. I read and drink water out of cups. And I talk to people who need company. . . . Happy birthday Grandpa. I hope you have a nice time for your birthday. I hope this gets in the mail in time for your birthday. Love, Leah [Leah died on July 9, her grandfather's birthday.]

Her father and I summed up Leah's short "eight and three-quarter" years with these simple words engraved on the stone covering her grave: "She brought love and joy to our world."

During those first years after Leah's death, I experienced the intense and varied emotions that accompany acute grief, as well as physical symptoms—chest pains and insomnia. I went for counseling, took antidepressants and sleeping pills, and despite the warnings of my psychiatrist used alcohol to numb the pain. I continued working, finding work was the only place I could get any respite from grieving. It took every ounce of energy I had to focus my mind while at work. I often cried as I drove to and from my office each day. My nights were filled with images of Leah's death and funeral. An autopsy had revealed no specific cause for her death. The doctors could not explain why she had suffered a brain seizure when she did, just 10 minutes after a nurse had checked her, finding her vital signs normal. And so I struggled, as so many bereaved parents do, with the why question. My psychiatrist encouraged me to find a way to say goodbye, and I wrote the following poem:

To Leah
I remember so well the day they called to tell us
Someone cared enough to give you life
And give you away.
I remember like it was yesterday.

You cried when I first held you.
Until I rubbed your back
And told you your name.
Then you seemed to remember there was a reason why you came.

The doctors weren't quite sure why you couldn't see
And it really didn't matter much.
In your mind's eye you saw enough to teach us all
About "to be or not to be."

Nearly always you had a dimpled smile,
A confident, happy spirit.
And there was never any doubt the world was a better place
Because you were in it.

It's been five months now
Since you've gone.
No one knows exactly why,
And I don't know how to say goodbye.

Because despite the hard times we both endured
One thing I know for sure.
The nine years we shared together
Were worth far more than any other forever.

As the shock of Leah's sudden death began to wear off, the reality of her absence hit hard. This was not a bad dream that would soon be over. As my mind tried to grasp the enormity of my loss, my body rebelled at the constant stress. My muscles tensed and when I moved I could hear popping sounds; shooting pains down my arms and legs were diagnosed as tendinitis. I strained my back and developed a bladder infection. Physical pain intensified my extreme emotional pain and brought me to the brink of suicide. More than once I held a bottle of pills in my hand and asked God why I should bother to go on living. I was in existential and spiritual crisis. Eventually I got an answer. It came in the form of questions. "How could you ever face Leah again if you kill yourself? She lived with such courage and joy. How can you do any less? Do you really want to risk taking these pills that might not be strong enough to kill you, leaving you in a vegetative state suspended between this world and the next?"

For a long time I believed that I had failed in my duty as Leah's mother. I should have taken her home with me on July 4, the day her father and I visited her at camp and learned she had caught a cold. I was guilty of not being diligent enough. At the same time, there was the guilt I felt because of the freedom I now had from the exhausting challenges of being a divorced parent raising a child with special needs while working full-time in a demanding job. It was only through a long process of counseling and spiritual exploration that I eventually concluded my guilt was misconstrued. I did not have the power to keep anyone else alive, not even my beloved daughter. Sometimes it is easier to live with guilt than to feel powerless (Talbot, 1999).

It was many years before I began to feel I had truly survived Leah's death, before I was strong enough to wonder how my experiences might compare with other parents who had experienced such a loss. Two and a half years after Leah's death I remarried. The happiness this union brought was very healing. With my new husband's encouragement and support, I completed graduate school and was promoted to a challenging managerial position. I enjoyed the rewards that accompanied my career success and for several years found the work intellectually stimulating. Gradually, however, I began to recognize the symptoms of burnout. My academic and professional accomplishments distracted me from the existential questions I had not resolved. It felt like my soul was dying, but I didn't know why. Eventually alcohol no longer worked to deaden my pain. I returned to counseling, joined a church and a 12-step support group, and in 1990 left the corporate world to return to graduate school.

I spent the first year of my doctoral work studying human development and applying what I learned to my own life experiences. By 1992, 10 years after Leah's death, I was in transition toward an unknown future. I had moved beyond the why of Leah's death to the question, who am I now? It was during this time that I had an epiphany experience. Late one evening I was reading Helen Rose Ebaugh's research (1988) on the process of role exit. She had studied a wide variety of people who had left major roles: ex-cops, ex-prostitutes, ex-nuns, retirees, divorcées, and so on. She wanted to understand what it means to leave behind a major role and whether that role gets incorporated into a new identity. Included in her study were interviews with divorced mothers without custody of their children. They were struggling with the loss of a daily parenting role. Reading this was one of those great "ahah!" moments. When no one calls you mother anymore, what do you do with the part of you that has learned how to be and loved being a mother? Instantly I knew this was the missing piece, the reason my soul felt like it was dying.

Ebaugh's material on the process of role loss helped me understand the need to confront the loss of my parenting role as a separate loss. She pointed out that role loss creates multiple psychic realities and the need to confront role residual, the "hangover identity" from a previous status. I felt I had made peace with Leah's death in many ways and that that process would be ongoing for the rest of my life. I had come to believe she was where she was suppose to be, doing what she was suppose to be doing. I knew I would always miss her terribly, and that we would always be connected by love, which never dies. But I was still struggling with the loss of my parenting self. I did not know other bereaved parents and wondered how others felt about surviving this loss. I reviewed the thanatology literature and was surprised to learn there were no existing studies about the death of an only child. There were several studies of bereaved parents, but I could find no specific investigation of the loss of the role of parent after a child's death. If I wanted to know how other parents dealt with this loss, I would have to do the research myself. It was a life-changing call to action. I continued reading the bereavement literature, developing a lengthy list of questions.

Did other mothers who had been bereaved for many years see themselves as survivors, and if so, what did that mean for them? How had bereavement changed them, especially those who had been bereaved for many years? How were their experiences similar and how did they differ? Were there identifiable patterns to the experience of surviving such devastating trauma and loss? Did other bereaved parents choose to survive, and if so, did some pivotal incident or sudden realization influence their decisions?

I began looking for answers by deciding how I would select whom to ask. I felt that in order to understand what it means to survive, I also needed to understand what it means not to survive—to remain in a state of perpetual bereavement, defined by Rando (1993) as chronic mourning. Prior research had revealed there are bereaved parents who, despite the passage of time, seem only to go through the motions of living, remaining physically alive yet emotionally and spiritually dead. Others, however, were able to transcend acute grief to build new, productive and meaningful lives. I believed that those who viewed themselves as "survivors" held the potential for teaching, by example, how to overcome tragedy. The decisions they made and the reasons they made them could offer a key to greater awareness about the phenomenon of surviving a child's death. Such awareness would benefit not only bereaved parents but also those who attempt to help them. I learned, too, that many bereaved parents often complain that they feel isolated in their grief. Many perceive that their well-meaning friends and relatives become noticeably uncomfortable, even fearful, when they talk about their child and their loss. As I began my research I realized that above all else, I wanted to offer bereaved parents the opportunity of voice, assurance that they would be heard, and a forum for helping others through the example of their own painful experiences.

Acknowledgments

Two roads diverged in a wood, and I—
I took the one less traveled by.
And that has made all the difference!
—Robert Frost, 1930, "The Road Not Taken"

It is impossible to find words to thank all of the people who have traveled with me on the winding road that has led to the publishing of this book. But I will try.

My daughter, Leah Talbot, wanted to be a writer when she grew up. When she died three weeks before her ninth birthday, she left behind the table of contents for a book she planned to write. She has helped me write this book instead. She lives forever in my heart.

My husband, John Sandlin, shares the joy of completing this book with me. Although Leah died before he had the opportunity to become her stepfather, he has taken on that role anyway. He has encouraged me and believed I could do this work, sometimes when I didn't have the energy to believe it myself. Writing this book would not have been possible without his practical, emotional, and financial support. I am deeply thankful for his humor as well. When he tells others about his role as chauffeur during the 10,000 miles of travel required to conduct my research interviews, he tells them that I really did all the driving—all he had to do was sit there and hold the steering wheel! In addition to his wit and wisdom, he also has given me three wonderful stepdaughters. They were already grown and on their own when they came into my life, but they have become friends who love and accept me as the wounded mother I am. They have given us six grandchildren to nurture and cherish.

In a sense my writing career began many years ago. I will be eternally grateful to my parents, Clyde and Mary Breshears, who gave me the gift of books. Before I could walk they began reading to me. Somehow my father always managed to stretch the weekly budget to buy me a storybook. My mother used those books to teach me to read. She taught me about survival as well. She was born with a heart defect and battled illnesses all of her life. After several strokes, she spent the last 5 of her 78 years in a nursing home. She showed me what it is like to die an inch at a time but ultimately with grace and dignity. My father has encouraged me always, both by his faith in my abilities and by his example of always having goals in life. This year, at age 82, he completed the goal of personally installing a new roof on his house. Just as he had the help of friends during that construction process, I have had the help of many colleagues I am honored to call friends in writing this book.

My colleagues at The Fielding Institute provided thoughtful review, innovative guidance, and caring concern during my initial research. My mentor, Dr. Dorothy Blackmore, encouraged me with her enthusiasm and interest in my work while inspiring me with her scholarship and love of learning. Dr. Don Bushnell gave wise counsel and program guidance. Dr. Rich Appelbaum shared his insightful knowledge about conducting research and in so doing contributed greatly to both the design of the "Mothers Now Childless" study and the analysis of the data. Dr. Michele Harway helped me reach a better understanding of both qualitative and quantitative research methods, and Dr. Valerie Bentz introduced me to the power of phenomenology. Dr. Ruth Miller continues to be a kindred spirit, providing valuable perspectives and listening endlessly.

My admiration and thanks also go to my editors, Bernadette Capelle, Emily Epstein, and Kenneth J. Silver, and series editor Dr. Therese A. Rando, whose expertise and constructive comments improved the quality of this work. Dr. Gary Reker graciously permitted the use of the instruments included in my research. Dr. Catherine Sanders generously allowed me to include adaptations of her grief and bereavement model in this book. And Dr. Paul Rosenblatt offered important and insightful review comments.

I am grateful as well to Kay and Rodney Bevington, founders of Alive Alone, Inc., who provided contact information for participants in my research. The 80 women who participated in the "Mothers Now Childless" study shared both their happy memories of motherhood and their painful experiences of bereavement. They have my enduring gratitude and admiration, as do all the bereaved parents who have been my teachers and companions in grief.

Thanks also go to my colleagues at the Association for Death Education and Counseling (ADEC). From the day I arrived at my first ADEC conference not knowing anyone, ADEC members have welcomed me warmly and supported my continued learning. As is customary throughout the country of Nepal, I say to all of you: "Namaste" (I greet the God within you) and blessings for your important work. You all make a difference.

Chapter 1

What It Means to Be a Parent After a Child Has Died

"Your absence has gone through me like thread through a needle.
Everything I do is stitched with its color."
(Quoted by Bertman, 1997, author unknown).

Becoming a parent is a life-changing experience. Prospective parents prepare for the event in a variety of ways, but nothing totally prepares them for the multiple joys and challenges of parenting. Babies do not come with operating instructions. Parents learn by doing, by trial and error, building up a store of knowledge about what it means to create, sustain, and nurture a new life. For most mothers and fathers, parenting becomes a part of their identity—who they know themselves to be and who they are known to be by others in society.[1]

When women were asked in one study to name their most powerful learning experiences, "the mothers usually named childbearing or child rearing" (Belenky, Clinchy, Goldberger, & Tarule, 1986, p. 200). Motherhood has been shown to be associated with increased feelings of self-esteem. Having a child and performing the duties of motherhood can offer a new sense of purpose and contribute to a "sense of greater strength and maturity as a person" (Leifer, 1980, p. 167). Fathers also recognize the powerful impact becoming a parent makes on their identity. Many bereaved fathers have written about their experiences after their child has died. (See, for example: Allen, 1995; Bennett, 1998; Bramblett, 1991; Deford, 1983; Edler, 1996; Ford, 1985; Gunther, 1949; Hackett, 1986; Koppelman, 1994, 1998; Kushner, 1987; Livingston, 1999; McGovern, 1996; Morrell, 1988; Quezada,

---

[1]The sad fact that some parents kill their own children is beyond the scope of this book. The various causes and consequences of intrafamilial homicide are discussed in Charles Ewing's book: *Fatal Families* (1997).

1985; Ramsey & Ramsey, 2000; Robinson, 1998; Rouner, 1989; Sittser, 1996; Strommen & Strommen, 1993; Walsh, 1997; Wolterstorff, 1987.)

But what does it mean to parent a child who has died? What does it mean to parent the surviving child or children after a sibling has died? What does it mean when no one calls you "mother" or "father" again after the death of your only child or all of your children? These are the painful questions that confront bereaved parents in very personal ways on a daily basis. Anita,[2] who was interviewed 6 years after her son and only child died at age 15, provides an example:

> I'm always thinking of him. So, to me it's just the pure aggravation of hell. And I haven't enjoyed life since. I've tried to teach myself to somewhat enjoy it, but I don't enjoy it. I put on a fake face—because people think I'm doing fine—but they don't know how I feel. [As a result, she] feels like a time bomb ready to explode. I don't know from one moment to the next how I'm gonna react or think or do. And my mind, it seems like it doesn't center like it used to, on track. I wander. . . . I'm just totally a different person from it. Brad was my whole life. That was the one thing I wanted was to have a child. . . . I just suffer every day. I always think about it.

Frankl (1978), Bettelheim (1952), and others have pointed out that even suffering can have meaning if it changes oneself for the better. Changing oneself often means rising above oneself, growing beyond oneself. The death of a child presents the kind of suffering and challenge to self that creates an existential crisis—a search for the meaning of human existence. Attig (1996) called this a need to relearn the world. There is no prescriptive cure for this kind of existential suffering; however, there are responses that can promote healing and resolution. Bereaved parents commonly use two approaches as they struggle to make sense of their existential questions: logotherapy—therapy through meaning discovery (Frankl, 1955, 1963, 1969, 1978, 1997)—and meaning construction/reconstruction[3] (Raskin & Lewandowski, 2000).

Bereaved parents pursue so many painful questions and complex issues in their quest to understand what their child's death means for their lives. I am not alone in believing that both the lack of meaning and meaning-making efforts greatly influence the quality of life of bereaved parents. Researchers and clinicians are paying increasing attention to this crucial aspect of grieving, as discussed further in chapter 4.

---

[2]Pseudonyms are used throughout except when parents requested their actual names be used.

[3]A major philosophical difference between existentialists and constructionists lies in the epistemology of meaning. Existentialists believe in ultimate spiritual truth. Each person must discover how to responsibly apply spiritual truth to his or her unique life experiences. Constructionists believe each individual creates personal meaning in response to his or her unique life experiences. Whether discovered or created, meaning helps bereaved parents organize and make sense of painful and overwhelming experiences.

THE SEARCH FOR WHAT SURVIVAL MEANS

When I began to design my research of what it means to survive a child's death, I knew I needed to study parents who were not in the early years of acute grief. At that point, 10 years after my own daughter's death, I knew what surviving meant for me. But I didn't know how or whether my experiences might be like those of other bereaved parents. I wanted to understand what life many years later was like for them. How were their lives similar or different? What helped and what hindered them in living life and facing the future without their children?

To answer these questions I knew I would need to ask not just those bereaved parents who felt they had survived, but also those who felt they hadn't survived. Don't we really understand something by defining both what it is and also what it isn't? Isn't this true of all inquiry and learning related to human consciousness and behavior? Psychologist Lawrence LeShan (1990) described understanding as "an endless process of relating items of study to larger and larger sections of the organism, its history, and social environment" (p. 135). It seemed logical to me to begin my research by understanding others whose bereavement was most like my own. Thus, I began by limiting my study of survival to other mothers who had lost only children. In this chapter and those that follow you will read about these 80 "mothers now childless" and what their life-worlds were like 5 or more years after the death of their only child. You will be challenged, as I was, to then widen the lens of understanding and contrast how these women's experiences are similar to and/or different from those of other bereaved parents. *It is vitally important to remember as you read that there is no one way to survive the death of a child, no proven method of processing grief that ensures the best possible accommodation to this traumatic loss.* Please read that last sentence again. As many clinicians and researchers realize, it is our society's unrealistic expectations that parents should "accept" and "get over" their child's death that frequently cause secondary injury and anguish to many bereaved parents. The understanding gained about what it means to survive and what it means to remain in a perpetual state of chronic mourning many years after a child's death cannot be reduced to a treatment protocol. Rather, what we gain is greater empathy and multiple examples of the varied pathways traveled and detours sometimes taken by bereaved parents as their grief evolves.

What surprised me most about the 80 women in the "Mothers Now Childless" study, who had been bereaved for an average of 9 years, was that they clearly represented a bereavement continuum, with striking differences about what survival meant to those at opposite ends of that continuum. The overriding commonality among mothers who said they *had* survived their only child's death (versus those who said they hadn't survived and who were struggling with chronic, debilitating grief) was their ability to find meaning and purpose in life again. Extensive analysis of the study data (presented in chap. 2) highlighted various aspects of this meaning-making process, including the following (not in any specific order):

Sorting through and understanding the unique circumstances and aspects of their child's death.

Acknowledging and resolving any guilt related to the child's death and their inability to prevent it.

Coming to understand the unique impact of role loss on their personal identity.

Defining what being a parent meant and continues to mean to them.

Resolving any dissonance in their spiritual beliefs.

Redefining their beliefs about how the world works.

Consciously deciding to survive their child's death.

Pursuing multiple ways of coping with the pain of grief.

Learning from their evolving bereavement experiences.

Building a new and ongoing relationship with their deceased child.

Reconstructing their personal identity.

Searching for and finding or creating a new purpose for living.

Transcending the self to reconnect with and serve others.

Realizing that helping others brings hope and new meaning to life.

The outcome of this search for meaning and purpose in life was not recovery but resolution and adaptation: a healing of mind, body, and spirit to a degree that permits a new understanding of human existence, reinvestment in life, and discovery of meaningful ways to maintain an eternal connection with the deceased child. The following sections describe the structure and quality of life of the "mothers now childless" who courageously shared with me their happy memories of motherhood and their painful experiences of bereavement.

MOTHERS NOW CHILDLESS: STRUCTURES OF THE LIFE-WORLD

The 80 bereaved mothers studied demonstrated varying degrees of awareness about themselves, others, situations, and circumstances, as well as a broad range of attitudes about life. They shared "stocks of common knowledge" (Schutz, 1966), even as they also experienced and exhibited the "multiple realities" (Schutz, 1966) of their loss and bereavement. The focus or emphasis of each mother varied, along with the quality of her relationships with others, providing individualized pathways within the life-world. In the parlance of phenomenology, four underlying structures illuminate the life-world of these 80 women: stocks of common knowledge; multiple realities; varying levels of awareness and focus; and significant we-relationships.

Stocks of Common Knowledge

In our world of everyday life, we each have access to our own personal reservoir of socially derived knowledge. This knowledge consists of clear, consistent, and unquestionably valid "knowledge about" people, places, and things, knowledge that has been tested and passed on to us by others, and that explains the what, how, and why of social life (Schutz, 1966, p. 120). Individuals have varying degrees of familiarity with such knowledge. And we have the ability to discard knowledge that is no longer useful to us and "proceed from apperception to ever new apperceptions" (Schutz, 1966, p. 121).

There are two components that facilitate making sense of a given situation: the ontological framework of the situation (that which exists outside of and is imposed upon the individual, e.g., the irrevocable death of one's child), and the individual's own biographical reservoir of knowledge (e.g., past experiences with death and bereavement), which the individual, in turn, imposes on the situation in order to define its meaning. Repeatedly, the women studied stated how unprepared they were by prior life experiences to cope with the death of their child. Even in those cases where the child had been ill for years, nothing prepared the mother for what that child's death would mean to her life.

> We were never told anything. I mean people live with seizures their whole lives. We knew this was something we might have to deal with the rest of his life, but nobody ever told us it would be fatal. . . . His doctor . . . didn't even believe he was gonna die until he was gone. . . . The autopsy showed he had extra fluid around the brain . . . but there was no reason for any of it—nothing—no answers at all. [Doris, mother of 4-year-old who was diagnosed at age 2 with cerebral palsy]

At the outset of their bereavement, the 10 women interviewed in-depth had found nothing in their reservoir of socially derived knowledge which could help them understand their new reality. Over 85% of the 80 women studied had experienced a significant loss prior to their child's death. The 10 women interviewed did not perceive any of their prior losses as applicable to the overwhelming loss of their child. In addition, the women noted that lack of understanding from others around them often added to their grief and anxiety, and impeded their healing.

> It's like they try to deny that he existed. Well, that's the worst hurt that I think a parent has is when people try to shovel it to a back burner. It's because that child existed. Bobby existed. He was a pain in the ass for 18 of 18 years, you know. He was also loving. He was also fun, you know. But he existed. He was here. . . . It had been 18 years of him and I, and 18 years is a long time, and yet it goes by in the blink of an eye. . . . We battled a lot, as a mother and son are prone to do, but he was so precious to me. I couldn't fathom the world without him in it. [Irene, divorced mother of 18-year-old who was a passenger in a single-car accident; his fiancée, the driver, was unhurt]

The experiences of these women and those of many other bereaved parents support Brice's (1987, 1991) conclusion that in order to mourn, it is necessary to mourn *to* someone else. When this need is frustrated, parents begin to see their grief as pathological and question their own sanity. Lacking understanding listeners in their existing social world, all five of the women I interviewed who represented the "survival" end of the bereavement continuum sought out other bereaved parents and began to build a stock of common knowledge based on their shared experiences. The knowledge shared by the women studied demonstrates how bereaved parents come to understand, in varying degrees of awareness, that:

Life is *not* always fair and does *not* always live up to expectations. There are some things in life that parents cannot control no matter how hard they or others try.

> I have an incredible fear and have had since the minute Evan died that all I have left of him is in this house, and I have a fear of leaving my house. 'Cause I can take care of it when I'm here but when I'm gone, who knows what could happen. . . . Sometimes I can just be going to, I don't know, get an adjustment on my neck at the chiropractor or something and have a full-fledged panic attack in the car on the way to town. I don't know if I only feel safe right here, right now, and everything else is a challenge. I don't know. I think it's when I'm in a situation over which I have no control. . . . The one thing I should have been able—it was my job to be Mommy and now—. And I told one woman I lost my son. And she said, I know, my husband got my son in the divorce. And then I learned, well if they're lost, there's a chance you can find 'em. So I don't call it lost anymore. He died; he's gone; there's no—you know, he hasn't been missing for 6 months, and the police could still come to the door. There's no lost to it. It's a loss but he's not lost; I know where he is. It's [feeling out of] control. I guess that is it, the more I realize. [Doris, mother of 4-year-old who was diagnosed at age 2 with cerebral palsy]

Virtually all aspects of these women's lives have changed since the death of their child, including their feelings, beliefs, attitudes, values, assumptions, identities, activities, work, plans, priorities, goals, relationships with others, perceptions of the past, and motivations for the future. Over time their grief has not automatically gotten better; it has gotten different. Their experiences demonstrate that time alone does not heal, nor does sympathy. Rather, bereaved parents must consciously decide to survive their child's death and find their own personally meaningful ways to "live life alive" again.

> I'm sure that as the years go on I'll get more and more in touch with all those things about me that aren't all that wonderful, but they don't scare me anymore. I mean, my son died, I can go through anything now. It's okay. I was always afraid to love anybody because they'd leave me . . . and this is only a recent realization—probably in the last 6 months—that yeah, if I love somebody they may die and they may leave, but you know what, I'm gonna be okay anyway. . . . It doesn't scare me so much anymore to be alone, so it doesn't scare me as much to be with somebody either. [Gail, divorced mother of 16-year-old who died in a single-car accident while driving to work in the rain]

Losing a child and the role as that child's parent is not a "typical thing," but all parents know that this can and sometimes does happen. Today's news coverage often contains reports of children dying traumatic deaths, not just in far-off lands but throughout the United States, and sometimes in communities least expected to experience violence. Multiple deaths from the terrorist attacks on the World

Trade Center and Pentagon in 2001, the 1999 school shootings at Columbine High School in Colorado, and the Oklahoma City bombing in 1995, have raised national awareness that children die not just by accident, illness, or suicide in our society, but also by mass murder. A recent survey commissioned by The Compassionate Friends (1999), a national organization, found that "19 percent of the adult population in this country has experienced the death of a child,[4] and 22 percent the death of a sibling."

The unfair and atypical reality that confronts bereaved parents forces them to sort through their personal spiritual beliefs in an attempt to make sense of why bad things happen in our world. To survive, parents must reconcile their loss with their worldview and their belief in God or a power greater than themselves. Parents must be able to place their child somewhere beyond the grave. Irene's conclusion provides one example of this:

> I've also realized that while losing Bobby was painful, that he's on another plane of existence and he's got work to do, and if you grieve too much, you hold their spirit to this earth and they can never go the next step that they need to go. [Irene, divorced mother of 18-year-old who was a passenger in a single car accident; his fiancée, the driver, was unhurt]

To reinvest in life, most parents must overcome the fear that they and others will forget their child. They must reconstruct their experiences, both good and bad, as the child's parent, find new ways to maintain a connection with their child, and incorporate what they have learned from parenthood and bereavement into a new identity which encompasses both caring for others and caring for themselves. Julie found that as she reinvested in life by helping other bereaved parents, her fear that her son would be forgotten diminished:

> [And why do you think you don't have that fear anymore of forgetting your son?] I think because all that stuff that you go through in the early stages—the anger, the guilt, all that other stuff—that kind of clouds what you really need to hang onto. I think all that has left me. Um, more or less I have, I don't know, like peace with what I'm able to remember. In fact, the other day I remembered something that he had done that I don't think I had remembered in a long time . . . and it was just so vivid. It was something he had said, just the reaction on his face. So I think when all that stuff leaves you you're able to remember more vividly and a lot easier too. {Julie, mother of 9-year-old run over by a drunk driver while standing at the end of his driveway]

Julie had been co-leader for the local chapter of The Compassionate Friends for over 6 years. "I have a job here," she said, "and I'm doing my best in helping others through the valley of grief." She demonstrates how many of the women

---

[4]This figure includes all child deaths, from miscarriage through death of an adult child. Source: "When A Child Dies: A Survey of Bereaved Parents Conducted by NFO Research, Inc. on behalf of The Compassionate Friends, Inc.," June 1999.

studied were able to reach out to help others in ways that also keep their child a part of their daily life.

Multiple Realities

Bereaved parents experience the multiple realities of living with an ongoing identity as the dead child's parent, while at the same time taking on the new persona of a bereaved mother or father without that child to parent. Bridging such different provinces of meaning requires a conscious shift of mind, awareness, and energy. Several of the bereaved mothers studied had been able to make such shifts:

> I still have the need to be a mother. . . . It's like with Compassionate Friends when I took over co-leading [the local support group]—this is my baby. [Julie, mother of 9-year-old run over by a drunk driver while standing at the end of his driveway]

In studying the process of role exit, Ebaugh (1988) found that role residual was common to all who exited a role, voluntarily or not. Role residual is "the identification that an individual maintains with a prior role such that the individual experiences certain aspects of the role after he or she has in fact exited from it" (Ebaugh, 1988, p. 173). Further, "the more personal involvement and commitment an individual had in a former role, that is, the more self-identity was equated with role definitions, the more role residual tended to manifest itself after the exit" (p. 178).

Bereaved parents lose those roles that accompanied parenting the unique child who died. Sanders (1999, p. 96) provides an example: "One parent told me that in relinquishing one small aspect of his role as a father—that of being father to a son who played in Little League—he gave up the role of armchair coach, adviser, and team rooter—in that one situation alone." Presumably, this father's relationships with other Little League parents and his son's team mates also changed after his son's death. He would have to decide whether to continue attending games and what to do about his residual identities of "coach," "adviser," and "rooter."

Role residual can be a pivotal issue impacting parents' ability to reinvest in life. The five bereaved mothers I interviewed who had the *highest* life attitude scores (see chap. 2) each had incorporated volunteering to help others as a part of their new identity. Volunteering allows them to utilize the residual learnings from their role as a mother by caring for others while also meeting their own need to remember their child. Significantly, the five women I interviewed who had the *lowest* life attitude scores were not involved in such volunteer activities. At the time of the interview they remained ambivalent about living and unable to find new purpose and meaning for their lives.

Varying Levels of Awareness and Focus

Phenomenologists have pointed out that although we add to our sensory impressions without being aware that we do so, consciousness is intentional. We don't "see" something; rather, we intentionally "look for" something (Wagner, 1983, pp. 53–56). We give direction to our senses and willfully select what we will pay attention to in our life-world. Such selection is based on what interests us.[5] We are profoundly interested in the subject of death. Often we are also greatly frightened and confused by death and by our responses to it.

There was a stark contrast between the life-worlds of the two groups of women interviewed who represent opposite ends of the bereavement continuum. The examples that follow demonstrate the two groups' levels of awareness about their responses to the death of their only child and the quality of life they were experiencing at the time of the interview.

Participants With Lowest Life Attitude Scores

The five women who represented the "perpetual bereavement" end of the continuum were focused on how their child's death and their ongoing acute grief changed everything. The following quotes from each of these women demonstrate the degree of anguish they were struggling with at the time they were interviewed.

The best way to put it, since Edward died, I died! Everything that it seems like I used to know, used to do, the way I used to live, the way I felt, was all gone. I just, I completely became an empty person, and there really was nothing that mattered to me at all. And I'm still struggling with that. . . . I don't feel I can ever get myself back again to who I was when I had my boy. [Bev, divorced mother of 6-year-old run over by a car after the bike he was riding hit a sewer grate; she was riding behind him and witnessed the accident]

I tend to stay away from all friends, especially the ones that are married and have families and have grandkids. Because I have nothing to chat with them about. . . . I'm thinking, their kids can't be with us because Brad's not here. I don't say it to anyone but I think it. . . . That was never me before. . . . And I don't like that. That's not me, but yet it's become me. It's hard for me to handle, or to know how to accept it, or to know how to react. And so far I'm not doing a very good job of it except to run away and ignore it. [Anita, mother of 15-year-old who died following open heart surgery]

I keep thinking one of these days it's just gonna hit me like somebody slapped me in the face and then I'm gonna think, that's why I'm here. That's why all this has happened. But it's just kind of strange that you get up ever morning and you go to work. You work, you come home, you eat, you watch television and you go to bed. You get up and do the same thing over and over and over. It's like you're not going

---

[5]This development of self based on inborn personal preferences that direct each individual's attention is a central tenet of Jungian psychology. The Myers–Briggs Personality Inventory (MBTI) is a highly reliable instrument that identifies personality preferences and is useful in a variety of counseling situations. However it is not recommended for those in the midst of trauma or acute grief. See chapter 11.

anywhere. Everthing's just at a standstill. [Ellen, mother of 20-year-old run over by a car while riding his motorcycle]

I'm an unemployed mother. He was my *job*, period. Everything! And it came he was gone and—you know—nothing [tears]. . . . [If you could talk to Evan and ask him anything you wanted to ask him?] I'd wanta know if he's okay, that's all. That's all. That's all I've ever meant, is to make sure he's okay. I know he would want to know if I was okay too, and I'm working on it. Um, at the same time, then again you feel guilty—about feeling good [tears]. [Doris, mother of 4-year-old who was diagnosed at age 2 with cerebral palsy]

It's really hard to explain what it does to you. I'm not the same person at all. . . . I'm more prone to anger. I'm more aggressive with my work, the people at work. . . . I used to do quite a bit of stuff by myself. And I'm more, well, it's like I just really don't want to do anything. . . . I still have periods that I have to take off work, and I have migraines really bad then. . . . I just get really depressed. I get really, really down, and it's hard for me to get back up. . . . I think I hate everybody and everything and just go in with a chip on my shoulder. Any little thing and I'll fly off the handle. I think it's just mostly anger that he's gone. It's like I just have to pull myself up out of the ridges and just keep plugging along until it finally just kind of ebbs away. . . . Sometimes you think, man, is this ever gonna get over with. But then you think, well, you don't want it over with 'cause you think if you do, then you'll forget. [Fran, mother of 19-year-old who died from brain injuries 4 months after an auto accident]

These women were aware that their child's death had changed them into "a totally different person" who is confused by why this tragic event happened and unable to envision a future without their child. Holding onto their grief had become the price they were paying for not forgetting their child and their life as a mother. As such, their grief had become the focus of their lives, just as their child once was the center of their attention.

Participants With Highest Life Attitude Scores

The five women representing the "survival" end of the bereavement continuum were also well aware of how their child's death had changed their lives forever, but as the following quotes demonstrate, their focus had shifted to understanding who they had become as a result of their child's death.

The loss hit on so many levels because the loss hit in terms of my no longer having the role of being a mother. . . . I didn't know who Gail was. I was a mother. I was an exemplary employee, and you know, I had tried to be a mate. But I didn't know who I was, and so when he died I certainly lost the role of mother, but I lost a friend. . . . I died when he died. Gradually I've birthed a new me. I'm totally different. I have an identity beyond being a mother. It's a part of who I am and my experience, but it's not the total me. . . . It has just been a very slow, painful process to make the decision to live life "alive," to actually risk caring about others again, to learn to take care of myself. [Gail, divorced mother of 16-year-old who died in a single-car accident while driving to work in the rain]

I'm a totally changed person—more assertive, more open. I'm less fearful of allowing others to see deep inside of me. I will never allow anyone to hurt me unnecessarily or purposely again. I've taken more control of what I allow. Before I would listen and allow others their thinking, and not say anything. It was the fear of ever making decisions again after what happened at my son's bedside [having to decide not to let doctors resuscitate]. I had to realize that because of this one helpless event in my life, I had to gain control again. [Carol, mother of son who died at age 15 from muscular dystrophy]

I have been in Compassionate Friends meetings where I knew that there were people there that I could identify that were never gonna heal. They were never going to get over their grief because it had been an only child that they had lost and their entire identity was as the mother. They had no identity other than mother and wife, and I could tell by looking at 'em they weren't gonna make it, because they weren't maybe strong enough or whatever to reach down way deep inside where you have to find that strength. And you find it a little bit at a time. And I knew by looking at 'em, and my heart would break because I would think, they're not gonna survive it. I'm gonna survive it, you know. . . . Bobby would of wanted me to let go and to go on in another direction even, but to go on with my life and find some meaning apart from him, you know, which I would have done had he gone off, gotten married, had kids. I would have been a grandmother, and I would have talked to him a lot, and I would have gotten maybe flowers on Mother's Day or whatever, but I would have made another life. [Irene, divorced mother of 18-year-old who was a passenger in a single-car accident; his fiancée, the driver, was unhurt]

A lot of the people that come to the meeting [of the support group for bereaved parents with no surviving children, which she started] . . . they'll want to know: "What's your purpose now? What do you feel? What are you still here for?" I say, I hope to find out too, someday. But in the meantime, this is what I'm doing. This is what I've got to do. And this doing what I'm doing now is so rewarding for me. And I know it's helping other people. I've gotten so many cards and letters and gifts and things. It blows me away to think that what I do comes from my heart and they appreciate it so much. . . . Life is exciting again. . . . I've never felt so at peace as I do now. And I believe the group has a lot to do with it. They keep me going with, well, what do you think? I'm needed. [Helen, mother of 20-year-old son who died in a single-car accident on his way home from work late at night]

I have a job here, and I'm doing my best in helping others through the valley of grief. . . . They never met him [her son] but they know him [through her poetry and discussions with the bereaved parents support group]. And to me that's important. [Julie, mother of 9-year-old run over by a drunk driver while standing at the end of his driveway]

These five mothers realized that their child was the center of their life and that they had been "totally changed" by their child's death. However, they also were aware of having regained control of their lives, resolving their anger at God and/or nonsupportive friends and family, making a conscious decision to survive, and looking for and finding new reasons to live. They were directing their energy toward preserving memories of their child and motherhood, while at the same time building a new life by nurturing themselves and others.

Significant We-Relationships

When we are involved with one another, we share a common experience that phenomenologists characterize as "self-transcending" and "living in our common stream of consciousness." The "act of grasping the thoughts and feelings of others" happens within the intersubjective experience of face-to-face relationships (Wagner, 1983, p. 88). Such grasping includes our perceptions of bodily presence and movements such as speech, gesture, and facial expressions. This interactive process of relating to one another includes each individual's perception of the other's motivations and a corresponding reorienting of actions.

In order to reflect on our relationships, we must stop interacting and focus our attention on the process of how we have been relating. This is somewhat analogous to stepping out from between the trees in order to view the shape of the forest. Being able to do so gives us a new perspective from which to view our relational experiences and the feelings they create.

For bereaved parents, reflection offers the potential for changing the locus of control within their relationships. Lefcourt (1982) described locus of control as "a circumscribed self-appraisal pertaining to the degree to which individuals view themselves as having some causal role in determining *specified events*" (p. 183). Further:

> Locus of control can be viewed as a mediator of involved commitment in life pursuits. If one feels helpless to affect important events, then resignation or at least benign indifference should become evident, with fewer signs of concern, involvement, and vitality. (p. 184)

The following examples from the two groups of women at opposite ends of the bereavement continuum show how they differ in their perception of locus of control and how their relationships seemed to be influencing their ability to find peace and resolution. Doris, one of the five women with the *lowest* life attitude scores, said:

> She [her mother-in-law] blatantly blamed me—never in front of a witness—she called me the day after he died and accused me of killing him. She said, "He died 'cause you didn't give him his medicine, didn't he?" And at the time I was so in shock. Now, I could have something to say to her. . . .
>
> It hurt and it still does that, you know, I couldn't be first on his [her husband's] list. And in a lot of ways—most ways—I am, but a lot of times it feels like I'm not,

because of the work. But he loves it. . . . Most of the time I don't complain, but he has a lot to keep his mind busy and I don't, and I think I'm jealous of that sometimes. It's like he has a life and I don't, 'cause my job was taken away when Evan died you know. . . . That's my purpose on earth . . . to have that child and take care of him [crying], and I didn't do it right.

Doris provides examples of how relationships can reinforce a feeling of powerlessness. She continues to hold herself accountable for not being able to save her son and instead of directly confronting her mother-in-law, continues to feel blamed. Likewise, she does not acknowledge that she has any power to change the fact that her husband "has a life and I don't."

Fran provides another example. She said:

It's like my anger just kept building and building and building, and finally I just screamed [at her husband]: "You don't care that David is dead, you know, you didn't love him. It doesn't matter to you. You never say his name." He'd never go to the grave. It's like he was never born. And he said, "I can't believe you said that." And I said, "Well, that's the way I see it. You don't talk about it. You don't." If I'd say anything, or say, he'd done this, it's like a curtain would close. And it was just like he didn't even want to admit that he'd ever existed. I couldn't understand. It was like I was scared to death I would forget him. I had to keep saying his name and looking at his picture because I was afraid I would forget how he was. And I couldn't understand that he wasn't doing the same thing. . . . But finally he told me that he just couldn't bear to talk about it; it was too painful. And then after I got to understanding how he felt, then it didn't bother me as much that he didn't talk about him.

In contrast to Doris, Fran confronted her husband with her belief that he didn't care about their son and learned that her perceptions were not correct; that he does, in fact, mourn the loss of their son but has been defending himself from the pain of grieving.

Irene and Gail were among the five women with the *highest* life attitude scores. For Irene, the caring support of a friend helped her through early bereavement and provided the catalyst so she could reach inside herself to find the strength to gain control of her life again.

I thought, well, if he [a former employer] cares that much about me to worry about getting me back into the world [by insisting she come to work for him part-time], then I've got to cooperate and I've got to find that strength within me to continue on that path. And it took a while, but I made it, and I had to consciously say to myself, "You must get out. You must quit hiding." [Irene, divorced mother of 18-year-old who was a passenger in a single-car accident; his fiancée, the driver, was unhurt]

Irene's experience is similar to Gail's decision during the first year of her bereavement to ask a friend to call her every day for 3 months and make her promise not to commit suicide. This temporary support gave Gail the strength to "do some other things" to help her regain control.

She'd just talk to me and talk to me and talk to me until finally I'd say, "okay, stop harping on me, I'll promise you for today." . . . And in the meantime I got involved in Overeaters Anonymous, and the Big Book just made so much sense to me. . . . It was just like going home. . . . 'Cause I was so angry at God that there was no way I could talk about a God, but a higher power I could talk about, that made sense to me. . . . I ended up having a circle of friends there and a sense of community, to look at all this stuff from childhood [she was sexually abused by her grandfather during her childhood]. [Gail, divorced mother of 16-year-old who died in a single-car accident while driving to work in the rain]

These examples demonstrate how important it can be for the bereaved to be able to step outside of their relationships and evaluate how those relationships may be influencing their grief and vice versa. An understanding friend, support group, or counselor can serve to facilitate such reflection.

CONTRASTING THE LIFE-WORLDS

There were four major themes that showed the marked contrast between the five women interviewed who had the *lowest* life attitude scores and the five who had the *highest* life attitude scores. These themes are presented in summary form in Table 1.1 and discussed next.

THE THEMES OF CHRONIC MOURNING

Loss of Motherhood Experienced as Identity Disintegration.

The five women with the *lowest* life attitude scores, experienced the loss of their only child as a loss of self, goals, purpose for living, and hopes for the future. At the time of the interviews, all five demonstrated this level of identity disintegration. They could not envision a future without their child. And they perceived that pursuing a new, purposeful life would mean forgetting their child, denying the child's existence, and invalidating their life as a mother. This was the message that these mothers heard when those around them urged them to "get over" their loss and build a new life. Thus they resisted when others encouraged them to go for counseling or attend bereavement support groups. All but Fran talked of how painful it was to be around other parents with children. Thus, although these mothers clung to the memories of their child and themselves as a mother, they shut themselves off from any new mothering experiences with other children. This also was mentioned as a factor preventing them from seeking help from support groups that included bereaved parents with surviving children.

Need for an Understanding Support System Remained Unmet

All of these women voiced a desire to be understood and heard. These women had given of themselves to their children and families, and at the time of the interviews they felt emotionally and physically depleted and alone. Being understood

Table 1.1 Summary of Major Life-World Themes

Loss of Motherhood
Chronic mourning: Loss of only child was experienced as identity disintegration: loss of self, goals, purpose for living, and future. Living a new, purposeful life would mean forgetting the child, denying the child's existence, and invalidating past life as a mother.

Survival: Loss of only child was experienced as identity crisis: loss of part of the self, goals, purpose for living, and future. Child seen as separate and distinct personality, and self was seen as possessing unique attributes and strengths.

Bereavement Process
Chronic mourning: Mothers lacked adequate support system and coping skills. They were hesitant to reach out to others for help and continued to experience recurrent grief, helplessness, mental instability, and physical ailments related to stress.

Survival: Mothers had made a conscious decision to survive and to reinvest in life. All sought and accepted help from others and learned to use a wide variety of coping skills to deal with their grief and take care of themselves. Nonsupportive family and friends had been replaced with new, understanding others. All continued to experience periodic shadow grief and see bereavement as an evolving, lifelong learning process with some positive benefits.

Life Today: At Time of Interview
Chronic mourning: Mothers demonstrated ongoing ambivalence about living, remained angry at God and/or church, and had been unable to incorporate child's death into a beneficial belief system. No purpose for living had been discovered since the child's death. Focus was on reviewing aspects of the loss and the effect that unresolved grief was having on their lives.

Survival: Mothers had regained self-control and integrated what they had learned from bereavement into a new identity and a new worldview. Purpose in life was now focused on maintaining a connection with the child and using mothering skills to nurture themselves and others through volunteer activities. Mothers interviewed saw themselves as having become better people.

Hope for the Future
Chronic mourning: Having made difficult choices or decisions in the past may indicate the potential for being able to make a future decision to survive the death of their child and live life "alive" again.

Survival: Mothers interviewed all learned from prior life crises, which may have strengthened their self-esteem. All had acted courageously in confronting their grief by finding or creating opportunities to maintain a connection with their child and their identity as a mother while reinvesting in a purposeful life. All had taken responsibility for their own healing.

by others—friends, family, doctors, counselors, and/or clergy—seemed to be a necessary precursor for them to be able to understand and make sense of their multiple losses. Their bereavement was characterized by helplessness, anger, blame, regrets, guilt, recurrent physical illness, unresolved conflicts in current relationships, and concern about their mental stability. Cumulative prior losses of family and/or friends appeared to have complicated the bereavement of Bev, Ellen, and Fran. Three of the women, Doris, Ellen, and Fran, had had family or friends die or become seriously ill since their child's death, and this had compounded their grief.

Conflicts Related to the Death Remained Unresolved

These five women continued to experience ongoing separation anxiety evidenced by pining, yearning, and searching (in dreams) for their child. They continued to reexperience the trauma associated with the child's death and to search for causes and meaning of events surrounding the child's illness or accident. Anita, Bev, and Fran remained ambivalent about their decisions and actions at the time of the death. Both Anita and Doris (and possibly also Bev) blamed themselves for not being able to prevent their child's death. Three of the women (Bev, Doris, and Fran) had suffered the added trauma of being blamed by others for their child's death.

Life Is Purposeless and Meaningless

These women demonstrated that chronic mourning means remaining ambivalent about living. They had been unable to find new purpose and meaning for their lives. They remained angry at God and/or their church and had been unable to incorporate their child's death into any spiritual belief system that could bring peace and resolution. They were prevented from searching for new goals, purpose and meaning in life by their belief that doing so would mean forgetting their child and invalidating their life and identity as a mother.

Past Courageous Acts Demonstrate Hope for the Future

Although these women continued to suffer profound grief, I also found reason to hope that each of them would make a conscious choice to survive and reinvest in life in the future. All spoke of past actions they had taken that demonstrated an ability to make such a choice. Such actions included leaving a bad marriage and divorcing the child's father (Anita), beginning to assert herself in her marriage (Doris and Fran), cutting off contact with nonsupportive family members (Bev), beginning to search for a new self (Bev, Doris, and Ellen), and participating in bereavement research (all five women).

THE THEMES OF SURVIVAL

Loss of Motherhood Experienced as Identity Crisis

The five women with the *highest* life attitude scores experienced the loss of their only child as an identity crisis, a loss of an important part of themselves. These women were all very devoted to their child, yet they also considered their child a separate, unique person—a part of, yet apart from, themselves. All but Carol were or had been divorced mothers who had met many challenges in raising their child alone. Although not a divorced mother, Carol had built up her physical and emotional strength by coping with her son's debilitating illness and becoming his advocate. When their child died, each of these women had to confront a loss of meaning, purpose, and future in their lives; each had struggled in her own way to find the inner strength to build a new life. For Gail, the struggle required a return to the wounds of her early childhood, and learning to reparent herself. For Carol, Helen, Irene, and Julie, the struggle meant reaching out to find others to nurture, and being nurtured in return. Each found ways to maintain a connection with her deceased child through memorials, "messages" from the child, and reinvesting in life in ways that permit the child to remain a part of daily activities. All expected to be reunited with their child after death.

Confronting Grief With a Variety of Coping Strategies

In unique, individual ways, all of the five women with the *highest* life attitude scores had gradually regained control of themselves and their lives since the death of their only child. Gail began the process of gaining control as her son lay in a coma in the hospital, when she took charge of how he would be treated by staff and visitors. Carol and Helen both confronted unsupportive family members, and replaced them with a new extended family of other bereaved parents who both understood their loss and needed them. Julie and Irene received strength and direction from their sons' spirits, urging them to carry on and find new purpose in living.

The ongoing healing of these women was characterized by their use of multiple coping strategies to confront and manage their grief. These included praying; keeping a journal; voicing their anger, resentments, and fears; visiting the grave and talking with the child; finding symbols that represent messages from the child; preserving the child's memory by creating memory albums, establishing scholarships and memorials, and making donations to worthy causes; seeking and accepting help from others; telling the story of the child's death to others and gaining new perspectives about their experiences; celebrating the child's life on anniversary dates and holidays; engaging in reciprocal grieving with other bereaved parents; trusting their own feelings, experiences, and judgment; learning to take care of themselves; recognizing and accepting that their grief process may differ from others who also loved their child; and helping themselves by reaching out to help others.

Life Has New Meaning and New Purpose

All five of these women had survived crises in their lives prior to their sons' deaths: sexual abuse (Gail), father's death (Carol and Irene), and divorce (Gail, Helen, Irene, and Julie). Four of the women, Carol, Gail, Irene, and Julie, found ways to incorporate their child's death into a spiritual belief system that allowed them to acknowledge and then work through their anger at God. Each of these women made a conscious choice to survive. Helen talked of an "awakening" in the fifth year after her son's death; Irene of "turning points" on two separate occasions during the early years; and Carol of confronting her "unacceptable reality" by "building a dream on sorrow." Gail experienced this conscious choice to survive as a metanoia (a profound change of mind) brought about by her "higher power," and Julie survived by "grasping onto" the Biblical promise of being reunited with her son in Heaven, "never to be separated again."

As their bereavement progressed, each of these women reached an understanding of their new purpose in living. For Gail, this was "being the best person I can be and . . . going about God's business"; for Carol, Helen, and Julie it was celebrating their sons' memory and "helping others through the valley of grief"; and for Irene it was "the development of my soul" and "making my son proud of me." These women felt that positive benefits had accompanied the painful process of surviving their child's death. They had become better people and were now willing and able to help others. Each considered her bereavement to be a lifelong, evolving journey, and none expected to ever "get over" missing her child and her life as the child's mother.

Courageous Acts Inspired by the Bereavement Experience

All five of the *highest* life attitude women had taken courageous action in surviving the death of their only child. Gail joined a 12-step recovery program and continued to confront her dysfunctional childhood and her son's death through a program of self-development. When they could not find the help they needed in their communities, Carol and Helen began their own support groups for other bereaved parents and continued to take leadership roles in those groups. Irene became a hospice volunteer and worked with several other community groups. Julie persevered through the trial of the driver who killed her son, recovered her health after two major surgeries, and became a leader in her local Compassionate Friends group. In each case these women took responsibility for their own healing and either found or created opportunities to overcome the identity crisis they experienced in losing their only child.

SUMMARY

Looking at the structures of the life-worlds of the women in the "Mothers Now Childless" study draws attention to those elements that impact the derivation of meaning of their experiences. They demonstrate how important it can be for bereaved parents to seek out each other in order to build and draw support from their combined *common stocks of knowledge*. The *multiple realities* of the women studied highlight the pivotal importance of role residual and how helping others can provide the meaning and new direction necessary for survival by allowing parents to retain and use the nurturing part of their identity. The similarities and differences in the *level of awareness and focus* between the two groups of women interviewed demonstrate the intentionality of consciousness. Although they had had the similar experience of becoming "totally changed" people, the focus of those with the *lowest* life attitude scores remained aimed at feeling and defining the pain of their loss. Those with the *highest* life attitude scores, however, had seen not only a change in themselves but also a change in how they approached life and in their *significant relationships,* following a conscious decision to survive their loss.

The examples provided in this introductory chapter highlight elements that can characterize and give structure to the world of bereaved parents, a world that frequently feels and looks like "landscape without gravity" (Ascher, 1993). My experiences with bereaved parents have shown me that healing often begins when parents take action to combat their sense of powerlessness and losing control. For many, the motivation to act comes from a search for meaning, a need to make some sense of their child's death, their grief, and their irrevocably changed life-world. It is very difficult, if not impossible, for parents in the early years of acute grief to find positive (versus negative) meanings resulting from their child's death. It is important for them to know that most bereaved parents do survive this tragedy and eventually find purpose and meaning in life again. Donna Michaud Berger is a bereaved mother who provides a compelling example of what it means to survive extreme trauma and loss. Her husband and three children were killed in 1989 when a tractor-trailer ran over their parked car. She suffered severe burns and nearly died as well. Many people are helped by her description of what grief work is like. "Grief will not be denied," she says. "If you refuse to deal with it, you will never find peace. Grief is like an enormous boulder that must be ground into pebbles. There is no schedule. Each day you do what you can to chisel away at it. When you finally get down to the very last pebble, you put it in your pocket and carry it with you always and forever" (Berger, 1996, p. 12). Bereaved parents need to know that it is possible to learn ways to chisel away at that boulder, to eventually live a different yet meaningful life despite the sacred pebble of grief they will carry with them forever.

HELPING BEREAVED PARENTS SURVIVE

All researchers know that what appears to explain or be associated with particular outcomes when studying groups of people, such as my study of bereaved mothers of only children, may or may not be applicable to individuals whose experiences are similar. We know that the map is not the territory. The challenge is to use new understandings gained from research—the map—in ways that respond appropriately to the circumstances of individuals living in complex human territories.

The intent of this book is *not* to offer assessment guidelines to clinicians and caregivers who work with bereaved parents. There are excellent resources that provide extensive assessment criteria, such as Rando's (1993) *Treatment of Complicated Mourning,* and Worden's (1991) *Grief Counseling and Grief Therapy: A Handbook for the Mental Health Practitioner.* There are other sources, such as

Horowitz's (2001) *Stress Response Syndromes: Personality Styles and Interventions*, 4th edition, and Rothschild's (2001) *The Body Remembers: The Psychophysiology of Trauma and Trauma Treatment*, that outline interventions useful in relieving the intolerable levels of distress and despair that can accompany trauma and acute grief. Such interventions include eye movement desensitization and reprocessing therapy (cf. Shapiro & Forrest, 1997, pp. 151–170), thought field therapy (Callahan & Callahan, 1997), and the judicious use of antidepressants and/or anti-anxiety medications (cf. Raskin, 1997).

The intent of this book is to augment the uniquely personal approaches that clinicians and caregivers use to assist bereaved parents by highlighting key factors that bereaved parents identify as crucial to their evolving grief process. As in all kinds of therapy, the relationship between client and therapist is crucial. It is vitally important that clinicians not imply to bereaved parents that their grief reflects a mental disorder. This is like telling them their love for their child is somehow aberrant and out of bounds. Most bereaved parents have certain expectations for their therapist, including:

1 Empathy and a willingness to listen and try to understand their unique loss and experiences.
2 Acknowledgment that their child's death is a catastrophic, life-changing loss that will take enormous energy and incredible courage to survive.
3 Encouragement that they can survive and eventually find meaning in life again, even though they may not feel this is possible or even desirable from time to time as their grief evolves.
4 Confirmation that they are not, in fact, abnormal or "going crazy"—that grief is by nature idiosyncratic, unpredictable, and often makes people "feel crazy."
5 Information about the various grief responses and experiences of other bereaved parents who have survived and learned to live with their ongoing loss.

It has been said that the death of a loved one can make you either bitter or better. Gently acknowledging this harsh reality validates the enormity of the challenge facing bereaved parents. Surviving a child's death is a choice parents must make, sometimes several times, sometimes a day or an hour at a time. As clinicians and caregivers, we can help bereaved parents identify ways in which their love for their child is stronger than the pain of their grief. If the grief in front of them can be visualized, as Donna Berger said, as "an enormous boulder," can they also visualize their child's love as the power behind them helping to chip away at that boulder? Can they learn from other parents who have survived this loss that a desire to change, to move beyond pain, brings hope?

Some parents equate healing their pain with forgetting their child. Clinicians need to know whether this is true for individual clients. Years after her son's death, Fran's grief was accompanied by recurring depression, migraine headaches, anxiety attacks, and insomnia—all symptoms being treated by medication. There was an underlying condition, however, that contributed to the intensity of her pain—her attitude. "Sometimes you think, man, is this ever gonna get over with?" Fran said. "But then you think, well, you don't want it over with, because if you do, then you'll forget." It was essential for Fran to understand that she could heal her overwhelming pain without giving up her memories and connection with her son. As clinicians and caregivers, we help to normalize this loss when we convey to parents that the goal is not to "detach" from or "let go" of their child, but to acknowledge the reality of the child's physical death while also building new connections to the child's spirit. Similarly, it is important to stress that *healing after the death of a child does not mean becoming totally pain free. Healing means integrating and learning how to live with the ongoing loss. It means becoming able to love others and actively reinvest in life again. Healing often comes when bereaved parents decide they will not permit pain to be the only expression of their continuing love for their child.*

The following chapter summarizes the "Mothers Now Childless" study. It provides details about the participants, the questions they were asked, and analysis of the responses they gave. Although this chapter has presented my conclusions about the life-worlds of the women in the "Mothers Now Childless" study, chapter 2 provides the data that led to those conclusions. It is different from the other chapters in this book and provides extensive details about the study design and findings. Readers not interested in this level of research detail may wish to proceed to chapter 3, which continues the discussion of how grief evolves after a child dies.

The "Mothers Now Childless" Study: Research Design and Findings

The women I asked to participate in my study of survival after the death of an only child were mothers whose only child, ages 1 to 21, had died due to illness or accident 5 or more years previously. Selection was limited to not less than 5 years of bereavement because of earlier findings in the literature regarding the length of time it takes many bereaved parents to move beyond acute grief when a child dies. I excluded women whose children died from suicide or murder because these types of death generally present added complications to grief resolution. Similarly, I did not include bereaved fathers because of prior research that indicated that gender may influence bereavement processes and/or outcomes. I felt that limiting the selection criteria in this first study of surviving the death of an only child would help to ensure a more homologous sample, a baseline which could then be compared and contrasted with the experiences of other bereaved parents. This chapter is divided into two parts. The first describes the study participants and the research process; the second presents the detailed statistical findings and limitations of the study.

RESEARCH DESIGN

Participant Recruitment

The women who participated in the "Mothers Now Childless" study were contacted by means of a computerized mailing list provided by the organization Alive Alone (see Resources).

> Alive Alone, Inc. is a non-profit, tax deductible corporation, organized for such educational and charitable purposes as will benefit bereaved parents whose only child or all children are deceased, by providing a self-help network and publica-

tions to promote communication and healing, to assist in resolving their grief, and a means to reinvest their lives for a positive future. (Bevington, 1992)

Alive Alone has published a newsletter for bereaved parents with no surviving children since 1988. Bereaved parents learn of the newsletter through The Compassionate Friends support groups and/or referrals from grief counselors, ministers, or other caregivers. Parents can contact the newsletter editor to request contact information for other parents who are willing to provide support by phone or through the mails. The organization does not conduct support groups; however, members are invited to attend a biannual In Loving Memory Conference, which began in 1993, where workshops and discussion groups are held for parents with no surviving children. Alive Alone, Inc. and In Loving Memory are separate organizations working together to support parents now childless (see Resources).

Participant Characteristics

One hundred and fourteen women responded to a recruitment letter (53% of those contacted), and 80 met the study criteria (the others had either had additional children or their child died from murder or suicide). The 80 participants lived in 32 different states, and were predominantly white (94%), married (66%), and college graduates (51%).

These 80 women had been bereaved an average of 9 years, with 68% bereaved from 5 to 13 years. Seventy-seven percent of the children who died were between the ages of 14 and 21, and 73% of the deaths were accidental, predominantly automobile related. The personal characteristics of the 80 women and their children are summarized in Tables 2.1 and 2.2.

The Research Process

As discussed in chapter 1, bereaved parents face a severe crisis of meaning. Parenting and loving a child add meaning and purpose to life for most parents. When the ability to parent that child is taken away, life can seem suddenly meaningless and parents often struggle to find reasons to go on living. Many bereaved parents eventually work through this crisis, but some do not (Miles, 1979; Wheeler, 1990). As I began my research, I postulated that the criterion of life attitude (whether life has meaning and purpose) could represent a bereavement survival continuum. Participants completed a standardized instrument, the Life Attitude Profile–Revised (LAP–R)—see Appendix. Their responses approximated a normal distribution curve. The LAP–R was developed by psychologist Gary Reker (1992) to operationalize Viktor Frankl's concepts of will to meaning, existential vacuum, personal choice and responsibleness, realities and potentialities, and death transcendence (Frankl, 1963).

Women whose LAP–R scores fell at the high end of the bereavement continuum were classified a priori as representing "survival." Women whose LAP–R

Table 2.1 Personal Characteristics of the Participants (*n* = 80)

Characteristic	Frequency (*n*)	Percentage (%)[a]
Marital status at time of study:		
Married, to child's father	37	46
Divorced	19	24
Married, not to child's father	16	20
Widowed	6	8
Single, never married	2	3
Ethnic background		
Anglo/White	75	94
Black/African American	2	3
Hispanic	2	3
Other	1	1
Religion:		
Protestant/Christian	45	56
Catholic	26	33
Other	6	8
None	3	4
Education:		
High school graduate	38	48
College graduate	22	28
Advanced college degree(s)	18	23
Less than high school	2	3
Employment at time of study:		
Full time	45	56
Part time	17	21
Not currently employed	18	23
Occupation:		
Professional	18	23
Service/sales	16	20
Clerical	15	19
Managerial	11	14
Technical/arts	2	3
Not currently employed	18	23
Volunteer work:		
Currently volunteer	50	63
Do not currently volunteer	30	38
Annual family income:		
$25,000–$49,999	32	40
$50,000–$99,999	25	31
$100,000 and above	11	14
$10,000–$24,999	10	13
Less than $10,000	2	3

[a]*Percentages are rounded and may not add to 100.*

Table 2.2   Personal Characteristics of the Participants Children (*n* = 80)

Characteristic	Frequency (*n*)	Percentage (%)*
Gender of child:		
Male	49	61
Female	31	39
Age at death:		
14–18 years	41	51
19–21 years	21	26
5–10 years	8	10
11–13 years	6	8
3–4 years	4	5
Type of death:		
Accident	58	73
Illness/disease	22	28
Number of years since death at time of study:		
8 years	15	19
7 years	13	16
6 years	12	15
9 years	10	13
12 years	9	11
11 years	6	8
10 years	5	6
14 years or more	4	5
13 years	3	4
5 years	3	4
Range of years since death:	5 to 33	
Average number of years since death:	9	
Standard deviation:	3.77	

*Percentages are rounded and may not add to 100.

scores fell at the low end of the continuum were classified a priori as representing "a state of perpetual bereavement." Thus the LAP–R instrument was used as a means of purposive sampling to select bereaved mothers at opposite ends of the bereavement continuum to interview personally in their homes: five who had the *highest* life attitude scores and five who had the *lowest* life attitude scores. All 80 participants completed the LAP–R, along with an instrument called the Perceived Well-Being Scale (Reker & Wong, 1984) and a participant questionnaire. The instruments, questionnaire, and interview protocol are described next.

The Life Attitude Profile–Revised (LAP–R)

A copy of the LAP–R, information about its history and validity, and details about scoring the six scales that it measures are included in the Appendix. Dimensions of the six LAP–R scales are outlined in Table 2.3. Each of the six scales on the LAP–R has eight questions, making a total of 48 questions.

Scores from these six LAP–R scales were used to calculate a Life Attitude Balance Index (LABI), which takes into account both the degree to which meaning and purpose in life have been discovered and the motivation to find meaning and purpose (Reker, 1992, p. 20). Five women were selected on the basis of their LABI scores to represent the "survival" end of the bereavement continuum and to be interviewed in depth. These women scored *high* on four scales, indicating that they:

1 Have goals and a sense of direction in their life (the Purpose scale).
2 Demonstrate a consistent understanding of self, others, and life in general (the Coherence scale).
3 Acknowledge the freedom to make life choices (the Life Control scale).
4 Accept death as a natural aspect of life (the Death Acceptance scale).

Table 2.3 Dimensions of the Life Attitude Profile–Revised (LAP–R)

Scale	Measures	Conceptual Correlations
Purpose (PU)	Having life goals, sense of direction, worthwhileness	Self-transcendence; collectivism: internal locus of control
Coherence (CO)	Understanding self, others, and life in general; clear sense of personal identity; greater social consciousness; reason for existence	Self-transcendence: collectivism; lack of hedonistic values
Life Control (LC)	Perception of freedom to make life choices, exercise of personal responsibility	Internal locus of control
Death Acceptance (DA)	Absence of fear and anxiety about death; death transcendence	Semantic differential rating of death
Existential Vacuum (EV)	Lack of purpose, goals, direction; free-floating anxiety	Alienation; negative perceptions of life at present; negative self-concept; death anxiety
Goal Seeking (GS)	Desire to search for new experiences, be on the move	Restlessness; alienation; future orientation

Source. The content of this table has been extrapolated from information contained in the LAP–R Procedures Manual (Reker, 1992), used with permission.

These women also scored *low* on two scales, indicating that they do <u>*not*</u>:

5   Lack meaning, purpose, and direction in life and feel bored, apathetic, or indifferent (the Existential Vacuum scale).
6   Desire to get away from the routine of life and to be on the move, restlessly searching for new and different experiences; lack goals; and are future oriented (the Goal Seeking scale).

Conversely, five women were selected for personal interviews to represent the other end of the conceptualized bereavement continuum based on their LABI scores. These women: (a) scored *low* on scales 1 through 4, as described, and (b) scored *high* on scales 5 and 6, as described.

Endpoint scoring of the conceptualized bereavement continuum as measured by the Life Attitude Balance Index is shown in Table 2.4.

Life Attitude Balance Index Scores

When the LABI scores of all 80 participants were calculated, the *highest* score at the *survival* end of the continuum was 162, and the *lowest* score at the perpetual bereavement end of the continuum was –8. Those with the five *highest* LABI scores were contacted and asked to be interviewed. One of these five women declined and the woman with the sixth highest score was selected to take her place. Those with the five lowest LABI scores were also contacted and asked to be interviewed. One of these five women declined and the woman with the sixth lowest score was selected to take her place. LABI scores for the 10 women interviewed are shown in Table 2.5.

The Distribution of LABI scores for the 80 participants in the study is shown in Fig. 2.1. Note that the mean score for this sample is 84.6, with a standard deviation of 38.62. This compares to a mean score of 94.1 and a standard deviation of 29.98 for the normative sample (number of women = 491; $p < .01$; Reker, 1992, p. 46). Thus, the range of LABI scores within one standard deviation for the women in this study (68%) is 46 to 123, compared to a range of 64 to 124 for women in the normative sample. As expected, the LABI scores from this sample

Table 2.4 Endpoint Scoring of Conceptualized Bereavement Continuum as Measured by Life Attitude Balance Index (LABI) Scores

Perpetual Bereavement						Survival					
LAP–R dimension scores						LAP–R dimension scores					
PU	CO	LC	DA	EV	GS	PU	CO	LC	DA	EV	GS
L = 8	L = 8	L = 8	L = 8	H = 56	H = 56	H = 56	H = 56	H = 56	H = 56	L = 8	L = 8
Total possible LABI score:						Total possible LABI score:					
(32) – (112) = –80						(224) – (16) = 208					

Note. L = lowest possible score; H = highest possible score.

Table 2.5   LABI Scores of Interview Participants

Perpetual Bereavement <——— BEREAVEMENT CONTINUUM ———> Survival	
LABI = –8 (Ellen)	LABI = 162 (Carol)
LABI = –4 (Anita)	LABI = 145 (Julie)
LABI = 17 (Fran)	LABI = 143 (Helen)
LABI = 26 (Bev)	LABI = 140 (Irene)
LABI = 29 (Doris)	LABI = 140 (Gail)

of bereaved women were somewhat negatively skewed from the normative sample.

The Perceived Well-Being Index–Revised (PWB–R)

Research participants also completed the PWB–R, a two-scale measure of perceived psychological and physical well-being (Reker & Wong, 1984; Reker, 1995. The PWB–R was included as an added measure to clarify which participants to interview, if necessary. A copy of the PWB–R and information about its content, prior use, validity, and scoring can be found in the Appendix. Participants' LAP–R scores and PWB–R scores correlated highly ($r = .7691$; $p < .0005$). Accordingly, it was not necessary to use this second instrument to identify women to interview.

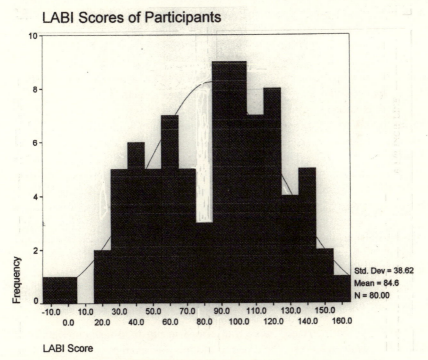

Figure 2.1 Life Attitude Balance Index scores of study participants ($N = 80$).

Participant Questionnaire

The participant questionnaire (see Appendix) consisted of demographic information and variables related to grief resolution. Items included those described in
the literature as being associated with or predictive of the course of parental bereavement, such as circumstances of the death, length of child's illness prior to
the death, perceived social support, additional losses, grief state, current involvement in meaningful pursuits, presence of a sustaining belief system, current existence of "mothering" behaviors, memorialization of the child's life, evidence of a
"turning-point decision" (Sanders, 1999), altruistic activities, and socio-demo-
graphic factors.

Interview Process

In-depth, interactive interviews were conducted with 10 women chosen on the basis
of their LABI scores to represent each end of the bereavement continuum: five
who scored *highest* and five who scored *lowest*. The intent of each interview was
to understand each mother's experience of surviving the death of her only child.
My role as interviewer was to help reconstruct her experiences (physical, emotional, cognitive, behavioral, and spiritual) of what it means to survive this loss.
My aim was to assist each participant in uncovering and discovering the choices
she had made during bereavement and the meaning she attached to her experiences. Did these women see themselves as survivors, and if so, what did that
mean to them? The interviews took place in the participants' homes, each located
in a different state around the U.S.A. Interviews lasted from 2½ to 5½ hours.

Following an initial explanation about the interview and the study, each interview began with the question: "What do I need to know in order to understand
what it has been like for you to survive your child's death?" Follow-up probes
were used as necessary; however, the form of the interviews was dynamic and
conversational, with the answers given to my questions continually informing the
evolving conversation. It was rarely necessary to pose the additional questions
included in the Interview Guide (see Appendix), as most of the participants covered these areas with little or no probing on my part. I shared my own bereavement experience with the participants when it seemed appropriate during our con-
versations. However, my goal was to encourage each participant to tell her own
story, and I carefully chose the points at which I spoke because doing so could
potentially change the topic of discussion. The content of the interviews was comprised of "stories, asides, hesitations, expressions of feeling, and spontaneous
associations" (Paget, 1983, p. 78).

Phenomenological Content Analysis of Interview Data

The tape-recorded interviews were transcribed in unedited fashion. Details of
enunciation were included in the typed transcripts. For example, words that were

emphasized verbally were capitalized and words that were elongated in speech were typed with the last syllable repeated twice (e.g., "not MEE"). The natural dialect of the conversation was reproduced by the use of compressed words when applicable (e.g., "mustov" rather than "must have"). All of these conventions of transcription aimed to achieve a written version that accurately portrayed the dialogue. This is important for the generation of meaning. As Paget noted: "In-depth interviews are contextual rather than abstract in their organization. . . . They respond to features of the ongoing interaction, to nuances of mood, and to the context of the evolving conversation. Yet they create knowledge" (Paget, 1983, p. 69). "The display of speech, not as a grammatical text but as a prosodic system . . . preserves the dynamic construction of talk. Meaning can be seen as it is constituted in the act of saying something and in the way it is said. The complexity, openness, and richness of talk then appear" (Paget, 1983, p. 87).

Preserving this dynamic construction of what was said is an essential part of the interactive, phenomenological interview. "Knowledge in in-depth interviewing means coming to understand, achieving a resolution of puzzlement." It also "means illuminating human experience: the complexity, opaqueness, and mystery of an essentially subjective species" (Paget, 1983, p. 88).

The content of each interview transcript was analyzed phenomenologically. This method of analysis was developed by Fischer (1974) and Giorgi (1975) of Duquesne University, explicated by Hycner (1985), and used by Brice (1987) to study one mother's mourning during the first year after the death of her only child. The analysis was hermeneutic in that it sought "to understand the meaning of processes and experiences rather than to discover causes," and it was phenomenological in that it also sought "to describe the essential intentional and conscious structures of these experiences in addition to their meanings" (Bentz, 1989, p. 15).

The phenomenological analysis followed six steps:

Step 1: First Reading of Interview Transcript—Bracketing Interviewer's Experience   Each interview transcript was read with an attitude of openness, while listening to the audiotape of the interview and paying attention to intonations, emphases, and pauses. I adopted an attitude of openness to the phenomenon by bracketing my response to separate parts of the conversation, by suspending my own meanings and interpretations as much as possible and letting the event emerge as a meaningful whole. This process revealed an overall sense of each participant's experience as reflected in the interview—a gestalt.

Step 2. Delineation of Meaning Units   Each transcript was reread to allow shifts of meaning to show themselves. Using the literal words of the participant, what was said was condensed and crystallized into individual units that expressed unique and coherent meanings that were clearly differentiated from each other.

Step 3. Delineation of Central Themes   These individual meaning units were reviewed vis-à-vis the central question: What does this statement reveal about this participant's life-world as a bereaved mother who has lost her only child? Redundant comments and any not related to the research were deleted. Units that naturally clustered together were identified by a central theme. At this stage the clusters were still quite situation specific. Also, some individual meaning units were listed under more than one cluster/central theme.

Step 4. Delineation of Major Themes   The meaning units and central themes were then reread with the central research question in mind: What is the experience of surviving the death of an only child that is revealed in this particular meaning unit and theme? At this point, a hermeneutical analysis was performed on the data that utilized my own disciplined biases (e.g., I considered the content of the interview data in the light of my knowledge of human development, personality theories, and bereavement research). This allowed me to organize the previously derived central themes around larger major themes. A master list of these major themes was compiled for each participant.

Step 5. Life-World Synopsis   The meaning units, central themes, and major themes were reflected upon with the following questions in mind: What is the participant's world of surviving the death of her child and what meaning does the participant attach to her experiences? Is this mother conscious of changes in herself that have come about during bereavement? If so, what kinds of changes? Does she speculate on what may have produced such changes?

Step 6. Participant Profiles   A participant profile was developed for each interview participant. The profile consisted of the life-world synopsis, responses to the participant questionnaire, and instrument scores.

Summary of Study Design

Using both qualitative and quantitative methods made it possible to gather and analyze data from the entire sample of 80 women and then to take an in-depth look at the experiences of women at opposite ends of the bereavement continuum. The study design is summarized in Fig. 2.2.

OVERVIEW OF STATISTICAL FINDINGS

Statistical analysis was also used to understand the commonalties and differences among the women in the study. Responses to the participant questionnaire were analyzed statistically as described below. The statistical findings are introduced here as an overview and are discussed further as they relate to key aspects covered within the following chapters.

Prior Research: The death of a child presents parents with a severe crisis of meaning.

Hypotheses:

1. Life attitude (whether life has meaning and purpose) reflects whether a bereaved mother has overcome the severe crisis of meaning caused by the death of her only child.

2. Life attitude (whether life has meaning and purpose) is associated with survival for mothers who have lost their only child.

Study Participants (n = 80)   mothers whose only child (age 1–21) died 5 or more years prior due to accident or illness

Interview Sample Selection: based on results of instruments completed by all:

Life Attitude Profile–Revised (LAP–R) and

Perceived Well-Being Scale–Revised (PWB–R)

Interview Sample (n = 10):   represents both ends of conceptualized bereavement continuum:

5 mothers selected a priori to represent "survival"

5 mothers selected a priori to represent "perpetual bereavement"

Conceptualized Bereavement Continuum Based on Life Attitude

<"PERPETUAL BEREAVEMENT" <		> "SURVIVAL">	
LAP–R Scores	PWB–R Scores	PWB–R Scores	LAP–R Scores
LOW:	LOW:	HIGH:	HIGH:
Purpose	Psychological	Psychological	Purpose
Coherence	well-being	well-being	Coherence
Control			Control
Death			Death
acceptance			acceptance
HIGH:	LOW:	HIGH:	LOW:
Existential	Physical	Physical	Existential
vacuum	well-being	well-being	vacuum
Goal seeking			Goal seeking

5 mothers interviewed:	5 mothers interviewed:
Ellen, Anita, Fran, Bev, Doris	Gail, Irene, Helen, Julie, Gail

Participant Questionnaire: Demographic information and variables related to grief resolution.

Statistical Analyses: correlation, discriminant, multiple regression, chi square.

(Continued)

Figure 2.2   Study design, (Sheet 1 of 2).

In-depth Interviews: interactive—conversational—tape-recorded

> >intent: to understand each mother's experience of surviving the death of her only child

> >researcher's role: help participant reconstruct her life-world experiences:

> inside experiences = thoughts and feelings that arise in consciousness
                          to the level of awareness and reflection

> outside experiences = conscious behavior and decisions in relationship to
                          significant others in her life

> >interview transcript: typed unedited, with nonverbal and paralinguistic communications added

Phenomenological Content Analysis (Giorgi, 1975):

> > bracket researcher's experience—adopt attitude of openness
> > read transcript while listening to interview tape
> > delineate individual meaning units of conversation
> > delineate central themes
> > delineate major themes
> > develop life-world synopsis:

> What is this participant's world of surviving the death of her only child?
   What meaning does she attach to her experiences?

Study Data: Individual Participant Profiles

> interviewees = instrument scores, questionnaire data, and
                   life-world synopsis
   all others = instrument scores and questionnaire data

Findings: > results of statistical analysis of questionnaire data
              > descriptions of "survival" and "perpetual (chronic) bereavement"

Discussion: > contrast the life-worlds: Is there a pattern(s) of survival?
                > answer hypotheses and research questions
                > contrast findings with prior research

Conclusions: > implications of the study
                 > limitations of the study
                 > recommendations for further research

Figure 2.2   Study design, (Sheet 2 of 2).

Discriminant Analysis

Question 27 on the participant questionnaire asked participants whether or not they felt they had survived the death of their child. Sixty women answered yes and 12 women answered no. The remaining eight women said "yes and no" and gave written responses indicating they weren't sure if they had survived. What were the differences between the women who said "yes, I have survived," and those who said "no, I haven't survived"? How and why did these two groups differ? Discriminant analysis is a technique that makes it possible to extract from the data a weighted combination of measures (independent variables) that will maximally distinguish groups (Kerlinger, 1979, p. 219)—in this case between those who said they had survived and those who said they hadn't survived.

Thus, using survival as the grouping variable, those who responded "no" to question 27 were coded as 0 and those who responded "yes" were coded as 1. Those who were unsure were coded as 2 and were left ungrouped in the analysis. The independent variables with the highest potential of discriminating between the two groups of women were identified by performing zero-sum correlation analyses between responses to questions on the questionnaire and the participants' Life Attitude Balance Index (LABI) scores. Seven variables correlated strongly with the LABI and were selected as the independent variables for the discriminant analysis. These seven "discriminating" variables, with corresponding discriminant function coefficients shown in parenthesis, were:

1   How helpful participants felt their friends were (.54276).
2   Participants' involvement in volunteer activities (.44579).
3   Participants' level of education (−.15753).
4   Amount of time elapsed between when the participant first realized the child might die and the child's death (.24877).
5   Annual family income level (.46705).
6   How helpful participants felt their religious or spiritual beliefs were (.05863).
7   How frequently participants discussed their grief with others (.41836).

Results of the discriminant analysis are shown in Table 2.6. Table 2.6 indicates

Table 2.6   Discriminant Analysis Groups: "Survival" Versus "Perpetual Bereavement."

Actual Group	Number of Cases	Predicted Group Membership	
		Perpetual Bereavement	Survival
Perpetual bereavement	12	9 (75%)	3 (25%)
Survival	60	7 (11.7%)	53 (88.3%)
Ungrouped cases	8	2 (25%)	6 (75%)
Total	80	18	62

Note. Percent of "grouped" cases correctly classified = 86.11%.

that 86% of the women were correctly classified by the seven independent variables. In other words, for 86% of the participants, the selected variables correctly identified the participant's answer to the question, "Do you believe you have survived the experience of losing your only child?" For those eight women who were unsure whether they had survived, their responses to the seven independent variables predicted that two belonged in the "perpetual bereavement" group and six belonged in the "survival" group.

Comparison of Discriminant Group Responses

The predicted group membership defined by the discriminant analysis was used to divide the 80 participants into two groups: one representing "perpetual bereavement" ($n = 18$) and one representing "survival" ($n = 62$). The frequency of responses to questions on the participant questionnaire was calculated for each predicted group to determine which questions helped to describe the differences between the groups. Chi-square analysis was performed to determine statistical significance. Results are shown in Table 2.7, with statistically significant questions marked with asterisks.

It is important to remember that using discriminant analysis to separate study participants into one group versus another is not done in order to judge the quality of individual participants' survival; rather, it is done in order to identify differences between two groups of participants.

Table 2.7 Comparison of Responses to Participant Questionnaire by Discriminant Groups

Response to Questionnaire	Perpetual Bereavement ($n = 18$) Frequency (%)	Survival ($n = 62$) Frequency (%)	χ^2 (80)
Believe survived child's death:			23.03**
No	9 (50.0)[b]	3 (4.8)	
Yes	7 38.9)	53 (85.5)[b]	
Yes and no	2 (11.1)	6 (9.7)[b]	
Type of Death:			0.00
Disease or illness	5 (27.8)	17 (27.4)	
Accident	13 (72.2)	45 (72.6)	
Time between diagnosis/ accident and child's death:			6.53
No warning	9 (50.0)	34 (54.8)	
Hours	4 (22.2)	11 (17.7)	
Days	0 (0)	7 (11.3)	
Weeks	0 (0)	1 (1.6)	
Months	3 (16.7)	2 (3.2)	
Years	2 (11.1)	6 (9.7)	
No response	0 (0)	1 (1.6)	
Time between realization child might die and actual death:[a]			3.88
No warning	13 (72.2)	39 (62.9)	
Hours	3 (16.7)	11 (17.7)	
Days	0 (0)	6 (9.7)	
Weeks	1 (5.6)	1 (1.6)	
Months	1 (5.6)	2 (3.2)	
Years	0 (0)	3 (4.8)	
Years bereaved:			14.38
5 years	0 (0)	3 (4.8)	
6 years	5 (27.8)	7 (11.3)	
7 years	2 (11.1)	11 (17.7)	
8 years	2 (11.1)	13 (21.0)	
9 years	2 (11.1)	8 (12.9)	
10 years	0 (0)	5 (8.1)	
11 years	1 (5.6)	5 (8.1)	
12 years	3 (16.7)	6 (9.7)	
13 years	2 (11.1)	1 (1.6)	
14 years	0 (0)	1 (1.6)	
17 years	0 (0)	1 (1.6)	
18 years	1 (5.6)	0 (0)	
33 years	0 (0)	1 (1.6)	
Sex of child:			2.67
Female	4 (22.2)	27 (43.5)	
Male	14 (77.8)	35 (56.5)	

(Continued)

Table 2.7   Continued

Response to Questionnaire	Perpetual Bereavement ($n = 18$) Frequency (%)	Survival ($n = 62$) Frequency (%)	χ^2 (80)
Age of child:			12.39
3 years	1 (5.6)	2 (3.2)	
4 years	0 (0)	1 (1.6)	
5 years	0 (0)	1 (1.6)	
6 years	1 (5.6)	2 (3.2)	
7 years	0 (0)	1 (1.6)	
8 years	0 (0)	1 (1.6)	
9 years	1 (5.6)	0 (0)	
10 years	0 (0)	1 (1.6)	
11 years	0 (0)	2 (3.2)	
12 years	1 (5.6)	2 (3.2)	
13 years	0 (0)	1 (1.6)	
14 years	0 (0)	2 (3.2)	
15 years	3 (16.7)	5 (8.1)	
16 years	1 (5.6)	9 (14.5)	
17 years	2 (11.1)	8 (12.9)	
18 years	2 (11.1)	9 (14.5)	
19 years	2 (11.1)	7 (11.3)	
20 years	2 (11.1)	7 (11.3)	
21 years	2 (11.1)	1 (1.6)	
Level of grief felt now:			15.96**
Grief dominates life	3 (16.7)[b]	0 (0)	
Feel grief daily	8 (44.4)[b]	24 (38.7)	
Feel grief weekly	3 (16.7)	16 (25.8)[b]	
Feel grief occasionally	3 (16.7)	22 (35.5)[b]	
No longer grieve	1 (5.6)	0 (0)[b]	
Discuss grief with others today:[a]			25.12**
Never	3 (16.7)[b]	1 (1.6)	
Rarely	8 (44.4)[b]	4 (6.5)	
Occasionally	4 (22.2)	42 (67.7)[b]	
Often	3 (16.7)	15 (24.2)[b]	
Helpfulness of family:			13.17**
Very unhelpful	6 (33.3)[b]	3 (4.8)	
Unhelpful	4 (22.2)[b]	9 (14.5)	
Somewhat helpful	4 (22.2)	22 (35.5)[b]	
Very helpful	4 (22.2)	28 (45.2)[b]	
Helpfulness of friends:[a]			47.89**
Very unhelpful	8 (44.4)[b]	0 (0)	
Unhelpful	6 (33.3)[b]	3 (4.8)	
Somewhat helpful	3 (16.7)	21 (33.9)[b]	
Very helpful	1 (5.6)	38 (61.3)[b]	

(*Continued*)

Table 2.7   Continued

Response to Questionnaire	Perpetual Bereavement ($n = 18$) Frequency (%)	Survival ($n = 62$) Frequency (%)	χ^2 (80)
Attend support group(s):			12.99**
Never attended	3 (16.7)[b]	2 (3.2)	
Once or twice	2 (11.1)[b]	7 (11.3)	
Occasionally	10 (55.6)	16 (25.8)[b]	
Regularly	3 (16.7)	37 (59.7)[b]	
Still attend support group(s):			1.24
No	11 (61.1)	34 (54.8)	
Yes	4 (22.2)	25 (40.3)	
N/A or missing	3 (16.7)	3 (4.8)	
Grief therapy:			4.19
Never	5 (27.8)	22 (35.5)	
Once or twice	3 (16.7)	11 (17.7)	
Occasionally	6 (33.3)	8 (12.9)	
Regularly	4 (22.2)	21 (33.9)	
Significant losses before child's death:			0.14
Yes	16 (88.9)	53 (85.5)	
No	2 (11.1)	9 (14.5)	
Significant life changes 2 years prior:			0.32
No	10 (55.6)	39 (62.9)	
Yes	8 (44.4)	23 (37.1)	
Significant losses after child's death:			5.36*
Yes	18 (10.0)[b]	47 (75.8)[b]	
No	0 (0)	15 (24.2)	
Spiritual/religious beliefs helpful:[a]			3.86
No	6 (33.3)	11 (17.7)	
Both helpful and unhelpful	5 (27.8)	11 (17.7)	
Yes	7 (38.9)	40 (64.5)	
Religion:			0.90
Catholic	7 (38.9)	19 (30.6)	
Protestant/Christian	8 (44.4)	37 (59.7)	
Other	1 (5.6)	5 (8.1)	
No response	0 (0)	1 (1.6)	
Changed religion after death:			1.15
No	7 (38.9)	33 (53.2)	
Yes	11 (61.1)	29 (46.8)	
Importance of religion:			2.76
Not very important	6 (33.3)	17 (27.4)	
Somewhat important	4 (22.2)	9 (14.5)	
Important	5 (27.8)	13 (21.0)	
Very important	3 (16.7)	23 (37.1)	

(Continued)

Table 2.7   Continued

Response to Questionnaire	Perpetual Bereavement (n = 18) Frequency (%)	Survival (n = 62) Frequency (%)	χ^2 (80)
Volunteer work:[a]			22.94**
Does not currently volunteer	14 (77.8)[b]	12 (19.4)	
Volunteered before death, not now	1 (5.6)[b]	2 (3.2)	
Started volunteering after death	2 (11.1)	29 (46.8)[b]	
Volunteered before and after death	1 (5.6)	19 (30.6)[b]	
Volunteer organizations:			33.69
Charities	0 (0)	6 (9.7)	
Church	1 (5.6)	12 (19.4)	
Bereavement support	2 (11.1)	13 (21.0)	
Schools/public education	0 (0)	5 (8.1)	
Community service/hospitals	0 (0)	12 (19.4)	
Does not currently volunteer	15 (83.3)	14 (22.4)	
Find volunteering meaningful:			0.06
No	0 (0)	1 (1.6)	
Yes	3 (16.7)	46 (74.2)	
No response/not applicable	15 (83.3)	15 (24.2)	
Employment:			2.62
Not currently employed	2 (11.1)	16 (25.8)	
Started work after death	3 (16.7)	14 (22.6)	
Worked before and after death	13 (72.2)	32 (51.6)	
Occupation:			7.16
Clerical	6 (33.3)	9 (14.5)	
Service/sales	4 (22.2)	12 (19.4)	
Technical/arts	0 (0)	2 (3.2)	
Professional	2 (11.1)	16 (25.8)	
Managerial	4 (22.2)	7 (11.3)	
Not currently employed	2 (11.1)	16 (25.8)	
Find work meaningful:			0.44
No	4 (22.2)	8 (12.9)	
Yes	12 (66.7)	38 (61.3)	
No response	2 (11.1)	16 (25.8)	
Memorials for child:			0.02
No	1 (5.6)	3 (4.8)	
Yes	17 (94.4)	59 (95.2)	
Learned from motherhood:			0.89
No	1 (5.6)	1 (1.6)	
Yes	17 (94.4)	61 (98.4)	
Current relationships with children:			7.80*
No	9 (50.0)	17 (27.4)	
Yes and no	2 (11.1)	(1.6)	
Yes	7 (38.9)	44 (71.0)	

(Continued)

Table 2.7   Continued

Response to Questionnaire	Perpetual Bereavement ($n = 18$) Frequency (%)	Survival ($n = 62$) Frequency (%)	χ^2 (80)
Marital status:			11.49*
Married—to father of child	5 (27.8)	32 (51.6)	
Married—not to father of child	3 (16.7)	13 (21.0)	
Single—divorced	5 (27.8)	14 (22.6)	
Single—never married	2 (11.1)	0 (0)	
Widowed	3 (16.7)	3 (4.8)	
Ethnicity:			1.55
Caucasian	18(100.0)	57 (92.0)	
African American	0	2 (3.2)	
Hispanic	0	2 (3.2)	
Other	0	1 (1.6)	
Education[a]:			1.13
Less than high school	1 (5.6)	1 (1.6)	
High school graduate	9 (50.0)	29 (46.8)	
College graduate	4 (22.2)	18 (29.0)	
Advanced degree(s)	4 (22.2)	14 (22.6)	
Annual family income:[a]			10.93*
Less than $10,000	1 (5.6)[b]	1 (1.6)	
$10,000–$24,999	6 (33.3)[b]	4 (6.5)	
$25,000–$49,999	6 (33.3)[b]	26 (41.9)	
$50,000–$99,999	4 (22.2)	21 (33.9)[b]	
$100,000 and above	1 (5.6)	10 (16.1)[b]	

[a]Discriminating variable used to determine group membership. [b]These results highlight and contrast statistically significant differences between responses from the two groups. For example, a total of 72.2% of those in the group representing perpetual bereavement had an annual family income of less than $50,000, while half (50%) of those in the survival group had an annual family income of $50,000 or more.
* $p < .05$
** $p < .01$

In addition to multiple-choice and short fill-in responses, the questionnaires provided space for participants to explain their answers. Review of these narrative responses produced four factors that were common among those participants who felt they had survived their loss and grown in positive ways. These "transformative factors" are shown in Table 2.8 and discussed in detail in chapters 6, 8, 10, and 11.

Table 2.8   Transformative Factors by Discriminant Groups

Questionnaire Narrative Responses	Perpetual Bereavement ($n = 18$) Frequency (%)	Survival ($n = 62$) Frequency (%)	χ^2 (80)
Reported experiencing a spiritual crisis following child's death:			6.39*
No crisis reported	5 (27.8)	29 (46.8)[b]	
Yes—Crisis has been resolved	3 (16.7)	18 (29.0)[b]	
Yes—Crisis remains unresolved	10 (55.6)[b]	15 (24.2)	
Reported making a conscious decision to survive:			6.96**
No	11 (61.1)[b]	17 (27.4)	
Yes	7 (38.9)	45 (72.6)[b]	
Reaches out to help others by volunteering or working in a helping profession:			8.66**
No	11 (61.1)[b]	15 (24.2)	
Yes	7 (38.9)	47 (75.8)[b]	
Types of changes in personal identity:			12.17**
Negative identity changes	10 (55.6)[b]	12 (19.4)	
Both negative and positive changes	1 (5.6)	8 (12.9)	
Positive identity changes	4 (22.2)	37 (59.7)[b]	
No identity changes reported	3 (16.7)	5 (8.1)	

[a]*p < .05. ** = p < .01. [b]These results highlight and contrast statistically signficiant differences between responses from the two groups. For example, 55.6% of those in the group representing perpetual bereavement had experienced a spiritual crisis as a result of their child's death that remained unresolved at the time of contact. This contrasts to a total of 75.8% of those in the survival group who either had not experienced a spiritual crisis or if so, had resolved that crisis by the time they were contacted.

Multiple-Regression Analysis

Multiple-regression analysis is a technique that assesses the joint or combined effect of independent variables on a dependent variable (Kerlinger, 1979, p. 167). How might the seven variables included in the discriminant analysis work to-gether to explain the difference (variance observed) in how participants scored on the Life Attitude Balance Index? Results of the regression analysis (forward method) are shown in Table 2.9. Four of the seven variables entered the equation ($p < .05$). As shown in Table 2.9, these four independent variables account for a total of 39% of the variance in LABI scores. In other words, 39% of a participant's LABI score may be accounted for by how she answered the questions represented by the four independent variables listed in Table 2.9.

The results of the multiple-regression analysis shown in Table 2.9 predict that participants' LABI scores were influenced by: (a) how helpful they perceived their friends had been since their child's death (very helpful, somewhat helpful,

Table 2.9 Stepwise Multiple-Regression Analysis Predicting Life Attitude (LABI Score) by Sociodemographic and Bereavement Variables: R^2 = .39

Independent Variable	Pearson R	Beta	Change in R^2
Helpfulness of friends	.45	.32**	.20
Volunteer activities of participants	.44	.29**	.09
Amount of time to anticipate child might die	.26	.25**	.06
Annual family income	.26	.22*	.04

$*p < .05. ** p < .01.$

unhelpful, or very unhelpful); (b) whether they participated in volunteer activities within their community; (c) how much time they had to anticipate their child might die (no warning, hours, days, weeks, months, or years); and (d) the level of their annual family income.

For example, those who said their friends were very helpful or helpful tended to score *high* on the LABI, whereas those who said their friends were unhelpful or very unhelpful tended to score *low*. In those few cases where participants with low LABI scores said their friends were very helpful, they also reported that their family was very unhelpful, and this may have contributed to their lower life attitude score. As was evident from the interviews, support (or nonsupport) from friends and family was mentioned frequently and given considerable importance by mothers as they described what survival has been like for them since their child's death.

Bereavement Continuum Endpoint Profiles

The "predicted" groups identified by statistical analysis, as well as the qualitative analysis of individual interviews, suggest the following prototypical profiles of each end of the bereavement continuum. It is important to remember that these are *group* profiles based on the results of the discriminant analysis presented in Tables 2.7 and 2.8. This means that the "survival" group in Tables 2.7 and 2.8 includes 3 of the women who said they did *not* think they have survived their child's death and 6 who were unsure about survival, as well as 53 who said they had survived. Likewise, the "perpetual bereavement" group includes 7 women who said they *do* think they have survived their child's death, 2 who are unsure, and 9 who said they haven't survived.

These findings are *not* generalizable to the entire population of bereaved parents, nor should they be used to classify bereaved parents into one group or another. They are included here to introduce some of the factors that illuminate the qualitative difference between what it means to survive and reinvest in life again and what it means to remain in a state of chronic mourning after a child dies.

Profile of Chronic Mourning

Those in the "perpetual bereavement" group continued to experience high levels of grief, yet generally they did not discuss their grief with others. They were not actively involved in a grief support group, and they perceived their family and/or friends as unhelpful to them. Most did not have significant relationships with other children, and were not involved in volunteer activities within their community. Many were struggling with a spiritual crisis that had not been resolved, and some believed they had changed in negative ways since their child's death. Many had a low standard of living.

The five women interviewed who had the *lowest* life attitude scores all lacked an adequate support system and coping skills. They were hesitant to reach out to others for help and continued to experience recurrent acute grief, helplessness, psychological instability, and stress-related physical ailments. These women experienced the loss of their parenting role as identity disintegration: loss of self, goals, purpose for living, and future. Living a new, purposeful life would mean forgetting the child, denying the child's existence, and invalidating their past life as the child's mother. All five women demonstrated ongoing ambivalence about living. They remained angry at God and/or their church and had been unable to incorporate their child's death into a beneficial belief system. Their focus was on reviewing aspects of the loss and the effect that unresolved grief was having on their lives. All five, however, had made difficult choices or decisions prior to their child's death that indicated their potential to decide to survive and reinvest in life again at some point in the future.

Profile of Survival

Grief was present but no longer dominated the lives of those representing "survival." They were apt to discuss the grief they did feel with others, often at grief support groups. They perceived their family and friends as helpful to them. They were likely to have remained married to their child's father and to have established significant relationships with other children since their child's death. They were also very likely to be involved in some type of volunteer activity within their community. These women had found their spiritual beliefs helpful to them or they had confronted and worked through a spiritual crisis, resulting in a redefining of their spiritual beliefs. They were likely to have perceived some positive changes in their identity as a result of coping with their grief and loss. Their family income level was likely to be above $50,000 per year.

The five women interviewed who had the *highest* life attitude scores had all made a conscious decision to survive and to reinvest in life. All had sought and accepted help from others and learned to use a wide variety of coping skills to deal with their grief and take care of themselves. Some had replaced nonsupportive family and friends with new, understanding others. All continued to experience periodic shadow grief and saw bereavement as an evolving, lifelong learning process with some positive benefits.

These five women experienced the death of their only child as identity crisis: the loss of part of the self, goals, purpose for living, and future. However, they saw their child as a separate and distinct personality and they saw themselves as possessing unique attributes and strengths. All five had learned from life crises prior to their child's death, that may have strengthened their self-esteem. These women had struggled severely with acute trauma and grief, but when interviewed they had regained self-control and integrated what they had learned from bereavement into a new identity and a new worldview. Their purpose for living was focused on maintaining a connection with their child and using mothering skills to nurture themselves and others, often through volunteer activities and/or employment in a "helping" profession. They had consciously taken responsibility for their own healing, and saw themselves as becoming better people.

Limitations of the "Mothers Now Childless" Study

The participants in this study were women who sought out and received support in the form of a newsletter for bereaved parents with no surviving children. In addition, half of these women had attended a bereavement support group regularly after the death of their child and another 26% had attended occasionally. A quarter of the sample received regular grief therapy after their child's death, and another 17% received occasional grief therapy after their loss. We do not know how many or how frequently those in the larger population of bereaved parents seek help, attend support groups, and/or participate in grief therapy. Likewise, we do not know how the incidence of volunteering and other characteristics demonstrated by this sample of 80 women compare to the general population of bereaved mothers and fathers. Psychological and spiritual experiences are never exactly predictable, nor repeatable. This is because "our inner experience differs from that of all others and is constantly changing" (LeShan, 1990, p. 135). Thus these findings cannot be generalized to the entire population of bereaved parents. However, it is equally true that what has been learned about survival, chronic mourning, personal transformation, and reinvestment in life following this traumatic loss is potentially transferable to other bereaved parents. This is especially true because it is in identifying both what they have in common and how they are different that parents learn what their unique loss of a special child means for their lives.

SUMMARY

What can we take away from the material presented here? First, we can focus on those variables that accounted for the disparity in these participants' life attitude scores and their belief about whether they had survived their child's death. These included:

The level of grief still being experienced and frequency of sharing it with
supportive others.

The perceived helpfulness of friends and family.

The impact of additional losses since the child's death.

Making a conscious decision to survive.

The perceived effect of changes in personal identity.

Marital status, income level, and relationships with other children.

Reaching out to help others by volunteering or working in helping professions.

Resolving spiritual questions brought about by the child's death.

Second, we can try to understand how these factors and perhaps others work
together over time as bereavement evolves. The following chapters discuss these
identified topics, providing quotes, examples, and discussion to add content and
context. Each chapter will likely bring up additional questions that may influence
whether and how the material is useful to other bereaved parents. We must ask
ourselves: What about this topic may be true for other parents? What is most
important and what is least important? What about this topic will be meaningful
to a father whose child was murdered; to a mother whose oldest son died by
suicide; to those who now find themselves parents of an only child whose sibling
has died? What seems to apply and what doesn't? This is exactly the same sort-
ing-through process that so often amazes and overwhelms bereaved parents: Everything about their lives is now seen in the light and darkness of the unrelenting
fact that their unique child died. Parents caught up in the painful waves of acute
grief often wonder if they are going crazy. We offer them hope when we help
them understand the severe and fluctuating yet "normal" symptoms that can characterize their grief process. Chapter 3 discusses how grief evolves after the death
of a child.

When a Child Dies, Does Grieving Ever End?

The poet Kahlil Gibran (1923, pp. 17–18) has described what it means to have children, to be a parent:

> Your children are not your children.
> They are the sons and daughters of Life's
>   longing for itself.
> They come through you but not from you,
> And though they are with you, yet they
>   belong not to you.
>
> You may give them your love but not your
>   thoughts,
> For they have their own thoughts.
> You may house their bodies but not
>   their souls,
> For their souls dwell in the house of
>   tomorrow, which you cannot visit,
>   not even in your dreams.
> You may strive to be like them, but seek
>   not to make them like you.
> For life goes not backward nor tarries
>   with yesterday.
>
> You are the bows from which your children
>   as living arrows are sent forth.
> The archer sees the mark upon the path of
>   the infinite, and He bends you with
>   His might that His arrows may go
>   swift and far.

> Let your bending in the archer's hand
> be for gladness;
> For even as He loves the arrow that flies,
> so He loves also the bow that is stable.

The poem speaks to the evolution of life, to the part parents and children play in creating the future together. When a child dies, the personal and unique future created by the relationship of parent and child is destroyed. Contrary to the poet's message, when a child dies life seems to go backward. The world suddenly is no longer what it has promised to be. The natural order of things has been violated and parents are left with only memories of yesterdays. Life as they have known it dies along with their child. Henceforth, they must take on a role not of their choosing—that of a bereaved parent.

THE WORST LOSS

Many researchers have concluded that bereaved parents are confronted with the most difficult form of bereavement (Cleiren, 1993; Knapp, 1986; Osterweis, Solomon, & Green, 1984; Rando, 1986; Rosof, 1994; Sanders, 1979–1980, 1999). This is because the loss is so multifaceted. Parents not only lose their unique relationship with a valued and loved child, they lose the part of them that that child represents. They lose the future that the child and they would otherwise have created together. They lose the immortality of being survived by the child and the child's descendants. And they lose their false illusions about the degree of control they have over life (Edelstein, 1984).

When there are surviving siblings, there is a reordering in the family structure. The roles filled by the child who died fall to those who are left or go unfilled. Parents no longer have the opportunity to physically parent the deceased child, and their relationships with the child's surviving siblings are changed forever as well. Six months after her 20-year-old son Aaron died from a fall while on a fishing trip, Nancy told his 18-year-old sister, Emily, "I never wanted you to be an only child." Theirs had always been a loving, close family, and both children had matured through their teenage years and developed deep friendships with their parents. Just weeks prior to her brother's accident, Emily had moved away from home to begin college. Nancy and Kurt, Aaron's father, encouraged Emily to return to school. They missed her greatly, looked forward to her frequent weekend visits, but also found it incredibly painful each time she would have to leave again. Emily missed and worried about both her parents and how they were coping without her. She struggled to grieve for her brother and go on with her new life in a busy college community. She thought that perhaps she would study psychology and some day help others who grieve. Nancy encouraged her daughter to not feel guilty about finding whatever happiness she can. At the same time, Nancy also worried about the possibility of losing Emily too. Bereaved parents live forever with this death of innocence, this knowledge that however unlikely, the worst could happen again.

Parents who have lost an only child or all their children face an additional loss. They lose the role of parent. No one calls them mother or father anymore. Their branch of the family tree suffers a total amputation. The word inheritance takes on an altogether different meaning. It is no longer possible to pass on to their descendants what they have worked hard to accumulate and learn. Many wonder who will be there to help them cope with the changes and challenges of old age.

A child's death irrevocably alters virtually every aspect of a bereaved parent's life. The emotional, cognitive, physical, social, and spiritual changes that take place work together to confront bereaved parents with a heightened responsibility for a new existence. Circumstances surrounding the child's death present unique issues that bereaved parents revisit, often repeatedly, as they face this new, unwanted existence.

Death After a Long Illness

Parents who have to watch their child die over a long period of time often are exhausted both physically and emotionally, and many describe themselves as initially "too numb to grieve." Many questions must be answered in order to understand what bereavement is like for these parents. For example: What was it like for them at the time the illness was diagnosed? How were treatment decisions made and what was involved in the treatment protocol? How did the child respond to the treatment? What were the family's relationships with the medical caregivers like? Did they have an opportunity to get all their questions answered about the child's illness? What was it like for the parents to function on a daily basis while the child was ill? What kind of support and resources did they have or lack? In what ways did the parents participate in daily caregiving for the child and how did this impact the rest of the family? Did they talk with their child about the possibility of death? Were they able to say goodbye? Were they present at the time of death? What regrets do they have about the ways they and their child fought the illness? What kinds of things are the parents telling themselves "if only" about? Are there things the parents were able to do to make their child's final days special and/or to work through unfinished business in the relationship? What are the most important things they learned from the uniqueness of their child's illness and death? How might they use what they have learned?

Some parents are able to sort through these questions in the early years of acute grief and move on to other aspects of their loss that are unrelated to the circumstances surrounding the child's death. Other parents find themselves emotionally overwhelmed by one or more of these issues and feel stuck in a repetitive cycle of intrusive images, blame and guilt. Some parents may disagree about circumstances and decisions made during the child's illness. They may need to realize when they have reached an impasse about this and then turn their focus toward areas in their relationship they do agree on that can help them move forward as a couple and as parents. Thus, when bereaved parents come for therapy it is important to ask what it was like for them before and during their child's illness and how these experiences have impacted their lives since the child's death.

It is also important to acknowledge that no matter how well the parents feel they and their child fought the illness, parents are never prepared for the death of their child. Lauraine talked about what it was like to care for her 21-year-old daughter Marie who died of bone cancer. "We did what we could for her . . . . We made pleasure trips out of going to the hospital. She knew she'd be throwing up a few hours later, so we tried to find something fun to do to make that day less of a bummer. My philosophy is to try to celebrate every little thing because you never know what tomorrow may bring." Marie died after 5 years in remission. "Living with the disease was hard," Lauraine said, "but nothing compared to what it was like after Marie's death . . . . You're never prepared for someone you love to die, and it's just as hard as any other kind of death" (Fox, 2001, p. 151).

Sudden Death

When a child dies as a result of a sudden accident or illness, time stands still and parents are overwhelmed by shock and disbelief. They must live forever knowing they did not have the opportunity to say goodbye, to say I love you one more time, to work through unfinished business, to say I'm sorry and thank you. Many questions confront these parents, who often are so traumatized they cannot hear or understand the details told to them when they are notified of their child's death. Some will never know the full story of what happened. What was their child's death like? Who was there? Who and/or what was responsible? Could the death have been prevented? What might have been different, if only . . . ? How could this have happened? Did it really happen or was it all a mistake, a bad dream?

Life feels surreal, and often those around them don't understand how much time parents need to even begin taking in their awful new reality. Later, as they reflect back, many parents say they honestly can't remember much of those first few months after their child died. They often describe going through the motions of living in a bewildering fog. When the fog begins to lift as the shock wears off, parents often awaken to a compelling and painful need to know what happened. This need to know often is accompanied by fear that they cannot bear to hear the answers.

When there has been conflict in the relationship with their child, as so often happens in the teenage years, parents can struggle with memories of harsh words and arguments. Don Hackett (1986), a bereaved father whose son Olin died at age 17, told what it was like for him to live with the unpleasant last words he and his son spoke to each other. In a Compassionate Friends newsletter article titled "Death During or Following Conflict," he wrote: "It took many months of soul-searching, with much time spent in the abyss of depression and despair, before I could come to terms with the conflict that seemed to cloud the loving nature of our relationship." His working through process helped him realize:

> The love between parent and child, before, during, and after the teenage years, keeps both vulnerable to disagreement or conflict. I finally came to understand that, had the situation been reversed, and I had died, Olin would feel a greater intensity of that same type of remorse and guilt. Like me, Olin would finally be forced to examine our years together, to remember other conflicts, and recall the constancy of the love and care with which all were ultimately resolved. I believe he would come to realize that I did not doubt his love, that a petty argument had no power to devastate what love had built between us.

When a sudden accident freezes their relationship, it takes time for parents to be able to step back and view the whole relationship. As they come to understand the circumstances of their child's death, parents must decide what weight to give them and how they fit into the larger context of the child's life.

Death by Suicide

The issues just described that accompany a sudden death are compounded by additional questions parents confront when their child dies by suicide. Thirteen years after her youngest son died by suicide, Ethel believed she had survived and grown in many ways. Yet she continued to live with the why questions, the unanswerable questions that haunt so many survivors of suicide. "It is difficult for me to know whether Billy was depressed or not at the time of his death," she said. "It is one of the questions which run through my mind over and over again as I try to figure out what is true, what was really going on with Billy, why he would do such a thing."

Many parents feel they should have been able to prevent their child's suicide. Many feel ashamed and abandoned. There is often less social support for these parents from those around them who do not know what to say or do to comfort them. The stigma of suicide can make parents feel ostracized. Survivors, including the child's siblings and close friends, can be at greater risk for suicide themselves. They need to understand that suicide results from the kind of extreme hopelessness that brings unbearable pain and makes it seem impossible to continue living. This inner struggle was eloquently described in a pastor's sermon as part of the eulogy of a teenager who shot himself. "Our friend died on his own battlefield. He was killed in action fighting a civil war. He fought against adversaries that were as real to him as his casket is real to us. They were powerful adversaries. They took toll of his energies and endurance. They exhausted the last vestiges of his courage, and only God knows how this child of His suffered in the silent skirmishes that took place in his soul." How important it must have been for this child's parents to hear this public acknowledgment of his private, overwhelming pain!

Homicidal Death

Five years after her 20-year-old daughter Nancy was murdered, Deborah Spungen published her personal account of surviving this nightmare. The book's title, *And I Don't Want to Live This Life* (Spungen, 1983), aptly describes the reality and rage of parents whose children are murdered. The intensity of pain these parents feel is impossible to put into words, but some have tried. Sixteen years after the kidnap and murder of his son Adam, John Walsh published *Tears of Rage* (1997), a brutally poignant account of a family's personal and public tragedy. "We were like two wounded, dying animals," John writes in describing the day he and his wife Reve learned of Adam's death. Slowly these two heartbroken parents began to channel the energy of their rage into founding the National Center for Missing and Exploited Children. Using their own unique gifts, the Walshes fought the inadequacies of the criminal justice system. Their efforts resulted in the passage of many new laws and the birth of the TV show "America's Most Wanted," which John Walsh hosts each week. Because of what happened to Adam Walsh and what his parents did about it, fugitives are being captured and other deaths prevented. Adam's mother, Reve, wrote: "I remember thinking, 'our son's been murdered, and now we've got to be the ones to do something about it?' It was a sad thing for this country that the fight had to be led by two broken-down parents of a murdered child. But we had to, because no one else was going to do it." And because they have shared their experiences, other parents who must endure the kidnap and/or murder of a child know they are not alone with their grief and that it is possible to survive such trauma.

There are so many aspects about a child's murder that add complexity to the parents' grief. The death is pointless, and parents are often tormented by what they think happened in their child's final hours. They may never know, or want to know, the details. They may have to endure and relive the details of their tragedy during a long courtroom trial. They may have to live knowing their child's murderer has not been caught, or that the murderer could someday be released from prison to murder again. These parents live forever with a need to understand how there can be such evil in this world. Their anger can harden into bitterness and destroy both past memories and current relationships. They may be terrified that the child's siblings or someone else they love could be murdered or victimized. The inept and hurtful responses of others, including those in the criminal justice system, can bring secondary injury to parents. This is especially true when others imply that the child precipitated his or her own death, such as by hitchhiking or being involved in drugs. Such "blaming the victim" translates into blame for parents who are themselves co-victims and already agonizing over their inability to protect their child.

The extreme circumstances unique to a child's murder cause these parents' grief to be traumatic, delayed, and complicated. The major characteristics experienced by homicide survivors are described by therapist Lula Redmond (1989, p. 31) as "cognitive dissonance, disbelief and murderous impulses, conflict of values and belief system, and withdrawal of support due to the stigma of murder. Survivors must deal with feelings of fear and vulnerability, anger, rage, shame, blame and guilt, and emotional withdrawal." She notes that "the lack of familiarity with and support by law enforcement, the criminal justice system, and media intrusion also lead to bereavement complications" for survivors. "The delays in resolution of the murder conviction, lack of adequate punishment for the crime, and lack of acknowledgment by society heighten the feelings of loss of control."

Like the Walshes, Deborah Spungen experienced all of these complications after her daughter was murdered. She began channeling her anger and rage into advocating for and working with other homicide survivors. She founded the on-going Families of Murder Victims program and continues to advocate for victims of crime. In 1997, 19 years after her daughter's death, Spungen published another book—*Homicide: The Hidden Victims—A Guide for Professionals*. It provides information and resources on how best to notify a family of the murder of a loved one and details the various effects of homicide on the family and friends of victims. The book includes useful interventions and advocacy techniques for those who help survivors, as well as coping strategies for caregivers who are themselves at risk for developing "vicarious traumatization" (McCann & Pearlman, 1990).

Each child's death brings unique circumstances, as noted earlier, which contribute in their own way to the grief of parents, family, and friends. But circumstances do not make some parents' pain worse than others. The pain that a child's death brings cannot be measured, classified, or evaluated and it is pointless, if not harmful, to try. Bereaved parents realize this instinctively, but it is important to acknowledge to them that no one else will ever totally understand their pain and grief. Likewise, parents need to know that everyone grieves in his or her own way: that there are no rules and no time limits. However, they may begin to feel some control over life again by learning more about their grief process, and how it differs from and/or is similiar to that of others who are grieving the same type of loss.

UNDERSTANDING THE GRIEF PROCESS

"What man can live and not see death, or save himself from the power of the grave?" (Psalm 89:48, *The New International Version of the Bible*). This timeless question goes to the heart of the interest in the subject of death. People are interested, often profoundly so, in things they cannot control. One way to gain some level of control over the fearsome finality of death is by trying to understand it. Numerous questions have been and continue to be investigated regarding the state of bereavement after the death of a loved one. First among these was the question of pathology.

The Question of Pathology

The intensity and diversity of grief symptoms cause many grievers and those around them to question their sanity, to need someone to reassure them their grief is normal. It could be said that the goal of psychology since its recognition as a discipline has been to discover and clarify what is "normal" about the human experience. Freud (1917/1957), the "father" of psychology, distinguished normal *mourning* from the disease of *melancholia*. He claimed that while the two shared certain affects, the distinguishing factor between them was that "the disturbance of self-regard" was absent in mourning (p. 244) and that "melancholia [unlike mourning] is in some way related to an object-loss which is withdrawn from consciousness" (p. 245). In today's parlance, Freud could be said to be differentiating between *situational depression* and *major (clinical) depression.*

The process of normal mourning, according to Freud, included recognition of the loss of a loved object through continual reality testing, leading to the unwilling, painful, and gradual withdrawal of the libido involved in attachment to the object. This withdrawal (commonly termed "letting go") would ultimately produce the freedom necessary to take up new attachments. If detachment was made unsuccessful by yearning for the lost object, however, Freud (1917/1957) predicted psychosis would result (pp. 244–245). Bowlby (1961) agreed with Freud that "insatiable and persistent yearning for the lost object" signals pathological mourning (p. 324). However, Bowlby (1980) also clarified that "searching and yearning behavior" is a part of normal mourning. He believed that "searching and yearning" must be expressed sufficiently (rather than repressed) so that the mourner's efforts to recover the lost loved one were repeatedly frustrated. The mourner would then admit defeat, thereby becoming able to accept the reality of the death.

Researchers have pointed out that neither Freud, who was mainly interested in depression, nor Bowlby, who studied the mother–infant relationship, was directly studying death. As Pollock (1961) noted, "Usually we assume that mourning and the reaction to permanent loss without death are equivalent. This equation, though not rejected, requires further demonstration. Differences may be present which allow for more precise description" (p. 343). Lindemann (1944/1965) studied the effects of deaths due to war and calamities of nature. He reached the conclusion that pathological grieving could to some extent be predicted by knowledge of the mourner's premorbid personality. For example, he believed those with an obsessive or depressive personality are more prone to distorted grief reactions. Bowlby (1969) added to this line of thinking by proposing that such a predisposed personality is often developed by the occurrence of less than satisfactory responses to losses provoked during infancy and childhood. These responses (e.g., persistent separation anxiety and angry, aggressive efforts to recover the lost object) occur "in such degree, over such length of time, or with such frequency, that a disposition is established to respond to all subsequent losses in a similar way" (pp. 317–318). Further, Bowlby pointed out that the quality of the relationship with the deceased can be a significant factor in determining the severity of grief reactions.

The question of pathology has evolved to focus on the multiple effects of bereavement, all of which must be understood within the context of the mourner's life-world. Pathological grief continues to be difficult to define. The current version of the *Diagnostic and Statistical Manual of Mental Disorders* (*DSM–IV*; American Psychiatric Association, 1994) includes a category (V62.82) that attempts to describe "normal bereavement" and to differentiate it from posttraumatic stress disorder and major depressive disorder. But it is common, if not arguably "normal," for bereaved parents to experience posttraumatic stress symptoms and major depression, especially after a sudden violent death (cf. Murphy et al., 1999). Rando's research and clinical experiences with bereaved parents led her to conclude:

> The simple fact is that what is considered abnormal or pathological in other losses is typical after the death of a child in the sense that it is experienced by the majority of bereaved parents. Failure to delineate a new, more appropriate model of mourning and to determine what constitutes pathology within this group has resulted in the development of inappropriate and unrealistic expectations for bereaved parents, who cannot and must not be expected to have the same bereavement experiences as other mourners. (Rando, 1993, p. 630)

A new diagnostic category, traumatic grief, has been proposed and is under study for the *DSM–V* (Jacobs, Mazure, & Prigerson, 2000; Neimeyer, 2000). This new category (see Table 3.1) includes a unidimensional cluster of symptoms that

Table 3.1 Criteria for Traumatic Grief (Proposed for *DSM-V*, Axis I)

Criterion A:
1. The person has experienced the death of a significant other.
2. The response involves intrusive, distressing preoccupation with the deceased person (e.g., yearning, longing, or searching).

Criterion B (at least 6 of 11): In response to the death, the following symptom(s) is/are marked and persistent:

1. Frequent efforts to avoid reminders of deceased (e.g., thoughts, feelings, activities, people, places).
2. Purposelessness or feelings of futility about future.
3. Subjective sense of numbness, detachment, or absence of emotional responsiveness.
4. Feeling stunned, dazed, or shocked.
5. Difficulty acknowledging the death (e.g., disbelief).
6. Feeling that life is empty or meaningless.
7. Difficulty in imagining a fulfilling life without deceased.
8. Feeling that a part of oneself has died.
9. Shattered worldview (e.g., lost sense of security, trust, or control).
10. Assumes symptoms or harmful behaviors of, or related to, the deceased person.
11. Excessive irritability, bitterness, or anger related to the death.

Criterion C: The duration of the disturbance (symptoms listed) is at least 2 months.

Criterion D: The disturbance causes clinically significant impairment in social, occupational, or other important areas of functioning.

Source. Jacobs et al. (2000).

are claimed to be empirically separate from depressive symptoms and that do not respond to medication.

The traumatic grief category, as proposed, does a better job of clarifying the debilitating symptoms often experienced by bereaved parents. It hopefully will result in more insurance coverage for parents who seek counseling. But when putting the diagnostic categories into practice, it is vitally important to convey to bereaved parents that *they* are not "disordered." Their grief is extreme, traumatic, debilitating, and frequently requires professional intervention. But it is *not* abnormal for this loss. Bereaved parents who seek or are sent for counseling are at risk for secondary injury when they are subjected to assessment and diagnosis. Bereaved mother and journalist Elizabeth Mehren (1997) provided an example:

> One of the many odd and unforgettable experiences that surrounded my daughter's death was my visit to a—how can I word this in a way that is both polite and accurate?—hmm, well, a member of the mental health profession. My husband and my primary care physician were worried. They felt my grief and sadness over Emily's death were out of bounds. They felt I had somehow changed (which I of course had, but it took me—not to mention them—a while to figure this out). They felt I was different (ditto). They decided that it might help if I "talked things over" with someone. In other words, a psychiatrist.
>
> . . . This is where the story gets interesting. Because after I poured out my heart to this large, overweight, bearded stranger who went to great lengths to avoid direct eye contact with me, he asked a series of questions to which I was supposed to answer yes or no, much as in a jury trial. But when he asked me if I heard "voices that are not there," I was stumped. Well, if I hear them, I mused, how do I know they're not there? This time he did make eye contact, shooting me an icy glare. "Logically," he said in a voice of clinical dispassion, "you are of course correct."
>
> Since I felt like Alice tumbling down the rabbit hole toward Wonderland—a sensation that many parents have described to me, although not always in those terms—it was strange to hear the concept of logic introduced into the conversation. Since when did logic have one single thing to do with the death of one's child!
>
> After tallying the yes and no answers, the mental health professional came up with the following conclusion: "It is impossible to determine," he intoned, "whether you are suffering from normal grief or from extreme pathological grief." As if there were one whit of distinction! And as if—if there were—it would make one shred of difference! (Mehren, 1997, pp. 105–107)

Parents who have experiences like this do not make return visits. Interestingly, we do not know how often bereaved parents leave a professional's office feeling unheard, misunderstood, and/or judged and never return. There has been no research of bereaved parents who leave counseling "against medical advice" or never consider it in the first place. We do know that some parents in acute grief find completing even brief questionnaires to be confusing and overwhelming. We also know that establishing rapport and trust with bereaved parents is critically important. Asking how we can best help them and what we need to know in order to understand their grief conveys our interest in and respect for each unique parent.

The Question of Duration

Another question central to the study of bereavement has been its duration. In later years, Freud experienced the death of his daughter and grandson and as a result modified his thinking about the resolution of grief. In a letter to his friend Binswanger, he noted that although the acute stage of grief eventually subsides, the bereaved are never able to fill the particular gap left by their loved one and do not wish to because this would mean relinquishing their love for the deceased (Binswanger, 1957, p. 106). Pollock (1961) pointed out the necessity of recognizing the significance of who and what are lost, as well as the degree of maturity of the mourner. He noted that "in all probability the purest form of the mourning process occurs in mature adults. Even here, however, the loss of a child can never be fully integrated and totally accepted by the mother or the father" (p. 353).

"Studies have shown that in comparison with other types of bereavement the grief of parents is particularly severe (Clayton, 1980; Clayton, Desmarais, & Winokur, 1968; Sanders, 1979–1980; Schwab, Chalmers, Conroy, Farris, & Markush, 1975; Shanfield & Swain, 1984; Singh & Raphael, 1981), complicated, and long lasting (Osterweis, Solomon, & Green, 1984), with major and unparalleled symptom fluctuations occurring over time (Fish & Whitty, 1983; Levav, 1982; Rando, 1983)" Rando, 1986, p. 6. Rando (1986) asserted that the loss of a child is sufficiently different from other types of bereavement "to warrant consideration of new norms for duration of parental grief response" (p. 351). She later identified seven syndromes indicative of complicated mourning. Three of these syndromes (absent, delayed, and inhibited mourning) involve problems in expression; three involve skewed aspects (distorted, conflicted, and unanticipated mourning); and the seventh (chronic mourning) represents problems with closure (1993, p. 156). Rando's (1993) guidelines and recommendations provide a useful framework for understanding, normalizing, and treating the varied, complex, and traumatic aspects of bereaved parents' grief.

Research indicates that individuals who are able to identify and incorporate what their experiences mean to their life are less likely to develop posttraumatic stress disorder even when stress reactions have been extreme right after the traumatic event (Neimeyer, 2000; Rando, 1993, p. 435). Therapeutic approaches that help bereaved parents understand and/or construct the meaning of their experiences are particularly useful. See, for example, chapter 9, "Narrative Disruptions in the Construction of the Self," in Neimeyer and Raskin (2000), and chapter 9, "Intervening in the Six 'R' Processes," in Rando (1993).

Just as Freud came to believe that some losses are grieved forever, others have reached similar conclusions (cf. Rosenblatt, 1996). After a child dies, it is doubtful that grief ever completely ends for bereaved parents, but there can be solace, adaptation, and resolution. Researchers have sought to understand what happens to bring about such healing.

THE GRIEF PROCESS AND THEORIES OF GRIEF RESOLUTION

Most bereavement theories describe grieving in terms of stages, phases, processes, or tasks, with discussions regarding its content and structure that relate to the questions of pathology and duration. Table 3.2 summarizes four well-known grief process theories.

APPLYING GRIEF THEORIES TO BEREAVED PARENTS

The Role of "Acceptance"

The most widely known grief theory comes from psychiatrist Elizabeth Kübler-Ross's work with the dying (1969). The grieving process she identified as common among patients who were anticipating their own death became known not as "the five stages of dying" but as "the five stages of grieving." Unfortunately, oversimplification and misinterpretation of Kübler-Ross's contributions have too often resulted in a prescriptive approach to grieving. The implication is that appropriate processing and working through will lead to the final grief stage she termed *acceptance*. This is not only an unrealistic expectation for bereaved parents, it frequently complicates their grief even further. Carol, whose only child died at age 15 from muscular dystrophy, provides an example:

> I will not accept the term acceptance. I feel this way and this is what I say to our [support group] members and when I speak to groups on grief. "What do you mean by acceptance? If you mean that I am to accept this unacceptable reality which is against all the laws of nature of burying your child before yourself, I'll say no. If you mean acceptance is letting go of some of the pain associated with the death, then I will say, ok. However, that isn't the way the term acceptance is used. So I have to look at things that will help us to reinvest into life, and that to me is coming to a resolution that my child always was and always will be a part of my life. And [if] you allow me to do that, then I can resolve myself to the fact that I will have to live without him physically the rest of my life. But if you don't allow him to remain a part of my life, then that's going to put a wedge in our relationship."

Carol was urged to accept her son's death by her best friend, who also insinuated that knowing his disease was terminal should have helped her to anticipate and accept his death.

> She has pained me so. . . . She said to me: "You knew Scott was going to die from the time you were told he had muscular dystrophy." She said: "Now put him away and put it aside and get on with your life." And she has 5 healthy children! And she never allowed me to say his name again.

Carol demonstrates how important it is to understand not only the derivation of grief theories but also how those theories are being operationalized. In explaining the stage of "acceptance" reached by dying patients, Kübler-Ross (1969) ad-

Table 3.2. Grief Process Theories (Sheet 1 of 2)

Elizabeth Kübler-Ross (1969, *On Death & Dying*)	John Bowlby (1980, *Attachment & Loss*, Vol. III)
NOTE: This theory applies to the dying and was not intended as a bereavement resolution theory.	**Phase 1: Numbing**
	The mourner's initial response is characterized by shock, panic, or anger. This phase is usually fairly brief.
Stage 1: Denial and Isolation	**Phase 2: Yearning and Searching**
"I favor talking about death and dying with patients long before it actually happens if the patient indicates that he wants to." (p. 39)	The mourner exhibits feelings and behaviors associated with the urge to recover the lost loved one: alternating belief and disbelief that the death has occurred, restless searching, intermittent hope, repeated disappointment.
Stage 2: Anger	**Phase 3: Disorganization and Despair**
"When the first stage of denial cannot be maintained any longer, it is replaced by feelings of anger, rage, envy, and resentment. The logical next question becomes: Why Me?" (p. 50)	Despair sets in when hopes of reunion gradually fade. Mourner is unable to maintain active interchange with the world and experiences restlessness or apathy, with concurrent anxiety and depression (differentiated from depressive illness).
Stage 3: Bargaining	**Phase 4: Reorganization**
"The bargaining is really an attempt to postpone; it has to include a prize offered 'for good behavior,' it also sets a self-imposed deadline (e.g., one more performance, the son's wedding), and it includes an implicit promise that the patient will not ask for more if this one postponement is granted." (P. 84)	The mourner must tolerate the pain of emotional detachment and alarm of disorganization in order to become open to new possibilities of a world without the deceased.
Stage 4: Depression	Gradually the mourner begins to adapt to the new environment by responding in appropriate ways to his or her new life.
Dying patients often experience two types of depression: Reactive Depression: related to losses associated with the illness Preparatory Depression: contemplation of impending death	
Stage 5: Acceptance	
"If a patient has had enough time (i.e., not a sudden, unexpected death) and has been given some help in working through the . . . stages, he will reach a stage during which he is neither depressed nor angry about his "fate. . . . Acceptance should not be mistaken for a happy stage. It is almost void of feelings." (p. 113)	

Table 3.2 Grief Process Theories (Sheet 2 of 2)

J. William Worden (1991, *Grief Counseling & Grief Therapy*, 2nd ed.)	Therese A. Rando (1993, *Treatment of Complicated Mourning*)
FOUR TASKS OF MOURNING:	**NOTE:** Complicated mourning is present whenever, considering the amount of time since the death, there is some compromise, distortion, or failure of one or more of these six processes:
1. To accept the reality of the loss.	**AVOIDANCE PHASE**
"When someone dies, even if the death is expected, there is always a sense that it hasn't happened. . . . Coming to an acceptance of the reality of the loss takes time since it involves not only an intellectual acceptance but also an emotional one. The bereaved person may be intellectually aware of the finality of the loss long before the emotions allow full acceptance of the information as true." (pp. 10, 12)	**1. Recognize** the loss. • Acknowledge the death. • Understand the death.
2. To work through the pain of grief.	**CONFRONTATION PHASE**
"If this task is not adequately completed, therapy may be needed later on, at which point it can be more difficult for the person to go back and work through the pain he or she has been avoiding. This is very often a more complex and difficult experience than dealing with it at the time of the loss. Also it can be complicated by having a less supportive social system than would have been available at the time of the original loss." (p. 14)	**2. React** to the separation. • Experience the pain. • Feel, identify, accept & give some form of expression to all the psychological reactions to the loss. • Identify and mourn secondary losses.
3. To adjust to an environment in which the deceased is missing.	**3. Recollect** and re-experience the deceased and the relationship. • Review and remember realistically. • Revive and re-experience the feelings.
The bereaved must adjust to the loss of old roles and take on new roles, as well as challenges to their fundamental life values and beliefs. "People work against themselves by promoting their own helplessness, by not developing the skills they need to cope, or by withdrawing from the world . . ." (pp. 15-16)	**4. Relinquish** the old attachments to the deceased and the old assumptive world.
4. To emotionally relocate the deceased and move on with life.	**ACCOMMODATION PHASE**
Incompletion of this task is best described as not *loving*—holding on to the past attachment rather than going on and forming new ones. Some people find loss so painful that they make a pact with themselves never to love again. ". . . the task for bereaved parents is to evolve some ongoing relationship with their child, but to do this in a way that would allow them to continue on with their lives after such a loss." (p. 17)	**5. Readjust** to move adaptively into the new world without forgetting the old. • Revise the assumptive world. • Develop a new relationship with the deceased. • Adopt new ways of being in the world. • Form a new identity.
	6. Reinvest in life.

monished that it "should not be mistaken for a happy stage. It is almost void of feelings" (p. 113). To expect bereaved parents to reach a state void of feelings about the death of their child is anathema to the very construct of parenting.

The Role of "Detachment"

Detachment is another frequently used term that can adversely affect the healing of bereaved parents. John Bowlby (1961, 1969, 1980) envisioned a final phase to the grief process, culminating in emotional detachment from the deceased and adaptation to a new life. He divided the grief process into four phases (see Table 3.2): 1) numbing, 2) yearning and searching, 3) disorganization and despair, and 4) reorganization. He noted that the numbness of the initial phase is often characterized by shock, panic, or anger and is usually fairly brief. During the second phase the mourner exhibits feelings and behaviors associated with the urge to recover the lost loved one. Alternating between belief and disbelief that the death has actually occurred, the mourner experiences "restless searching, intermittent hope, repeated disappointment, weeping, anger, guilt, and ingratitude" toward comforters, "which are to be understood as expressions of the strong urge to find and recover the lost person" (Bowlby, 1980, p. 92). This phase can last for months and sometimes years, and it is the role of mourning customs to help the bereaved tolerate the frustrations and painful emotions that accompany yearning and searching behavior. Bowlby believed that for mourning to have a favorable outcome, these emotions must be consciously experienced and processed. The mourner must come to understand that these emotions are expressions of attachment behavior aimed at maintaining closeness to and communication with the lost loved one (Bowlby, 1980).

When these feelings are thus identified and the mourner begins to recognize that the loved one can no longer reciprocate this attachment behavior, hopes of reunion gradually fade. Emotional expectations are then withdrawn from the deceased, behavior usually ceases to be focused on the lost loved one, despair sets in, and the mourner enters the third phase, where "behavior, lacking an object toward which to be organized, becomes disorganized" (Bowlby, 1961, p. 334). In this phase the mourner is unable to maintain an active interchange with the world and experiences "restlessness or apathy, with concurrent anxiety and depression," which Bowlby (1961) differentiated from depressive illness (p. 335). Gradually, as mourners gain an ability to tolerate the painful emotions, physical discomforts, and cognitive confusion of the third phase, they come to recognize and accept that the loss is in fact permanent and that their life must be shaped anew. Mourners must tolerate the pain of emotional detachment and the alarm of being unable to cope in order to become open to the possibilities provided by a world that no longer contains the deceased. When mourners begin to adapt to their environment by responding in ways appropriate to their new circumstances, the reorganization of the fourth phase has begun. Gradually mourners accept the facts related to the death and slowly they begin to realign their selves and their worldviews to their new situation of living without their loved one (Bowlby, 1980, p. 120).

Contrary to Bowlby's assertion, when bereaved parents "accept the facts" of their child's death and begin to adapt to their new world, they do *not* detach emotionally from their child and their role as that child's parent—just as parents do not detach emotionally from their living children when they grow up and leave home to live independent lives. Becoming a parent is forever, even when daily parenting tasks are no longer needed or possible. Richard and Kitty Edler provide an example. They became bereaved parents in 1992 when their 18-year-old son Mark was killed in an accident. After his death, they helped found a chapter of The Compassionate Friends (TCF), and Richard served as president of TCF's national Board of Directors. In his book *Into the Valley and Out Again* (Edler, 1996), he talked about how they have accepted the fact that Mark is dead and that their most important wish (to have him back again) can't come true (p. 112). He talked about how their tragic loss shaped their lives anew:

> It's almost as if grief mounts a radar antenna on your head, even though you never wanted it there. That antenna scans the world around you with a new clarity and a sensitivity to others you never had before. It gives you x-ray vision into other people's hurt. Most people rearrange their priorities in life. Many strengthen their faith. Some change careers, do more charity work, or find a cause with special meaning. These are all positive steps we take in our children's name. It doesn't make the hurt go away, but it helps us heal. (p. 108)
>
> We both feel we are living more on purpose, with a sense of what really matters. We are doing things that count beyond money, and trying to help others in Mark's name. Of all the "universal truths" of grief, the one most true is simply this: the more you give back to others, the more you heal. (p. 111)
>
> [But healing does not mean there won't be unexpected "flashbacks" that bring pain.] Flashbacks . . . become a part of your new self. For Kitty it was thoughts of different happy events—every time she drives by a little league field, by the intermediate school, or when she sees a child who looks like Mark at an earlier age. (p. 107)
>
> Part of coping with loss is taking those special memories and bringing them back into your consciousness in a positive way, and having them available for you whenever you want them. I like to think of it as not just putting memories in a drawer, but opening that drawer regularly and taking them out, holding them in your hands, and enjoying them. Too many people shut the drawer forever. (p. 107)

For bereaved parents, healing means both withstanding painful flashbacks and learning how to remain emotionally and spiritually connected with the child in comforting, positive ways.

The Role of "Identification"

One way that parents remain emotionally connected with their deceased child is through the process of *identification* (discussed in chaps. 9 and 11). This process was observed by Pollock (1961), who maintained that mourning is comprised of two stages, acute and chronic, and that it "has certain phenomena, utilizes certain mechanisms, and has a definite end point" (p. 355). The acute stage includes the three phases of shock, grief, and separation. Initially the mourner experiences shock, which may result in panic, moaning, wailing, or physical collapse. This shock phase "results when the ego is narcissistically immobilized by the suddenness and massiveness of the task that confronts it" (p. 346). Shortly thereafter, grief sets in as the mourner faces the reality of the loss and experiences deep despair and sorrow that create intense pain. During the separation phase, the mourner becomes increasingly able to differentiate herself from the deceased, resolves any feelings of ambivalence toward the deceased, relinquishes communication with the deceased, and begins to acknowledge the reality of their separateness. In the chronic stage of mourning, adaptation to life without the deceased continues and the mourner begins to make decisions without reference to the deceased. New people and external objects gain her attention. "These newer objects are seen not as exact substitutes for the lost object [loved one], but as figures which permit reality relations that are mutually satisfactory. The loss of the dead object [loved one] is assimilated, accepted, and the bereavement can come to an end" (Pollock, 1961, p. 354). This is not to say, however, that the deceased is forgotten. For through the process of identification, aspects of the deceased become integrated into the new personality of the mourner. Darlya, the bereaved mother of an adult child, provides an example of this process. In grieving for her son Dustin, she has found it important to remember what her son would tell her whenever she became upset and frustrated with her overly demanding and "socially retarded" boss. "Who's your employer Mom? Remember—God is your employer Mom!" This change in perspective had helped Dustin and it continues to help her on a daily basis. As Pollock put this: "Intra-psychically the object that is lost becomes part of the ego [of the bereaved] through *identification*" (p. 354). As previously noted, Pollock also believed that for parents "a child's death can never be fully accepted or integrated" (p. 353).

The Role of "Integration"

Recognizing that the death of a child is a "forever loss," how do bereaved parents work to achieve some degree of "resolution" and "healing" of their pain? Catherine Sanders's (1999) integrated theory of bereavement helps explain the complex process of integrating a loss. She studied various forms of adult bereavement (the death of a parent, spouse, or a child). Her study included 115 bereaved men and women in Tampa, Florida, who completed the Minnesota Multiphasic Personality Inventory (MMPI) and the Grief Experience Inventory (GEI). People who had not experienced the death of a family member within the previous 5 years provided matched controls for the study. Sanders's integrative theory is presented visually in Figure 3.1.

As shown in Figure 3.1, Sanders's theory considers both the internal and external factors impacting the bereaved, which act as moderators during the pro-

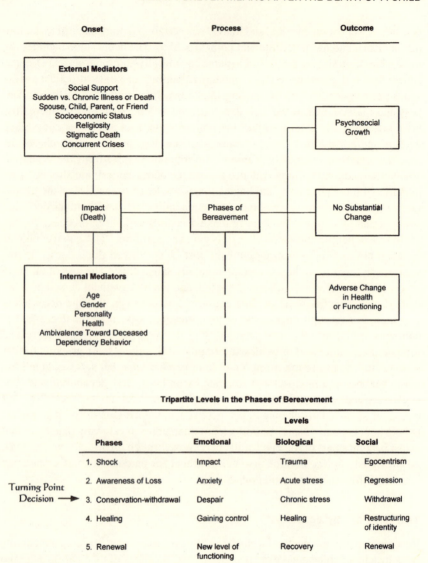

Figure 3.1 Sanders's integrative theory of bereavement. From Sanders (1999), with permission.

cess of bereavement and significantly affect the outcome of mourning. "Internal moderators describe elements that are endemic to covert personal state" (p. 44), whereas external moderators are factors surrounding the death and the socioeconomic environment of the bereaved. These moderator variables are constantly interacting during what Sanders presented as five phases of bereavement. These five phases comprise a free-flowing process, with symptoms of one phase often overlapping symptoms of the next, and with the potential of temporary regressions between phases. Stalled progress, "for many, . . . takes months or even years . . . to resume" (p. xv), and professional help may be needed to move forward and complete the process.

In her Tampa study, Sanders hypothesized that "the basic MMPI profile configurations are indicative of premorbid adjustment strategies that have been exacerbated by the stress of bereavement" (p. xiv). This hypothesis—in keeping with the ideas of Bowlby and Lindemann—was supported by her findings. The same "person who manifested disturbed reactions as a trait syndrome displayed the same disturbed reactions in an exaggerated form as a state syndrome. Similarly, those who used denial as a protective defense mechanism displayed those same characteristics to a greater degree when coping with a loss or inordinate stress" (p. xiv). Thus, Sanders concluded that individuals react to stress in ways that are truly personal yet functionally integral—ways that are consistent for them.

The first three phases of bereavement described by Sanders—shock, awareness, and conservation—are based primarily on biological needs. However, at the end of the third phase, she maintained, "the griever makes a decision, conscious or unconscious, to survive and begin a new life, or to remain in perpetual bereavement and, perhaps, die. If either of the latter decisions is made, bereavement becomes fixed in the third phase" (p. 44). Making a decision to survive, however, is not the end of the bereavement process. It is "not until one has reached a new level of functioning, incorporating the necessary changes [emotional control, physical healing, and identity restructuring] that one can feel ready to begin again, a new person in a new life" (p. 44). The turning-point decision defined by Sanders and also noted by Johnson (1987, pp. 27–30) is consistent with the experience of many of the "Mothers Now Childless" who had survived early trauma and grief after their child's death to become, eventually, new people with new lives. Bereaved parents often refer to this as "finding a new normal"—a level of functioning different from their life before their child's death and also different from other parents who have not lost a child.

The uniqueness of Sanders's bereavement theory lies in her emphasis on motivation and self-will. Although her theory is not linear, progression implies eventual movement from one phase to another. Motivation is the driving force "to move to the next phase, to cross the bridge and go forward" (p. xv). In her description of each phase, Sanders used examples from her study, as well as references from the literature, to demonstrate the psychological and accompanying biological reasons behind the movement from one phase to another. Sanders's model includes elements identified by Yalom (1980) as part of the psychological construct of *willing*, "the mental agency that transforms awareness and knowledge into action" (p. 289). Willing requires the ability to feel one's true feelings guiltlessly, recognize the reality of one's existence, define the multiple meanings associated with one's life choices, become conscious of one's wishes, and take responsibility for making one's own life decisions (Yalom, 1980). There is evidence of such willing within Sanders's description of movement through bereavement. Her model, as extrapolated from chapters 3 through 8 of her book (Sanders,

Table 3.3. Movement Through Sanders' Five Phases of Bereavement

Phase 1—Shock

General Characteristics

Disbelief—functions as a buffer that allows bereaved to process the reality of the loss gradually.

Confusion—bereaved is off-balance, unable to conceive of a world without that person.

Restlessness—defensive systems keep the bereaved in constant state of alert.

Feelings of unreality—how the death happens and how the bereaved is told of the death dramatically affect how the death is processed by the bereaved.

Regression and helplessness—uncontrollable events of bereavement bring about feelings of helplessness and regression, back to childlike dependency and weakness.

State of alarm—state of intense physiological alarm governed by the sympathetic part of the autonomic nervous system which is a natural reaction to a threat to security.

Physical Symptoms
  Dryness of the mouth
  Need for sighing
  Loss of muscular control
  Weeping
  Uncontrolled trembling
  Startle response
  Sleep disturbance
  Loss of appetite

Psychological Symptoms
  Egocentric phenomenon: cognitive awareness is narrowed and attention drawn to personal needs.
  Preoccupation with thoughts of the deceased.
  Psychological distancing: to protect themselves from pain, the bereaved gain distance even from themselves.

Moving on: Shock usually passes into next phase when rituals of death are over and constricted emotions begin to release and overflow.

Phase 2—Awareness of Loss

General Characteristics

Separation anxiety—bereaved suddenly realize everything that had been dependable has gone, leaving them vulnerable and afraid.

Conflicts—decisions of daily living often require changes that result in another loss of one kind or another, adding to the pain.

Acting out emotional expectations—awareness of death continues to produce raw pain as each expectation for life as it was is met with frustration and disappointment.

Prolonged stress—grief uses enormous quantities of psychic energy and creates undue stress, straining the bereaved both emotionally and physically.

Physical Symptoms
  Yearning
  Crying
  Anger
  Guilt
  Frustration
  Shame
  Sleep disturbance
  Fear of death

Psychological Symptoms
  Oversensitivity: reacting to others more quickly and negatively than the bereaved normally would.
  Searching for deceased in familiar places.
  Disbelief and denial.
  Sensing the presence of the deceased.
  Dreaming of the deceased.

Moving on: The limit to the amount of emotional arousal one can experience forces one into retreat. Exhaustion initiates the next phase of withdrawal, which gradually becomes the primary behavior during phase 3.

Table 3.3. Continued

Phase 3—Conservation

General Characteristics

Withdrawal—bereaved experience a daily pattern of fatigue and need for rest, as the body needs to conserve both physical and emotional energy.

Despair—a sense of utter despair pervades as the bereaved turn inward to review the loss and realize that life as before will never return and the lost person will never return.

Helplessness—the sheer frustration of uncontrollability leaves the bereaved despairing that nothing will ever matter again; some may overrely on others, giving up even more control over their lives by remaining in a state of learned helplessness.

Diminished support—friends/family provide less support and expect bereaved to "get over" their loss within 6 months to 1 year after the death.

Physical Symptoms	Psychological Symptoms
Weakness	Hibernation: a holding pattern where the bereaved become stagnant, unable to see or think about the future.
Fatigue	
Need for more sleep	
Weakened immune system	Obsessional review: bereaved grasp the loss by repeatedly mentally reviewing it and testing reality.
	Grief work: through rumination and unfocused concentration comes an acknowledgment that old conditions are no longer attainable.
	Turning point: decision (conscious or unconscious) either to move forward, remain in status quo, or become ill and possibly die.

Moving on: As feelings of hopelessness and helplessness begin to dissipate, bereaved begin to plan and look ahead. Bereaved begin to come to see a need to decide the direction of their new life. Each person chooses the right way for him or her. There is no good or bad way to resolve a significant loss.

Phase 4—Healing

General Characteristics

Turning point—the turning point decision barely contemplated at the end of phase 3 becomes conscious, usually gradually, and bereaved begin to act on it.

Assuming control—bereaved slowly gain a sense of control over their emotions and over the world around them.

Identity restructuring—bereaved begin to accept responsibility for a new and different existence; return of self-confidence and trust for the world is gradual and erratic; identity based on life with the deceased must be replaced with a new identity structured without the loved one.

Relinquishing roles—roles must be relinquished if growth is to develop; loss of a child may require most restructuring of identity; parent's roles have changed because that particular child is no longer there; when bereaved relinquish roles, the work of changing an identity begins to take place.

(Continued)

Table 3.3. Continued

Physical Symptoms	Psychological Symptoms
Physical healing	Forgiving: self-forgiveness by working through
Increased energy	guilt, anger, and shame associated with not
Sleep restoration	preventing the death.
Immune system restoration	Forgetting: letting go of the past and of grief.
	Search for meaning: taking time to process what the deceased has meant both to the bereaved and others; reviewing/renewing spiritual values.
	Closing the circle: rituals, symbols or actions that represent new ways of sharing life.
	Hope: beginning thoughts of a future; ability to look back past the death to see happy memories.

Moving on: It is important for bereaved to be able to see the deceased in realistic terms, recognizing frailties as well as strengths, in order to move to the final phase of renewal.

Phase 5—Renewal

General Characteristics

New self-awareness—ability to recognize the alternatives in life and the freedom to choose opens up possibilities and the bereaved experience a new sense of competence and inner strength.

Accepting responsibility—recognition that bereaved cannot depend on anyone else for their confirmation; that they alone must give meaning to their lives, finding their own answers as they go.

Learning to live without—learning to live without the resources once taken for granted and to find substitutions and replacements to fill the voids caused by the death.

Physical Symptoms	Psychological Symptoms
Revitalization	Living for oneself: discovering who one is and
Functional stability	focusing on being that person.
Caring for physical needs	Anniversary reactions: experiencing poignant memories and temporary grief flashbacks.
	Loneliness: bereaved begin to wish for significant others in their life.
	Reaching out: bereaved begin to reach out and build new relationships.
	Time for the process of bereavement: the amount of time to achieve renewal depends on the relationship of deceased, resources available to bereaved, internal and external mediators, and degree of shock at time of death.

Moving on: During the renewal phase, the bereaved achieve some level of success but they still need backup support systems. It is important to: (a) encourage the bereaved to try new directions, (b) help bereaved initiate new actions, or (c) provide comfort when things do not work out as planned.

1999, pp. 36–113), is outlined in Table 3.3.

Note that Sanders's five phases of bereavement culminate in what she termed *renewal*. Researchers have proposed a variety of terms to describe a positive outcome for bereavement. Parkes and Weiss (1983) used the term *recovery*, which they defined as replanning of the life situation and attaining a new, independent level of functioning. If recovery does not occur, they deemed the reaction abnormal. In his research, Cleiren (1993) used Bowlby's term *adaptation* ("to reengage and function adequately in daily life") and *debilitation* ("ongoing weakness in physical, psychological, and social functioning"). Doka (1993a) suggested the term *amelioration* as more appropriate because it implies "to make or become better." He compared bereavement to losing an arm and noted that there is a need to rebuild the spiritual or philosophical system that has been challenged by grief and to move into a new life without forgetting the old. Klass (1988) suggested using the term *resolution* as a goal for bereaved parents: "not a return to life as it was before, for there is no going back . . . but a sense of a new self" (p. 120). Those who find a new sense of self also find they have some things in common with other bereaved parents.

COMMONALITIES AMONG BEREAVED PARENTS

Bereaved parents experiences revolve around the issues of the parent–child relationship and the effects of the child's death on the individual parent, the marriage, the family, and society. Each parent has a unique and different relationship with the child who died, and thus each parent's bereavement is idiosyncratic and highly personalized. But there are some important commonalities among bereaved parents (Knapp, 1986; Oliver, 1990; Rosof, 1994; Sanders, 1999).

In interviews with over 300 parents, Knapp (1986) found that bereaved parents desire never to forget their dead child and that "mothers, particularly, harbor a great fear that what memories they have of the child may eventually fade away" (p. 29). He found that these parents frequently expressed a wish to die themselves, but did not act on that desire because they didn't want to hurt others they would leave behind (pp. 32–33). The parents he studied had a need to fit death into some kind of recognizable context, and 70% of them turned to their religious faiths for answers and comfort (p. 34). Over time the parents also experienced a change of values from traditional goals of success and personal achievement to more family-oriented values. "Doing things *with* the family rather than *for* the family, and taking a genuine interest in each other, eventually came to be defined as more important than trying to 'keep up with the Joneses'—perhaps a common behavior pattern in the 'predeath family'" (p. 37). Many of these parents reported they were more compassionate in their dealings with others, "more understanding of the problems of others, more forgiving of the transgressions of others, more open with their own feelings, more patient, and more loving" (p. 39). Many of these parents, however, also continued to experience episodes of shadow grief, "an emotional dullness where the person is unable to respond fully and completely to outer stimulation and where normal activity is moderately inhibited" (p. 41).

In examining the lives of 12 mothers from 4 to 19 years after the death of their children, Oliver (1990) reached conclusions similar to those of Knapp. A bereaved mother herself, Oliver concluded that the grief of the mothers she interviewed was idiosyncratic except for four areas of commonality. All of these bereaved mothers believed in life after death and the possibility of maintaining a relationship with their child. They all recognized a motive to live more fully and had consciously reformulated their values and priorities. They were also all involved in various actions of service to others that were spurred by the recognition of a broader connection to the pain of others. Their grief had decreased in intensity but shadow grief remained, and all expected to grieve forever (Oliver, 1990, p. 202).

THE CONTINUING ROLE OF GRIEF IN BEREAVED PARENTS' LIVES

If grieving never entirely ends for bereaved parents, what role does it play many years after their child's death? How is it expressed and how does it impact the quality of their lives? The women in the "Mothers Now Childless" study had diverse answers to these questions.

As the data in Table 3.4 show, the level of grief felt at time of contact, 5 or more years after the death of their only child, was one distinguishing factor between the opposite ends of the bereavement continuum for women in the "Mothers Now Childless" study. A total 61.3% in the group representing the "survival" end of the continuum said they still felt grief *weekly* or *occasionally.* This contrasted to 44.4% in the group representing "perpetual bereavement" who said they continued to feel grief *daily*, and grief still *dominated* the lives of 16.7% of this group.

Additional losses since their child's death appeared to have contributed to the ongoing grief of both groups. All 18 women in the "perpetual bereavement" group had suffered a significant loss after their child's death, as had 75.8% of those in the group representing "survival."

A few of the women commented that another loss exacerbated their ongoing grief for their child. Some had lost a parent and felt that the grief and stress of their child's death was a contributing factor to that parent's death. Others pointed out that the grief they felt after losing their parent or spouse was dramatically different from their grief for their child. Some said losing their parent was easier to accept because the parent had led a long and full life and/or death brought an end to the parent's suffering and pain.

Although it is unclear exactly how additional losses affected both groups, it is clear that grief continued to play a role, in varying degrees, in the lives of all 80 of the women in the "Mothers Now Childless" study. There was, however, a significant difference between the groups in whether they shared their grief with others. After their child's death, over 85% of those in the "survival" group had

Table 3.4 Excerpted Responses from Bereavement Questionnaire by Discriminant Group: Grief Level at Time of Study

Response to Questionnaire	Perpetual Bereavement ($n = 18$) Frequency (%)	Survival ($n = 62$) Frequency (%)	χ^2 (80)
Level of grief felt now:			15.96**
Grief dominates life	3 (16.7)[b]	0 (0)	
Feel grief daily	8 (44.4)[b]	24 (38.7)	
Feel grief weekly	3 (16.7)	16 (25.8)[b]	
Feel grief occasionally	3 (16.7)	22 (35.5)[b]	
No longer grieve	1 (5.6)	0 (0)[bb]	
Significant losses after child's death:			5.36*
Yes	18 (100)[b]	47 (75.8)[b]	
No	0 (0)	15 (24.2)	
Discuss grief with others today:[a]			25.12**
Never	3 (16.7)[b]	1 (1.6)	
Rarely	8 (44.4)[b]	4 (6.5)	
Occasionally	4 (22.2)	42 (67.7)[b]	
Often	3 (16.7)	15 (24.2)[b]	
Attend support group(s):			12.99**
Never attended	3 (16.7)[b]	2 (3.2)	
Once or twice	2 (11.1)[b]	7 (11.3)	
Occasionally	10 (55.6)	16 (25.8)[b]	
Regularly	3 (16.7)	37 (59.7)[b]	
Still attend support group(s):			1.24
No	11 (61.1)	34 (54.8)	
Yes	4 (22.2)	25 (40.3)	
N/A or missing	3 (16.7)	3 (4.8)	
Grief therapy:			4.19
Never	5 (27.8)	22 (35.5)	
Once or twice	3 (16.7)	11 (17.7)	
Occasionally	6 (33.3)	8 (12.9)	
Regularly	4 (22.2)	21 (33.9)	
Believe survived child's death:			23.03**
No	9 (50.0)[b]	3 (4.8)	
Yes	7 (38.9)	53 (85.5)[b]	
Yes and no	2 (11.1)	6 (9.7)[b]	

[a]Discriminating variable used to determine group membership. [b]These results highlight and contrast the statistically signficant differences between responses from the two groups.
*$p < .05$. **$p < .01$.

attended a support group either occasionally or regularly. Over 25% of the "perpetual bereavement" group, however, said they had never attended a support group or had done so only once or twice after their child died. The two groups also differed when asked: "Do you discuss your grief with friends and/or relatives in your life today?" Over 90% of the "survival" group said they continued to discuss their grief with others often or occasionally. This contrasted with 60% of the "perpetual bereavement" group who said they rarely or never discussed their grief with others. As discussed further in chapters 9 and 10, the varying ways of remembering and memorializing their child and of reaching out to help others provided opportunities for many of the women to share and discuss their grief and to keep their child a part of their daily lives.

If grieving can be expected to continue in varying levels for bereaved parents, what role does expressing that grief play vis-à-vis finding solace and resolution? It is not uncommon for parents who still grieve openly to others years after their child's death to be judged as "stuck" in their grief process. However, the findings shown in Table 3.4 suggest that parents who share their grief with others may be both demonstrating and facilitating their own healing. Those women who said they had survived their child's death felt grief less frequently but discussed the grief they did feel with others more frequently than the women who said they hadn't survived.

This is an important finding that can help to validate bereaved parents' experiences. These parents need to know that it is not realistic to expect to resolve their loss entirely and no longer feel any grief. They need to know that it is normal for new losses to bring flashbacks of their child's death and/or to be contrasted with their grief for their child. Further, they need to know that sharing their grief with supportive others is an indicator that they are continuing to heal, not that they are somehow stuck in grief and failing to go on with their lives.

Bereaved parents also need to know that grief is often unpredictable and they should expect sudden "grief attacks," especially during the early years of acute grief. For example, something as simple as seeing their child's favorite book at the book store can trigger sudden, excruciating pain. And unlike the response they would get if they had a heart attack while shopping, those around them most likely won't know what to do to help.

During early acute grief, many parents "return to work, school, or other activities feeling vulnerable, less confident about their capabilities, less able to concentrate, distracted by memories, and flooded with emotions that disrupt thinking. For others, work is the only place they are able to concentrate—focusing on tasks helps take their mind off their grief for awhile" (Talbot, 2000a). Yet rarely are bereaved parents offered accommodations to help their transition back into the workplace, unlike employees who receive leaves of absence for pregnancy or "limited duty" assignments based on a physician's "return to work order" after an accident. What it means to return to work or school during the first months and years after the death of a child is another aspect of parents' grief that has yet to receive appropriate attention, accommodation, and research.

It can help bereaved parents to be reassured that they can learn to live again by taking "one grief at a time," as one bereaved mother put it. Thinking too far ahead and trying to envision a pain-free future can be frightening and overwhelming. As when facing any difficult task, breaking grief up into individual pieces can make the pain more manageable.

SUMMARY

This chapter has reviewed research that acknowledges the severity and evolving nature of bereaved parents' grief. Resolution does not mean an end to grieving; parents continue to experience "flashbacks," "anniversary reactions," and new losses. For bereaved parents, resolution includes learning how to live with grief and finding ways to share that grief with others. Expectations for parents to "accept" the death and "detach" from their child are not only unrealistic but can be harmful. Instead, healing appears to be facilitated by "identification" with the child and "integration" of the loss in ways that honor the parents' past lives and build continuing connections with their children. Learning from prior research about how the grief process evolves can help parents start to regain control of their lives. Part of regaining control is becoming able to withstand the pain of acute grief as they sort through the unique circumstances of their child's life and death. Chapter 4 discusses how bereaved parents learn the painful and poignant lessons that their loss brings them.

Chapter 4

One Death—A Thousand Strands of Pain:
Finding the Meaning of Suffering

> The churning inside me never stops;
> days of suffering confront me.
> My harp is tuned to mourning,
> and my flute to the sound of wailing. (Job 30:27, 31)

> I just suffer every day. I always think about it. [Anita]

After Job had prayed for his friends, the Lord made him prosperous again and gave him twice as much as he had before. The Lord blessed the latter part of Job's life more than the first. (Job 42:10, 12)

It's not a journey any of us want to take but along the way there have been joyful moments—there have been sad moments—but it's a journey that in a way I feel blessed to be taking because it's another development of my soul. [Irene]

The biblical account of Job remains a prophetic preview of the kind of suffering and pain felt by bereaved parents around the world to this day. Parents ask many questions, of themselves, of others, and of God: Why? Why did our child die? Why has this happened to us? What caused this death? Why now? What does this death mean? Did we do something wrong? What could we have done to prevent this? Can the death of any child have meaning? What possible meanings could come from such pain and suffering?

    The search for meaning by bereaved parents has been identified by numerous researchers and practicing psychotherapists (Blank, 1998; Brice, 1987; Cleiren, 1993; Craig, 1977; Currier, 1982; Edelstein, 1984; Jozefowski, 1999; Klass, 1991; Knapp, 1986; Miles & Crandall, 1986; Miller, 1999; Nadeau, 1998; Oliver, 1990;

Peppers & Knapp, 1980; Rando, 1986; Rosenblatt, 2000a; Sanders, 1992, 1999; Savage, 1989; Schneider, 1994; Wheeler, 1990; Zenoff, 1986). The circumstances of the death and the relationship with the child are revisited and reevaluated, and new meanings (both positive and negative) are found or constructed (Braun & Berg, 1994; Frankl, 1963, 1969, 1978, 1997; Kelly, 1963; Miles & Crandall, 1986; Neimeyer, 1998; Wheeler, 1990).

MEANINGS DERIVED FROM THE PARENT–CHILD RELATIONSHIP

Two women from the "Mothers Now Childless" study, representing opposite ends of the bereavement continuum, demonstrate how complex and crucial this review of the relationship with the deceased child can be. Anita, whose son was born with multiple heart defects and died at age 16 after a second open heart surgery, provides an example of negative meaning-making. Anita blamed herself for Brad's heart disease and tells the story of how she cursed her unborn baby during an argument with his alcoholic father when she was pregnant.

> It was a very hot day and we had been arguing. And he came home and he'd been drinking and I said, "Oh God, let there be something wrong with this baby." And why did I say that? I don't know. Why should I take our problems and put it into a baby, an innocent baby, I don't know, but I did. Well, when Brad was born . . . he had like four very extensive defects . . . and they [the doctors] just couldn't come up with anything (any reason why). . . . And I thought, yeah, it's that prayer that I mumbled out of anger. So that's how I've always blamed myself. [Anita]

Anita's statement demonstrates symbolic interactionism, the theory that says when people define situations as real, they will be real in their consequences. Anita's experience also exemplifies how important it is for bereaved parents both to dissect the pain of their grief into individual strands of meaning and to question the reality and rationality of those meanings.

After Brad's death, Anita had been able to share her reason for blaming herself with a nun who helped her "to deal with it." This warm and sympathetic nun had encouraged Anita to keep telling herself that God did not inflict Brad's birth defects in answer to her angry prayer. But at the time of the interview, 6 years after Brad's death, Anita said she was still blaming herself. Guilt and self-blame seem to be a universal, and natural, part of grief for bereaved parents. In a sense, guilt represents a bereaved parent's power. "Sometimes it can be easier to live with guilt than to feel powerless" (Talbot, 1999). When this is the case, the use of "paradoxical intention" (Frankl, 1969) may be helpful. Parents can be encouraged to hold on to their guilt and/or self-blame (because it represents their power) for as long as it is useful to them. Doing so can help parents see that they create their guilt; that it is separate from them; and that they can choose when to transform this power (guilt) into something more useful.

So much is taken away from bereaved parents when their child dies. When they perceive those around them as attempting to take away their grief, too, they

often rebel—and rightly so. Some, however, become fixated in their rebellion, at least for awhile. Anita told me her therapist kept trying to get her to say aloud that her son was dead, and this became the focus of their sessions together. "After three years of counseling I finally said it to her and then she says, well, I think we've gone as far as we can go and she dismissed me. . . . Usually I say he passed away or I lost him. That's probably the second time I've said it. I DON'T LIKE THAT WORD!" Anita had not sought out a new counselor. She talked about her ongoing depression and her lack of will to live:

> I don't feel like I have survived hardly at all since I've lost him. I'm just struggling in the water. I can't envision myself functioning and actually living without him. . . . I think about it [suicide] occasionally. I'm not gonna say that I don't, or that I've wiped it out completely. . . . I'm living because I won't kill myself. I don't want to do that 'cause I don't want to screw up not gettin' to heaven. So I'm surviving basically for that reason, and for my family.

Gail provides a contrasting example of the importance of reevaluating the relationship with the child. She worked through the circumstances surrounding her son's death and her own guilt toward a more balanced and realistic under-standing of their relationship and her role as a single, divorced mother. It was raining the afternoon that Andy's car crashed into a utility pole one block from their home as he drove himself to work. At age 16 he'd had his driver's license only 1 month at the time of the accident. No drugs or alcohol were involved. He suffered severe head injuries and died 8 days later. Gail talked of the guilt she had about her son's accident because she was "pushing him out of the nest."

> He was not the one that was particularly anxious to start driving. I'm the one that pushed it. . . . He failed his driving test three times . . . the driving part. And I men-tion that 'cause I have a lot of guilt about that. . . . I was going through this thing where I was just tired of parenting. I was tired of the responsibility. . . . Looking back on it . . . I just felt like he was clinging to me a lot, not physically but emotion-ally, and it felt uncomfortable. But I now know that was just my own uncomfortableness with any kind of emotional intimacy. And once he did get his license and did get a car, and did get a job, he really liked it.

Gail explained how she had reevaluated her relationship with her son:

> Having Andy gave me a purpose for living. Until he was born I didn't have enough self-esteem to have the energy I think to, well, I can't exactly say that because I went to college. I was the first person in my family to ever do that. I made a decision when I was 12 that I wasn't gonna live the way that I was brought up [she was sexually abused by her grandfather]. . . . As I grew into parenting—as I grew into the role—a lot of what I did was based on providing Andy with different opportuni-ties than I had. . . . And looking back upon it, I was pretty unemotionally available to him for the 16 years of his life. Um, but I was sorting through lots of stuff, lots of stuff. And I couldn't, there was always a hole in me. There was always a hole. . . . And

as I look at it since I've sorted things out the last several years, I mean it was a very codependent relationship, and really very unfair to him.

For Gail, surviving her son's death meant returning to the wounds of her childhood and building a new self. "I died when he died," she said. "Gradually I've birthed a new me. I'm totally different. I have an identity beyond being a mother." At the time of the interview, Gail was teaching psychology and child development at a local community college and was a first-year doctoral student in a clinical psychology program. She also volunteered for numerous educational organizations and was an active member of her church. She described her life during the 8 years since Andy's death as "a very slow, painful process to make the decision to live life 'alive'—to actually risk caring about others again—to learn to take care of myself."

MEANINGS DERIVED FROM THE ONGOING TRAJECTORY OF THE CHILD'S LIFE

Bereaved parents also find the multiple meanings of their loss over time as they continue to see their dead child "grow up" vicariously in the life events of other families and as they confront reminders of what their child might have looked like or accomplished. Gail provides a compelling example of how she continues to find meaning from her "dance with the veil of death":

> I went in January to Hawaii to do a workshop for a week with the two people . . . I've done workshops with on and off since right after Andy died. And you know, I thought, oh a workshop in Hawaii—yeah, we'll get into some stuff but that's ok. Well the whole week I was grieving Andy's death. I never expected that to come up. But two things happened. One, there was a man there who looked very much like how I would imagine Andy would look as an adult. And another, there was an emergency physician there and I just wanted to chew his ass out. And he let me! And this other man that looked like Andy let me just smell him and touch him. I mean, I miss Andy's smell. And you know, all those feelings about that you're gonna forget him [tears]—that I'm gonna forget the exact color of his hair, the exact way it laid on his head. The exact way he smelled. The exact way he used to hug me. And I got to do all that with these guys. And it was just like I told them—it's like I have my own life now, and I've built a really good life for myself. It's full of so much richness and so many blessings. But it's like I'm always dancing with this veil of death, and so they asked me to share the veil with them and to let them take the veil for awhile and I could dance without it and they would carry the veil for me. And that was like, oh wow—gosh that's an interesting idea. I never thought about that before. So I mean this is seven years after he dies that this is still happening. And when I went over there I felt like you know, I was going on a week on the big island of Hawaii in January. I was thinking of all the fun. So you know I don't see that this is—I think that a parent's gonna get over their child's death is a myth. I mean it's kind of like the myth that we're gonna grow up and be an adult. I am going to be on a personal journey—a quest to find out who I am til the day I die. I am going to be processing

my son and what he meant to my life and what it's meant not to have him in my life til the day I die.

Meaning-making after the death of a child can be seen as taking separate but interrelated pathways: meaning-making that addresses issues, circumstances, and questions about the child's life and death, and meaning-making that focuses on the survivors' beliefs, worldviews, life purposes, and hopes for the future now that the child has died. There are various cross-connects between these two pathways and no obvious order or prescriptive approach to navigating such tough questions. Some parents say they cannot conceive of a future without their child, and their focus remains one of trying to make sense of the child's death. Some parents seem to weave interconnecting strands of meaning between the pathways.

MEANINGS ABOUT THE PAST THAT INFLUENCE THE FUTURE

Coming to understand certain circumstances related to the child's death can lead to better understanding of the child's life and contributions to the world, whether positive, negative, or both. Parents sometimes then choose new purposes and activities for their own lives that arise from these new understandings. Irene provides an example.

Irene's 18-year-old son Bobby was killed in a single-car accident. On their way to Irene's house, Bobby's fiancée lost control of the car and hit a tree. Bobby died instantly; his fiancée was not injured. No drugs or alcohol were involved.

> Bobby had had such a troubled year or so the year before he died, and I was glad that when he died it was on a happy note. They were coming to give me happy news that they were gonna get married and he didn't die when he was strung out on drugs, or he didn't die in an alcoholic daze. He died on an upbeat note, and that allowed me also to deal with some of the guilt that I felt because maybe I didn't do things right. Mothers, I think, always go through that.

Irene chose to focus on the one positive meaning she drew from Bobby's death—her gratitude that it was truly an accident and not the result of his using drugs or alcohol. As Irene worked through her parenting guilt and reviewed her son's life, she developed new reasons for her own life:

> I had to reinvent my life. I had to find a reason to go on, and one of the reasons that I finally said, Irene, you must get your shit together—in other words, get your act together—was because I didn't want my son when I see him again when I die, I didn't want him to turn away from me and say, "I'm ashamed of you Mamma, you wimped out. You didn't try to keep going." And I didn't want him turning his back on me and walking away. So I said, well, I've got to keep going, if only so Bobby will give me the thumbs up when I get to heaven (I hope I'm going to heaven anyway) and say "good for you Mamma, you hung in there and you survived." So that was also what kept me going. And then I got involved more. I got involved in some volunteer work at the hospital. I volunteered in hospice. . . . I just said, I have to

reach out and just keep going. Just one foot after the other. That's basically the way I thought Bobby would want me to be. . . . And it's not that I love him any less, it's just that you have to go on, and you have to make a life. You either have to make a life or you have to give up on life and just become a hermit and live with your . . . own pity party. I don't think that's healthy.

One reason Irene decided to volunteer as a hospice worker was because she wanted to work with AIDS patients. She said Bobby had been "as homophobic as they come. Where he got it from I will never know because he did not get it from me." She wanted to do something to compensate for this. "I said, well, if I work with AIDS patients somehow I'm erasing his homophobia." Through volunteering she met and became friends with a young man, another volunteer, who she now calls "my adopted child. And he helped me. Because of his bubbly personality; that helped." As Irene demonstrates, questions related to the child's death and life can eventually lead to questions about the meaning and purpose of life of the parents now that the unthinkable has happened. A painful search for meaning can result, as it did for Irene, in decisions to reinvest in life in ways that create a positive legacy and provide hope and new goals.

THE CRISIS OF MEANINGLESSNESS

In her research of the death of an adult child, Blank (1998) noted that parents who wrestle with the why questions related to their child's death "may really be facing a crisis of meaning, of what makes life worth living, what values we hold that give us personal satisfaction, what makes us feel that our having lived has had some significance, that our lives count for something, that the major investment of our energies has been worthy. The major investment parents make can be and often is in the lives of their children" (pp. 63–64). After a child dies, parents need to find a way to account for and place their loss within the structure of their own values, beliefs, and assumptions about how the world works. The meaning of life is reformulated as parents confront the reality of what has happened, search for understanding from others, and reevaluate their assumptions about how the world works.

Margaret Miles (1979; Miles & Crandall, 1986) conceptualized a phase of parental grief that included the search for new meaning in life. Meaning, she formulated, could be found in:

1   Adherence to religious and philosophical beliefs.
2   Identification of the uniqueness of the child's life and death.
3   Memorialization of the child's memory.
4   Becoming involved in activities that can help individuals and society (Miles & Crandall, 1986, p. 239).

Miles and Crandall reviewed open-ended questionnaire data from bereaved parents collected during three previous studies in order "to assess both the positive 'growth' resolutions and negative 'despair' resolutions following the profound experience of losing a child through death" (p. 237). The parents were not directly asked about their search for meaning or personal growth because "it was felt that directly asking parents these questions would bias their responses toward the negative pole, since bereaved parents are sensitive about the idea that growth could occur because of their child's death" (p. 241). It was unclear how long the parents in these three studies had been bereaved but since most were members of support groups it seems likely the majority would have been bereaved less than five years. Miles and Crandall found it "interesting to note that so many of the parents indicated they had found some meaning and had grown in some important ways following the deaths of their children" (pp. 241–242). The parents' responses were summarized into two groups:

Positive ("growth resolution") comments:

Learning to prioritize and reorganize my goals
Becoming more sensitive and helpful to people who hurt
Losing my fear of death
Learning to appreciate young people
Realizing the importance of spending more time with my family
Cherishing memories
Feeling more positive about life
Being more compassionate and more caring of others
Being more spiritual
Feeling stronger
Being grateful
Becoming aware of the fragility of life
Having a greater understanding of life and death
Learning to live each day to the fullest

Negative ("despair") comments:

Life has stopped
No good will ever come from the death
Not being able to forget or recover
Having a negative, meaningless view of life
Just existing
Feeling suicidal
Lacking trust

THE IMPACT OF MEANING-MAKING ON LIFE PURPOSE

In another study, Wheeler (1990) investigated the relationship between parents' perceptions of purpose in life and characteristics related to the parents, the children, type of death, and level of grief. Time since the child's death was found to be a significant factor influencing parents' purpose in life scores. Wheeler administered the Purpose in Life Test (PIL) (Crumbaugh & Maholick, 1969/1981), the

Grief Experience Inventory (Sanders, Mauger, & Strong, 1977), and a questionnaire devised to measure meaning to 203 bereaved parents nationwide who were
recruited through The Compassionate Friends newsletter. Thirty-five percent of
the participating parents had been bereaved for up to 24 months; 28% had been
bereaved between 24 and 48 months; and 37% had been bereaved over 48 months.
"The time periods were chosen because studies by Rando (1983) and Fish (1986)
have suggested that critical differences in grief may be found in the three time
periods" (p. 59). Wheeler's (1990) study showed that the purpose in life of bereaved parents is affected by the following variables (pp. 101–103):

1   Loss of more than one child.
2   Loss of an only child.
3   Death by suicide.
4   Certain types of meaning-making: (a) no meaning, (b) meaning related
    to specific people or activities, (c) meaning related to beliefs or values.
5   Time since death of child.

Parents bereaved for less than 4 years had significantly lower Purpose in
Life scores. "There were some indications in the data that the relationship between PIL and time since death was not linear" (p. 65). Wheeler performed a least
square means analysis for the three time periods, and the results indicated a significant difference at the .05 level between the PIL scores in the first time period
(score = 100.14) and the third time period (score = 108.11). There was also a
significant difference ($p = .0002$) between the second time period (score = 100.14)
and the third time period (score = 108.11). There was no significant difference
between the first and second time periods (pp. 69–70). This curvilinear relationship between time periods for the participants in the study was charted in a line
graph (see Fig. 4.1).

The graph suggests a drop in purpose in life between the second and fourth
years of bereavement. Other studies that have measured level of grief have shown
that bereavement is not a linear experience. For example, in his study of 77 women
and 35 men, Fish (1986) found that the grief of mothers was more intense after 2
years than it was in the beginning, and it did not taper off until after 5 years (p.
419). Likewise, in a study of 54 parents following the death of their child from
cancer, Rando (1983) found that grief actually intensified in the third year.

Wheeler (1990) reported that the descriptive data collected in her study support suggestions in the literature that parental bereavement can create a severe
crisis of meaning; however, the data also suggest many parents are able to reinvest
in life. She found that most of the parents in her study reported some positive
changes in themselves as a result of the bereavement (pp. 110–112). Fathers ($n =
45$) had lower grief scores than mothers ($n = 158$) but similar Purpose in Life
scores (p. 107).

When asked what had given their life meaning since the death of their child,
the parents in Wheeler's study frequently responded "surviving children" (p. 105).

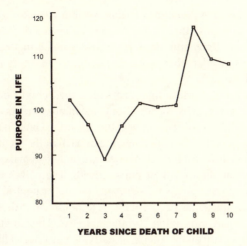

Figure 4.1 Wheeler's line graph of Purpose in Life Test means for the first 10 years after bereavement (*n* = 203). From Wheeler (1990, p. 67), with permission.

Fifteen of the 203 children who died were only children (p. 50). Wheeler noted that "the lower purpose in life scores for parents who lost an only child and those who had experienced the death of more than one child affirm the difficult nature of these losses" (p. 105). In other words, losing the role of parent negatively impacted parents' Purpose in Life scores.

In addition to "surviving children," the following *sources of meaning* were mentioned by the parents in Wheeler's study: "contact with people; activities, often altruistic in nature; beliefs and values about life and afterlife; connections with the dead child; and personal growth" (p. 109).

The parents reported positive, negative, and mixed *changes* resulting from their child's death. Positive changes included becoming more caring, valuing life more, becoming less materialistic, being less concerned about insignificant things, discovering the importance of close relationships, not taking things for granted, and becoming a stronger person. Negative changes included being sadder, feeling depressed, disillusionment, less tolerance, and becoming less trusting in relationships. (p. 110)

Those parents in Wheeler's study who reported not finding any meaning had the lowest PIL scores. Those parents who reported specific meanings (related to specific people or activities) had higher PIL scores than those with no meaning but lower than parents who reported meanings related to beliefs and values (p. 105). Wheeler attributed the lower scores for parents who reported finding no meaning in life to the presence of the "existential vacuum" described by Frankl (1969).[1] She explained the difference between the other two groups of parents as

[1]The "existential vacuum" is one of the six scales measured by the Life Attitude Profile–Revised, which was completed by the 80 women who participated in the author's research of death of an only child. See Appendix.

support for the theory that "a belief or value system provides a more effective antidote to meaninglessness than a specific person or activity" (p. 105). Citing Kelly's (1963) personal construct system, Wheeler noted that beliefs or values "may contribute a more adaptable construct system for meaning in life than specific people or activities."

Confronting a crisis of meaninglessness after their child's death is one way bereaved parents shape their lives anew. Some meanings parents derive are positive, some negative. Both positive and negative meanings push parents to decide what to do next, given their new understanding of each of the meanings related to their unique loss. It is different for parents who are unable to make any sense of or find any positive meaning after their child's death. Their lives are also shaped anew because they remain indecisive—as Anita put it, "struggling in the waters," and yet they are not the same people they were before. For these parents, "no meaning" and/or "negative meaning" bring emptiness. This emptiness is not the numbness so often a part of the shock of early, acute grief. This emptiness is characterized by frenzied frustration and frozen despair that inhibits further action. As they journey through the barren valley of the shadow of death, some parents just seem to have to set up camp at times along the way. As we have seen, meaning can provide the motivation to break camp and move forward.

MEANING-MAKING AS AN EVOLVING PROCESS

Although bereaved parents experience great challenges in making any sense of their child's death, doing so can be critical to becoming able to reinvest in life. Bereavement research has led thanatologists to view meaning-making as a central process of grieving (Attig, 1996; Nadeau, 1998; Neimeyer, 1998; Prend, 1997). Rando (1993) noted that "the search for meaning can be a major part of mourning, especially, but not exclusively, after the death of a child (because the death of a child violates the very order of nature) and after sudden, unexpected deaths; suicides; homicides; or deaths occurring under other very traumatic or mutilating circumstances" (p. 433).

Soren Kierkegaard drew attention to the tension that exists between the need to understand one's past while also pursuing an uncertain future. He said: "It is perfectly true, as philosophers say, that life must be understood backwards. But they forget the other proposition, that it must be lived forwards" (quoted in Groopman, 1997, p. 38). The death of a child is a life-changing event that forever divides parents' lives into a before and after. Parents often feel that their world stops when their child dies while for others the world goes on much as before. Many parents find that in the early years of acute grief they go through the motions of living, but this is a life lived in response to the external world and those in it, not a life lived purposefully. Many cannot go forward until they have, in fact, "understood backwards" what has happened and what this death means. Bereaved parents can be encouraged to explore and reflect on what their loss means by gently asking them open-ended, "what" questions. For example:

What is it like for you to _____?
What does _____ mean to you?
What are you feeling _____ about?
What is different now about _____?
What changes have you made in _____?
What has been helpful to you? hurtful to you?
What do you need in order to _____?
What is your role of _____ like now?
What is still possible?
What have you learned from _____?
What is your relationship with _____ like now?
What would _____ be like if _____?
What action(s) do you need to take to _____?

Understanding can become a catalyst for action when parents consciously realize they cannot change what has happened and it's up to them whether and how they go forward. Doris provides an example. She talked about having a job during the first 4 years after Evan's death and said during the interview she was beginning to see some changes from those early years.

> So I don't know, in the beginning life happened and I was there, and now maybe I've changed the things that are happening. Life made me get up every morning and now I am the one who gets up. [It sounds to me like you've decided that you're gonna live again.] And I feel guilty about that [voice breaking]. And there are times I don't know why. Why I want to. And there are still days when I don't want to.

As Doris exemplifies, understanding what has happened, regaining control, and finding meaning in life again is an ongoing, up-and-down process. Ambivalence is common. It takes time, usually a great deal of time, for the heart to acknowledge and absorb what the head knows and has come to believe. This absorption of what the loss means is pervasive; it takes place at the cellular level as well as the social level. Bereaved parents' interactions with family and friends can greatly influence their meaning-making process. Sometimes parents no longer find old relationships meaningful, and this is especially true when friends or family members don't mention or include memories of the child who died. These parents frequently seek out new relationships, often with other bereaved parents, with people who continue to acknowledge their loss and remember their child. Parents often say they never would have imagined how much their loss would effect all of the other relationships in their lives. Thus, meaning-making is both an inner, psychological process and an external, sociological process.

Janice Nadeau (1998) studied extensively how families make sense of death. Her research demonstrates that individuals do not just make or find their own meanings, they do so both as part of and apart from family and friends. Individuals are both stimulated and inhibited by others in how they make sense of their experiences. Meaning-making *stimulators* include, for example, such things as comparing one's beliefs with others, telling stories, sharing dreams, asking questions, and noticing coincidences that create shared understanding. Meaning-making *inhibitors* are features that impede the process, such as family rules that prohibit talking about sensitive issues, family dynamics that cut off input from certain members, and collaborations that aim to protect some members from pain by restricting information and sharing.

As Nadeau pointed out, knowing the meaning that the loss has to the bereaved is critical to the integrity and value of therapeutic interventions. "What does this mean to you?" is a critical question to ask bereaved parents. It's also important to assure them that they may not yet know what this means, that knowing is a process that takes time, that when they feel stuck about not knowing, they can begin by expressing what this loss does *not* mean. Parents need to be assured that it is normal to question, to search for meaning, to believe there can never be any sense made of a child's death, to decide to live with unanswerable questions. It is also normal to consider and discard several possible meanings, leaving only those they find acceptable from their current perspectives. It is important to stress that acknowledging positive meanings does *not* mean that they condone their child's death. When parents feel like their world has stopped and is meaningless, they need to be encouraged to remain open to the idea that change is still possible. New meanings can be discovered; old meanings can be discarded. Parents create their own hope when they recognize that meanings and behavior patterns which were once important are no longer useful and they can decide to take action to initiate change. When grief leaves parents numb and unable to even fathom what meaning could be made of such pain, it's important to provide assurance that sometimes meaning comes in its own time, without conscious effort and when least expected. Thus, meaning-making is a process that can be consciously initiated and influenced by various interventions but it is also a phenomenon that can be intuitive, mysterious and sudden. Symbolism is one example of how meaning-making can be both conscious and unconscious.

The Role of Symbolism

Symbolism is frequently a part of bereaved parents' search for meaning. Acute pain and agony are difficult to express in words; symbols can create and convey a deeper, more personal yet universal understanding and connection. Benoliel (1985) noted that loss can be an initiator of creative personal expression. Such expression takes many different and symbolic forms, some of which are discussed here.

Sometimes new meanings come to bereaved parents through dreams and/or during times of prayer and meditation. This "coming through" is often experienced as a "coming from"—a special message from God and/or from the deceased child. The dictionary defines *numen* as an indwelling, guiding force or spirit and *numinous* as having a deeply spiritual or mystical effect. In her psychological study of childbearing loss, Savage (1989) explored the experience of mourning using a numinous paradigm: "Like ancient man's initiation mysteries [rituals, rites of passage], grief also seeks to understand and experience the healing, transformative nature of the numinous" (p. 47). The paradigm Savage used in her analysis of mourning follows Neumann's (1970) "archetype of the way," a guiding process that proceeds from birth to death to search, recovery, and rebirth. Within this paradigm there is recognition of the human "will to meaning" (Frankl, 1969), the desire to understand the significance of the experience of suffering and death. Critical to this understanding, Savage asserted, is the analysis of dreams about the deceased. She provided numerous examples of dreams of bereaved mothers in which the figure of the dead child could be seen as a symbol for some inner reality of the bereaved mother. When this symbolic phenomenon was brought to consciousness through analysis, Savage found that bereaved mothers experienced sudden and meaningful clarity regarding the significance of their loss.

Julie provides an example of how a dream helped her understand her own "destiny" and integrate her past and the loss of her son, her only child, with her new life.

My Nanna died when I was six, but she was like the matriarch of the family. And at one of the masses we had for my Dad [after his death], I think it was his birthday or death anniversary, a cousin, who's a Deacon, said the gospel and he spoke about my Nanna. He said how being a bereaved mother, she had a dream one night where she dreamt of her daughter Mary. [In the dream] she says: "Mary, you have a heart condition"—she was carrying a bucket of water in each hand—and my Nanna says to her, "Mary you shouldn't be doing that, you have a heart condition." She said "you shouldn't be lifting that, it's heavy." And Mary said, "Mama, that's your tears. You have to let go of your tears so that I don't have to carry them around." And after that, my cousin said that Nanna used to help everyone on the block—cause we lived in Brooklyn in brownstone houses and she used to help everyone then who was experiencing the loss of a job, or the loss of a child, or whatever—people would go to listen to her. So my cousin in the church said how he had this cousin who's doing the same thing for other people, which was me. And when he said that, I thought GEE! And afterwards I went up to him and I said, "truly I have never heard that story before," and he said, "Why do you think you were named after Nanna?" Yeah, he said, "who would of known?" He said, "you're doing the same work that Nanna did, with your Compassionate Friends." [Julie had become a TCF chapter leader]

Hearing Julie's dream experience brought back my own memory of a healing dream I had after the death of my daughter. My dream occurred 9 years after Leah's death. At that time I had not read Savage's research nor studied dream analysis (cf. Moustakas, 1994). On April 28, 1991, I awoke with memory of the following dream, which I recorded in my journal:

In the dream I was anguished because Leah and I had been separated for a long time. I didn't know where she was but somehow I knew I wasn't suppose to see her. My mother was there, and she and I had an argument. She didn't want me to see Leah and I thought she had been hiding information about Leah. I pointed to several empty photo frames where Leah's pictures had been and insisted on going to see Leah. Next I was under water and brightly colored fish were going by. There were three channels with the largest fish in the center channel. I saw Leah coming towards me from the third channel, the one farthest away. She was holding someone's hand and she didn't have on her glasses. I didn't think she could see me. I crossed over the center channel to go to her and she knew me when I spoke to her. We held each other and cried and cried together. I awoke feeling peaceful, serene, forgiven.

Two weeks later I shared that dream with my therapist and wrote down my interpretation of it after our session. I decided that the sea in the dream represented Jung's "collective unconscious." Its rocking movement was soothing in the way that a mother rocks a child to comfort her. The fish were intensely beautiful and interesting. Crossing the channel to Leah, I felt lighthearted, almost like I was going on an adventure. I decided it was God holding Leah's hand. God was taking care of her; she no longer needed her glasses, which I had laid beside her in her casket and buried with her. Crossing over the center channel meant that I had left a "negative mother" behind; and perhaps the empty picture frames meant that I had left my negative self behind as well. This dream remains a vivid turning point in my grief. It allowed me to forgive myself for not being able to prevent Leah's death, and it provided comforting assurance that she was with God and this was where she was supposed to be. Two months later, I reflected on this dream again. I saw that it was after this dream that I moved beyond the "Why?" questions of Leah's death to asking, "What now?"

The use of symbolism as a way of searching for meaning was also demonstrated by Luba Klot Slodov (1992), who used art therapy as a way of visually understanding her childhood survival of the Nazi concentration camps and affirming the meaning of her life. She wrote of the guilt she felt for having survived when a million and a half other children died: "Being spared gives one a tremendous feeling of responsibility. Before the war I need not have had a reason for being alive. Now I did" (p. 87). Finding meaning in becoming a teacher, an artist, and an art therapist, Slodov described the process of healing that she continued to experience through her artwork:

> In times of trouble, art pierces through my soul and presents itself as a trainload of images of a painful nature. Forgotten memories and present painful issues merge in concert into eruptive, volcanic explosions only to open old wounds that seek attention and healing. . . .
>
> For me, images surface when I am stimulated emotionally. When I seek solutions, significant imagery appears and reappears selectively. A dialogue occurs with the images as though they are my counselors. After gathering and selecting significant images, the [art] work begins. . . . The solutions are not obvious, nor do I feel any better until I go through the whole creative process and complete the likeness of my first perception.
>
> In my experience, giving birth to my children and creating new life and creating art is [sic] very much the same. As I am one with the child and then separate, so

it is in my art. One moment the art is part of the artist, the next it is separate. It is new, it is original, it is unique and separate, with new potential and new possibilities and new beginnings. Nurturing and loving and letting go is [sic] part of the process, the joy and pain equally significant. . . . I find my life and my art flowing from an inner urge motivated by my past to seek meaning in my life and be the best I can become. (pp. 116–118)

Whether through dream analysis, prayer and meditation, or art therapy, the intent is to expand the consciousness such that a spiritual attitude can be consciously realized and wholeness achieved. Savage (1989) argued that the process of grief resolution is a "cryptic analogue for the process of individuation" [ego development and the differentiation of the psyche], one that includes an expanded personal understanding of that which is collective and universal and that which is unique and individual (p. 46). Symbolism is a way of recognizing connections beyond the self. Bereaved parents feel disconnected from life as they have known it and disconnected from the child who contributed meaning to that life. Symbolism can help bereaved parents create a life that is meaningful again in new and different ways but one that also maintains a spiritual bond with their child.

The Role of Reframing

Meanings can also be found and/or created when bereaved parents reflect cognitively on individual aspects of their loss and grief. In her study of bereaved parents, Wheeler (1990) noted some evidence of reframing in the descriptive data she collected. "One father reported that what gave him meaning was, 'Realizing that, by turning the equation around, I can celebrate his *life* (our love, our good times together, his humor, courage and wisdom) instead of concentrating exclusively on his death'" (p. 118).

The power of reframing was eloquently portrayed by Frankl (1978) as he described the psychology of surviving the concentration camps of World War II:

Certainly we are used to discovering meaning in creating a work or doing a deed, or in experiencing something or encountering someone. But we must never forget that we may also find meaning in life even when confronted with a hopeless situation as its helpless victim, when facing a fate that cannot be changed. For what then counts and matters is to bear witness to the uniquely human potential at its best, which is to transform a tragedy into a personal triumph, to turn one's predicament into a human achievement. When we are no longer able to change a situation—just think of an incurable disease, say, an inoperable cancer—we are challenged to change ourselves. . . . This is brought home most beautifully by the words of Yehuda Bacon, an Israeli sculptor who was imprisoned in Auschwitz when he was a young boy and after the war wrote a paper from which I would like to quote a passage: "As a boy I thought: I will tell them what I saw, in the hope that people will change for the better. But people didn't change and didn't even want to know. It was much later that I really understood the meaning of suffering. It can have a meaning if it changes oneself for the better." He finally recognized the meaning of his suffering: he changed himself. Changing oneself often means rising above oneself, growing beyond oneself. (p. 39)

When bereaved parents are unable to make any sense of their child's death, they can still find or create meaning by what they decide to do in response to that death. It is a response only they can make. Expanding one's frame of reference in the wake of this tragedy comes from reflecting on painful questions: In what ways am I different because I parented this unique child? In what ways am I different because this unique child died? What thoughts keep coming to me about this loss? Are these thoughts rational—do they reflect the true reality of my child's life as well as her death? How are the world and the people in it different because this unique child lived? What would my child want me to feel and do now? What can I contribute to the world that would honor my child's life? What would it mean to others to see me respond to my loss in this way?

As parents reflect on questions like these they need others around them who can serve as "sounding boards." This is a role commonly taken by counselors and therapists as well as by trusted friends and family members. The process of cognitive restructuring is one of externalizing thoughts and reflections, hearing them rephrased by someone else, having one's meanings reality-tested and validated, and discovering new ways of looking at thoughts and experiences. Meanings come not just from what the heart feels; they come from what the mind says. It is important for bereaved parents to realize that meanings come from both their hearts and their minds and that meanings can change as their grief evolves.

THE ROLE OF SCRIPTOTHERAPY AND BIBLIOTHERAPY

When my daughter died in 1982 there were few books available that could help answer the many questions I had. But someone sent me Rabbi Kushner's just-published book *When Bad Things Happen to Good People* (1981). I found it comforting and helpful. Since that time there have been many books published about the death of a child, many written by bereaved parents reflecting on their process of trying to find meaning and make sense of their child's death. One example is George McGovern's (1996) book about the death of his daughter: *Terry: My Daughter's Life-and-Death Struggle with Alcoholism*. Scriptotherapy, also know as journaling or writing as a form of therapeutic expression, has become recognized as an effective part of self-help and therapy. As Riordan (2001) noted:

> When we verbally label and describe an event—such as trauma—by writing about it, we can sort through it and gain a sense of control. . . . Scriptotherapy also works by bringing the subconscious to the conscious. Poetry, in particular, seems to provide rich material from our subconscious. Writing about our troubles teases out remnants of other themes in our lives that may also bear on our trauma. (p. 6)

Bibliotherapy, reading selected literary resources, is another important tool be-reaved parents use to understand their grief as they contrast their experiences to those of others (cf. McCracken & Semel, 1998). I used scriptotherapy and biblio-therapy to address my feelings of guilt and anger after my daughter died. The process ultimately led me to study the concept of forgiveness.[2] Guilt and anger can be debilitating for bereaved parents and forgiveness is frequently misunder-stood. The conclusions I reached brought new meaning and perspective to my grief process. They are included as an example of how scriptotherapy and biblio-therapy can be cathartic and meaningful to the individual griever and useful to others who may be struggling with similar emotions or circumstances.

The Gift of Forgiveness (Talbot, 1999, 2001)

When Leah died, I felt like I'd landed on some unknown planet. I didn't know the language or the rules. I felt powerless, angry, betrayed, guilty, alone, and hopeless. Before Leah died, I had not thought a whole lot about forgiveness. But in the early years after her death I came to realize that guilt and anger were key emotions be-hind the pain that was searing my soul. Through a long process of study and reflec-tion, I came to realize that feelings of anger, resentment, and guilt are part of grief for most people. Often our anger is directed at others, such as doctors, nurses, clergy, police, family, friends, God, and/or the loved one who died and left us. This is especially true when the death was by suicide or murder or might have been pre-ventable in some way.

Like so many bereaved parents, I felt guilty for not being able to keep my daughter alive somehow. For a long time I believed that I had failed in my duty as Leah's mother. I should have taken her home with me the day I visited her at camp and learned she had caught a cold. I decided I was guilty of not being diligent enough. At the same time there was the guilt I felt because her death brought free-dom from the exhausting responsibility of being a single parent raising a child with special needs while working at a challenging full-time job. It was only after a long process of counseling, study, and spiritual exploration that I concluded my guilt was misconstrued. I did not have the power to keep anyone else alive, not even my beloved Leah. *Sometimes it is easier to live with guilt than to feel powerless.* That was such an imporant learning for me: *Sometimes it is easier to live with guilt than to feel powerless.* Gradually the process of re-examining and changing my thoughts and beliefs allowed me to relinquish my guilt and forgive myself. I came to believe that for reasons unknown to me, Leah had followed her own destiny.

Ultimately I had to admit that I was indeed powerless in many ways. One of the paradoxes of grief is that my guilt represented my power, at least for awhile. When I was able to let go of my guilt, my power to choose more positive and mean-ingful ways to grieve returned and strengthened me.

Anger is another emotion that commonly accompanies grief. We are angry at ourselves for things we did and/or didn't do or say, most often preceded in our thinking by the words "if only." Sometimes we use our anger to avoid the pain of our loss or to avoid communicating with others about what we are feeling. We can

[2]For guidelines in using intentional forgiveness as a counseling intervention, see Ferch, 1998.

find ourselves resenting people who don't understand us. When this happens, it helps me to remember how one person defined resentment. She said that *harboring resentment is like drinking a cup of poison and expecting the other person to die.* Another wise saying helps me remember to examine my expectations. That saying is: unrealistic expectations lead to premeditated resentments. *Unrealistic expectations lead to premeditated resentments.* Perhaps my most important resentment was at God. If I could not keep my daughter alive, why didn't God step in and do it for me? Was I being punished for the sin in my life? For a time I wished I was Catholic and could go to confession and be forgiven every week. Yet I knew many faithful Catholics also struggled with guilt and anger at God. I concluded that the loving God of my understanding would not punish my daughter to get even with me for my sins. So just where is God when bad things happen? (Talbot, 2000b). This was another question I lived with and worked through for a long time. Surprisingly, it even became the title of a sermon I was invited to preach many years later, after I had joined a twelve-step support group and become an ordained Presbyterian elder.

Actually, anger can be a useful emotion. My anger kept me in dialogue and relationship with God. Ultimately I came to believe that God did not choose for Leah to die, it was merely her time to leave this world and continue her spiritual journey in God's kingdom. God's promise is to be with and within me, supporting and comforting me during all the events of my life, those that bring joy and those that bring grief. I received this message in a dream several years after Leah's death. I awoke from that dream with a kind of peace I had never felt before. It is a feeling best described by our word forgiveness. That feeling dissolves anger and resentment like an antacid. Forgiveness, I now believe, is the process of identifying, claiming, and expressing anger, and becoming willing to forgive who and whatever is the source of that anger.

I found it essential to release my anger before it could harden into bitterness. It's often said that experiencing a loss will make us either bitter or better people. Bitterness hardens our hearts and we suffer another loss—we lose the ability to give and receive love. In his book *Seventy Times Seven—The Power of Forgiveness,* Johann Christoph Arnold (1997) wrote: "Bitterness destroys our souls, and it can destroy our bodies as well. We know that stress can cause an ulcer or a migraine, but we fail to see the relationship between bitterness and insomnia. Medical researchers have even shown a connection between unresolved anger and heart attacks; it seems that people who bottle up their resentment are far more susceptible than those who are able to defuse it by venting their emotions" (p. 8). I had to learn how to feel and release my anger. I also learned that an attitude of gratitude can be a powerful antidote for anxiety and a guard against unrealistic expectations. I found it impossible to feel anxious, afraid, or angry and grateful at the same time.

Today in my work with grieving people, I often find that forgiveness is misunderstood. What does forgiveness mean? First, let's look at what forgiveness doesn't mean. *Forgiveness does NOT mean* condoning or pardoning insensitive or abusive behavior, or acting like everything is OK when we feel it isn't. It does *not* mean forgetting what has happened, or naively trusting others who have shown themselves to be untrustworthy. Robin Casarjian explains this in her book *Forgiveness— A Bold Choice for a Peaceful Heart* (1992). She maintains that what we forgive is not the *act*, not the abuse or the insensitivity. What we forgive is the *people*, the people who could not manage to honor and cherish themselves, us, their families, their spouses, their children or others. What we forgive is their confusion and ignorance and desperation and whatever it happens to be. "Forgiveness is not about what we do," she says, "it is about the way we perceive people and circumstances" (p. 30). For example, we can forgive somebody and set boundaries and still take action. We can forgive someone and litigate against them. So forgiving myself for not being able to save Leah doesn't mean I don't have any regrets. It does mean that I view myself and my parenting role differently.

Thus, forgiveness is *a conscious decision* to stop hating both others and ourselves. It is an act of self-interest—something we do for ourselves to find greater freedom and peace. Even when we have suffered outrageous trauma, we can work through our appropriate anger and choose forgiveness as a powerful way to cast off the role of victim. Psychologist Richard Gayton journeyed through this difficult process after his wife was murdered in their home. He now shares his learnings about forgiveness with others. In his 1995 book *The Forgiving Place: Choosing Peace After Violent Trauma* he wrote: "I have found that, in my twenty years of working with survivors of assault, murder, rape, war, suicide, and other violent trauma, this dual approach, both psychological and spiritual, offers the best hope for full recovery. To cope with violent trauma, we must accept the primitive, self-destructive impulses of man. And we must also discover his powerful inner resources for love and regeneration. Tools of psychology help us heal the wounded emotions; spiritual practice allows us to reconnect with the source of life within us, an ancient memory of our value and essential goodness that propels us beyond our woundedness" (p. xvi).

So . . . when we choose forgiveness we consciously recognize that we cannot change what has happened. We cannot change the fact that our child died or how others react to that fact or to us. But we *can* change ourselves—gradually, over time, and with much difficult emotional work. Gayton noted that "this journey to forgiveness against what seems impossible odds teaches us of the ability of the human psyche to regenerate itself and return to life more capable of loving and receiving love than before" (p. xvi). To me, this means that increased love can be my daughter's legacy to the world. Gayton described the formation of what he called a "Forgiving Self." He maintained that "we will know our minds have changed and made the values of our Forgiving Self a habit when we see certain behavioral and attitudinal shifts in ourselves. We will feel at peace with the memories of the violence" (p. 92). Note that he doesn't say we accept or agree with what has happened—with the death of our child. Rather, we create a place inside ourselves where we can be "at peace with the memories" of what happened. The peace Gayton described reminds me of my favorite definition of forgiveness: *"Forgiveness is giving up all hope for a better past"* (source unknown). When we experience forgiveness, we receive hope for *today* and for *the future.*

Gayton stressed that "An important indicator that we have created a permanent peaceful place in our life for the traumatic event is the completion of a 'memorial.' A memorial is a symbolic and at times physical representation and expression of our love for someone who has died, but it can also be a concrete reminder of the joy and growth we have attained from having overcome violence to ourselves" (p. 92). And we bereaved parents know we have been violated. Our child's death has torn a huge hole in our heart that can never be filled again. For us, healing means cauterizing the torn edges around that hole. Forgiving and feeling forgiven helps us generate bypasses around that huge hole in our heart. Memorials and rituals are tools we use to continue the healing process.

It is also important to realize that forgiveness is a process and not a one-time event that absolves us of all future feelings of anger or guilt. Actually, guilt, like anger, can be a useful emotion. Appropriate guilt stirs up our conscience and makes us realize we need to ask for forgiveness—as I asked God to forgive me for blaming him for not saving Leah. But if we harbor inappropriate guilt, it keeps us from feeling forgiven and from creating a healthy future.

As I studied forgiveness, I discovered that there are many biblical figures who asked for and received forgiveness. For example, we read in Genesis (39:47) that Joseph forgave his brothers for selling him into slavery in Egypt. In 2nd Samuel, we learn that King David admitted his sins of adultery and murder to God and God forgave him and held him up as Israel's greatest king. Job prayed for his friends who did not understand his grief and God forgave them and "blessed the latter part of Job's life more than the first" (Job 42:10, 12). This part of the Book of Job was difficult for me; I had to read it very carefully. Notice that God gave Job twice as many material possessions as he had lost but not twice as many children. God gave Job another 7 sons and 3 daughters, not 14 sons and 6 daughters. I believe this is because Job's 10 children who died were safely in God's loving arms and waiting to be reunited with their parents when their time came to die.

The prophet Ezekiel proclaimed God's message of hope and restoration to the Israelites. God promised the wicked that if they turned away from sin, made amends, and did what is just and right, God would not remember any of their sins (Ezekiel 33:14–16). You just read that for humans forgiving does not mean forgetting, but in Ezekiel God says he will do just that—he will forget all our sins. I think that's an amazing promise! And then there's Jesus. Jesus forgave his disciple Simon Peter who had disowned him. Peter accepted forgiveness and went on to become a great church leader (Mark 14:27–72; John 20:19–23).

In my evolving grief process, I have learned to identify, express, and release anger and inappropriate guilt; to forgive; to seek and receive forgiveness. As Rabbi Kushner wrote in *When Bad Things Happen to Good People* (1981), I have come to realize that: "the ability to forgive and the ability to love are the weapons God has given us to enable us to live fully, bravely, and meaningfully in this less-than-perfect world" (p. 148). I also believe that the person I am becoming in this process is a gift from my daughter. Not one I would have chosen, but one I choose to cherish nonetheless.

SUMMARY

A child's death presents bereaved parents with a need to understand the meaning of life, now: now that they have been thrust out of their everyday, routine experiences into the new, unwelcome reality of pain and sorrow. Learning how to go on living as a bereaved parent depends a great deal on parents' ability to participate in a lengthy, evolving, and ongoing meaning-making process. The preceding discussion points out the elements of that process, the types of meanings derived by bereaved parents, the most common sources of those meanings, what facilitates meaning-making, and the quality of life that can come out of the process.

To recap, the meaning-making process consists of consciously recognizing key questions about the loss, confronting a crisis of meaninglessness, and evaluating potential meanings over time as grief evolves. Parents use words, symbols, dreams, prayers, meditation, contemplative study, and cognitive reframing to work towards a balanced perspective about their loss, one that is both realistic and rational. There are four potential types of meaning reported by bereaved parents: positive, negative, and/or mixed meanings, and no meaning. Types of meaning can be divided further into those related to specific people or activities and those related to the parent's beliefs or values. There are many sources of meanings. The most common are the parent–child relationship; the child's life experiences and achievements; the child's ongoing influence in the parent's life; the parent's personal development and how it influenced parenting experiences; the parent's beliefs, assumptions, worldview, and life goals; circumstances surrounding the child's death; the child's legacy and memorials honoring the child; and the parent's participation in altruistic activities. Meaning-making facilitators can be positive or negative. Meaning-making *inhibitors* include personal or family dynamics, rules, or collaborations that inhibit information gathering and sharing. Meaning-making *stimulators* include comparing and sharing information and experiences, asking questions, and noticing coincidences. The outcome of meaning-making can be despair; feelings of worthlessness and lack of goals; and/or fixation on certain affects related to the loss, such as guilt and self-blame. But meaning-making can also result in a decision to reinvest in life; in recognition of personal growth; participation in new activities; establishing new goals and relationships; developing new interests; setting different priorities; and finding valuable ways to maintain a spiritual connection with the child.

The process of individual change in response to the death of a child takes many forms. Those that appear to be especially important to bereaved parents contain examples of searching for and finding or creating meaning. The following chapters continue the discussion of how bereaved parents change as they find and create new meanings many years after their child's death.

Chapter 5

Bereaved Parents'
Search for Understanding:
The Paradox of Healing

At a seminar on grief, Doug Manning (retired pastor, grief expert, and author) shared a remarkable story. Apparently a funeral home had decided to sponsor a grief group for persons who had experienced stillbirths. The meetings were to be held at the funeral home, in a study, on the first Monday of every month. About the time the very first meeting was to start, a little old lady wandered into the funeral home. Thinking she had come for a viewing, the funeral director approached her.

"No," she asserted. "I'm here for the grief group. You see, sixty-one years ago I delivered a stillborn baby boy. My husband took him and buried him before I even got out of the hospital. I didn't even get to see him. My husband came into my room at the hospital and said, 'The baby's gone. I've buried him, and I never want to hear you mention it again.' So for the last six decades I've mourned for that little baby inside myself. Well, four months ago, my husband died . . . and I'm here to talk about my little boy . . . I named him Randy . . . and you're the first person I've ever told." (Used by permission of D. Manning; personal communication, October 12, 2001.)

When a child dies, whether in the womb, during childhood or adolescence, or as an adult, bereaved parents are overwhelmed by the intensity of the pain they must endure. Most search for people who can understand what it is like to live with this kind of life-changing loss. There is a need for the validation of feelings, for inspiration, and for reasons to hope that life can be less painful and meaningful once again. Sometimes the search for understanding results in new hurts and fractures in existing relationships with family and/or friends. For many parents, family, friends, and/or professionals play key supportive roles. The intent of this chapter is to demonstrate the impact that supportive and nonsupportive others can have on the life-worlds of bereaved parents.

SOCIETY'S REACTION TO BEREAVED PARENTS

In her study of death of a parent, spouse, or child, Sanders (1999) found that:

> Parental bereavement produced the greatest feelings of isolation and stigma. . . . Parents were aware that what they had experienced was one of the worst things that could ever happen to a person and that few other individuals wanted to connect with anyone who had experienced this kind of tragedy. One mother compared it to being a leper without a colony. Several spoke of walking down the street and seeing friends a distance away actually cross the street to avoid having to speak to them. Yet some of these parents would hesitate to mention these incidents for fear of sounding unduly paranoid. In reacting to their own projections as well as to the real reactions of friends and relatives, they created a world of sequestration that was akin to quarantine. (pp. 144–145)

Our society in general has not been particularly supportive of bereaved parents. For example, the women Oliver (1990) studied all claimed they would not have discussed certain aspects of the grieving process with anyone but another bereaved parent (p. 216). The experiences of these mothers following the deaths of their children confirmed "that there is little societal support available to the bereaved mother. The bereaved parent is met with fear, platitudes, an impatience with their grieving process and clear directives that their mourning is somehow aberrant" (Oliver, 1990, p. 209).

The need for and benefit of support from others for bereaved parents is undisputed in the literature, but the details—the type, timing, and efficacy of specific interventions—are less clear. Research has offered no prescriptive approach that can be said to totally meet the support needs of bereaved parents. There are obvious limitations to the number of measurements that can be included in research studies, and the need for longitudinal study of interventions adds to the complexity and cost of such research. The majority of bereavement research has been retrospective, and much of it has included parents during the early years of acute grief.

One recent exception is the 5-year "Parent Bereavement Stress and Nursing Intervention" study conducted in the state of Washington (Murphy, Lohan, Dimond, & Fan, 1998; Murphy, 2000). This study offered both informational and emotional support to 171 bereaved mothers and 90 fathers whose children aged 12 to 28 died sudden, violent deaths. A comparison group of 19 parents received no intervention. The parents were recruited into the study around 4 months after their child's death and took part in a 12-week intervention support program. Follow-up data were collected from the parents at 1, 2, and 5 years postdeath. The study findings demonstrated that offering support was helpful and positively influenced outcome, although parents' reduction in mental distress and trauma symptoms was "very slow." When they entered the study, about 33% of the parents met *DSM* criteria for posttraumatic stress disorder. Two years after the deaths, 21% of the mothers and 14% of the fathers met PTSD criteria. Five years after the deaths, 2% of the mothers and 6% of the fathers could still be diagnosed as positive for PTSD (Murphy, 2000, p. 593). The study investigators concluded that "referrals to support groups, bereavement counselors, and other services may need to be made at any time from early bereavement and even up to 5 years after the death of a child" (p. 596). Further, they recommended, "an important next step is to randomly assign parents to a variety of bereavement programs, i.e. telephone hotlines, parent-to-parent interactions, formal programs, and existing community resources, as an attempt to learn who needs what when" (Murphy, 2000, p. 599).

What seems clear from studies done to date is that "support" is necessary and important to bereaved parents' adaptation after the death of their child, but parents have diverse needs and perceptions about what is supportive. What some parents find helpful, others may not find helpful at all, and timing can be critical. This is an area much in need of additional study.

The following sections contain examples from women in the "Mothers Now Childless" study. Their experiences help us understand some of the ways bereaved parents' grief can be impacted by those around them.

Support From Others as Perceived by "Mothers Now Childless" Participants

Following the death of a child, most parents want and need supportive, nonjudgmental friends and family who will listen and try to understand their pain. Relationships played a significant role in either helping or hindering the healing of the women who participated in the "Mothers Now Childless" study. Participants were asked to indicate "to what degree you feel your family and friends have been helpful to you during your bereavement" and checked one of four responses: *very helpful, somewhat helpful, unhelpful,* or *very unhelpful.* They were also asked to write in examples of "the ways they have been helpful and/or unhelpful." It was surprising that so many of the women reported a dichotomy between their family and friends. Some said their family was very helpful but their friends were very unhelpful. For others the opposite was true. Thus, it was necessary to separate family and friends when tabulating the responses. It was clear that separating out unhelpful friends and/or family was a painful part of learning to live with their loss for many of the mothers in the study.

The perceived helpfulness of family and that of friends were factors that discriminated between the two groups of women who represented opposite ends of the bereavement continuum. As shown in Table 5.1, a majority of those in the group representing survival had felt supported by family and friends and had either regularly or occasionally attended a support group after their child died. The opposite was true for the majority of those in the group representing perpetual bereavement. It was clear from the written comments and the interviews that the women in the study had strong opinions and feelings about those closest to them and how they had offered or failed to offer needed and expected support. The stories of the women that follow highlight some of the factors that explain why the support of friends and family can be of critical importance to bereaved parents.

Parents' Fear of Forgetting the Child

One of the biggest fears bereaved parents have is that their child will be forgotten (Klass, 1988, 1993, 1996; Knapp, 1986; Rando, 1986, 1993; Rosenblatt, 2000a). How others react to the death of their child can perpetuate and heighten this fear or help to eliminate it. Anita and Helen provide contrasting examples.

Anita: No One Wants To Remember Him

 All of her son Brad's clothing and possessions were displayed in a basement "bedroom" in Anita's new home where she and her husband had moved after Brad's death. "I've not gotten rid of hardly anything . . . that way you don't feel like they've just been forgotten," she said. Anita talked about how her fear that her son will be forgotten was reinforced by many of those around her:

> The thing that gets me is that other people don't want to remember him. Do you find that to be true? It's almost a hundred percent across almost everybody I've ever talked to. I don't understand it. They'd say, "oh well gee, you're crying." Well, these are tears of . . . happy memories, let me cry a little bit. I need to. . . . When I try to talk about Brad it's just like they've been struck by an ice cube or something. They just get all cold and stiff, and "why are you talking about him?" And they don't know what to say back. And so I don't speak about him very much or very often or for a very long amount of time, and that hurts and I don't like that. He was and is a part of my life, and he always will be.

Many bereaved parents realize that others either cannot or will not meet their needs for keeping their child's memory alive and they search out other bereaved parents in groups like The Compassionate Friends (TCF). Anita attended TCF meetings a few times after Brad's death and was still on the newsletter mailing list.

> I don't go (to TCF meetings) because it seems like, there again, most of them still have more kids. It's not just them and them alone. So sometime in the evening they then start talking about the rest of their family, and I just chose not to go again.

Although Anita did learn at these meetings that "it's normal to still hurt, and miss, and cry," she reflected that "the one thing I was afraid of for a long time was the fact that gee, if I let myself go and smile, it was gonna mean I forgot Brad or that I don't love him anymore. And I still sometimes am finding myself doing that; I

Table 5.1   Excerpted Responses to Participant Questionnaire by Discriminant Groups: Support From Others

Response to Questionnaire	Perpetual Bereavement ($n = 18$) Frequency (%)	Survival ($n = 62$) Frequency (%)	χ^2 (80)
Level of grief felt now:			15.96**
Grief dominates life	3 (16.7)[b]	0 (0)	
Feel grief daily	8 (44.4)[b]	24 (38.7)	
Feel grief weekly	3 (16.7)	16 (25.8)[b]	
Feel grief occasionally	3 (16.7)	22 (35.5)[b]	
No longer grieve	1 (5.6)	0 (0)[b]	
Helpfulness of family:			13.17**
Very unhelpful	6 (33.3)[b]	3 (4.8)	
Unhelpful	4 (22.2)[b]	9 (14.5)	
Somewhat helpful	4 (22.2)	22 (35.5)[b]	
Very helpful	4 (22.2)	28 (45.2)[b]	
Helpfulness of friends:[a]			47.89**
Very unhelpful	8 (44.4)[b]	0 (0)	
Unhelpful	6 (33.3)[b]	3 (.8)	
Somewhat helpful	3 (16.7)	21 (33.9)[b]	
Very helpful	1 (5.6)	38 (61.3)[bb]	
Attend support group(s):			12.99**
Never attended	3 (16.7)[b]	2 (3.2)	
Once or twice	2 (11.1)[b]	7 (11.3)	
Occasionally	10 (55.6)	16 (25.8)[b]	
Regularly	3 (16.7)	37 (59.7)[b]	
Still attend support group(s):			1.24
No	11 (61.1)	34 (54.8)	
Yes	4 (22.2)	25 (40.3)	
N/A or missing	3 (16.7)	3 (4.8)	
Grief therapy:			4.19
Never	5 (27.8)	22 (35.5)	
Once or twice	3 (16.7)	11 (17.7)	
Occasionally	6 (33.3)	8 (12.9)	
Regularly	4 (22.2)	21 (33.9)	
Marital status:			11.49*
Married—to father of child	5 (27.8)	32 (51.6)[b]	
Married—not to father of child	3 (16.7)	13 (21.0)[b]	
Single—divorced	5 (27.8)[b]	14 (22.6)	
Single—never married	2 (11.1)[b]	0 (0)	
Widowed	3 (16.7)[b]	3 (4.8)	
Believe survived child's death:			23.03**
No	9 (50.0)[b]	3 (4.8)	
Yes	7 (38.9)	53 (85.5)[b]	
Yes and no	2 (11.1)	6 (9.7)[b]	

[a]Discriminating variable used to determine group membership. [b]These results highlight and contrast statistically significant differences between responses from the two groups. For example, a total of 72.6% of those representing the "survival" group were married, whereas a total of 55.6% of those in the "perpetual bereavement" group were either divorced, never married, or widowed at the time of contact.
* $p < .05$. ** $p < .01$.

do." Anita had found the TCF meetings painful, partly because she felt different from parents with surviving children. Her decision not to continue attending left Anita once again feeling alone with her grief and her fear that her son would be forgotten.

Helen: I Have a New Family Now

Helen had a similar experience of feeling different but had made choices that eventually resulted in a more positive outcome. "At the very beginning I was in total denial," Helen said. She and her husband Steve moved "clear across the state. . . . I figured if I changed everything . . . it'd get better. And it didn't. It was horrible." They moved to be near friends of Helen's from grade school who "eventually turned out to be just after what I was gonna do with my things. 'Now that you have no children, what are you gonna do with your house when you die?'" This prompted them to move again, and in her next town Helen found a Compassionate Friends group that she and Steve began to attend. Soon she found herself volunteering to make the coffee and bring snacks for the meeting.

> That nurturing or whatever part of me came back . . . then I had another reason, see. I had something to take care of, someone to take care of. And I think that's what happened. And I did get that satisfaction out of that part of it, but . . . I would go home and feel real alone and empty.

The group was meeting Helen's need to be needed, but not her need for understanding.

> After a while I didn't fit in because they do start talking about their other children, and our needs are different. Our futures have stopped; theirs continue to go on. The tragedy of their losing a child is no different than us losing our only one, but they have a purpose to get up eventually. . . . Going to The Compassionate Friends I could see them getting better—going up on a graph—and I could see us trying and just going like this, going down for no reason. We had no reason to go on. No reasons for any get-togethers or family reunions or anything anymore; it was gone. . . . And we *are* the ultimate loss. And we *are* spooky. We *are* different. And people don't know what to do about that, you know, they feel very uncomfortable.

Feeling different from and "jealous" of other bereaved parents with surviving children, Helen turned to her family for support, and found "they just disappeared. . . . They won't talk about him, and don't want to remember him, or acknowledge my loss."

During her fifth year of attending Compassionate Friends meetings, Helen met another mother who had also lost an only child. Together they decided to start their own support group for others like them. This group continues to grow, and Helen says, "I consider this group my family now." She still takes care of her

93-year-old mother, but has "cut off" the rest of her family, and others who "didn't understand."

> I started, I think, weeding out. Well, I did it. I didn't want to be around people that upset me or people that brought me down, or didn't understand. I just eliminated those people out of my life. I only wanted to be around people that I would feel the best around. I didn't waste my time anymore on trying to please somebody else, and not getting fed myself. . . . I've always been a people-pleaser. I've learned that the past 12 years, without knowing that before. I've always been a people-pleaser, but now I pick and choose the people I want to please.

In reviewing her relationship with the significant others in her life following the death of her son, Helen eventually was able to see the locus of control evident in their exchanges. Doing so helped her decide to begin changing her long-term pattern of "people-pleasing" behavior.

Helen talks of having "an awakening" during her fifth year of bereavement. In addition to starting the new support group, she began going to church with her husband and "started being around kids again, feeding them cookies." She took walks in the woods and began "to see the real beautiful things" in nature. She decided she wanted another dog as a Mother's Day present to herself. And she received a wonderful gift in memory of her son from his fiancée, Andrea, and her family.

> It was the fifth Christmas [after her son's death]. Andrea's mom made a vest of a pair of Bill's jeans. I have it and I gotta show you that. . . . [reading the accompanying note:] "Helen—This is made with all our love to help keep you warm. I used pants that I had of Bill's. Note the grease spots because they were a part of him. He tried to tear the Wrangler tag off and I left it as it was, so says Andrea. The pockets on the sleeve were Jason's [Andrea's little brother] because he wanted to keep you warm too. Hope you enjoy wearing this as much as I enjoyed making it for you," signed by the whole family. I mean, and they never forgot him. Five years later when most people don't even (mention him), they did this! . . . They ALL had a hand in this. They don't forget him; it's wonderful.

Helen also found support from another source that surprised her. Her husband's stepmother who lived in another town, encouraged her to write her feelings in weekly letters. In her stepmom's return letters Helen found "the most fantastic support I've ever had."

> For 10 years I wrote to her every Sunday and she wrote back every Wednesday . . . and she saved every one of my letters. She kept saying to me all along, "you have changed so much." [Years later, after her stepmom died, Helen's letters were returned to her and she began rereading them.] I read the first two years [of letters], and I didn't heal at all. . . . So two years was nothing. I thought there must have been a big change within there, but there wasn't . . . just denial and anger.

Helen remembered her stepmom told her that "since you got the (support) group started, *there's* been the biggest change in your grief." Helen talked about how the group helped meet her need for understanding and gave her a way to help others in memory of her son.

> What we've found [at the support group] is the fact that when we're amongst the people who truly understand that it takes care of all the other garbage. You're here. You all have lost your only child; you're all in the same situation; you're all in the same boat. Draw strength from this and then see if you can branch out, you know, as time goes on. You can't do it right off the bat, for sure. And I let them know that it will change. I don't like to say it gets better; it doesn't get better. You change. You accept this. You learn to live with this situation.

For Helen, as for many (but not all) bereaved parents, it was important to be with others who had had the same type of loss—in this case, the death of an only child. Feeling understood and accepted helped Helen learn to live with this nonnormative loss. "I've never felt so at peace as I do now," she said. "And I believe the group has a lot to do with it. They keep me going with, well, what do you think? I'm needed. I guess that's the thing. I guess I'm needed there." As she grew stronger, Helen became able to see her grief change and knew that others could be helped in the same way. She continued: "But also on the second hand, I can see now that I'm starting to delegate some things, and it's been a real pleasure. . . . It's, oh, I am so proud of myself to see that this is what's happening now. I'm real happy about that. Not that I don't have to do it anymore, it's the fact that *they*—they need to be needed. They need to be busy. [And it's helping them the same way it helped you?] That's right."

The Potential Risk in Reaching out for Help

When bereaved parents reach out for help from others, there is an inherent risk they will suffer additional emotional injuries. Ellen and Irene, representing opposite ends of the bereavement continuum, provide contrasting examples.

Ellen: Angry and Afraid to Risk Again

Ellen's family had been "very helpful" to her after her son Don's death and helped to keep his memory alive. She described how they helped: "If I wanted to talk, I could talk; if I didn't feel like talking, I didn't have to talk. I let them know at the beginning that I wanted Don remembered and I wanted to talk about Don, so there's never been an uncomfortable feeling amongst us when Don's name is spoken. They let me know they remember when his birthday and death anniversary dates roll around." Ellen's friends, however, had been "very unhelpful" and added to her grief.

> I had five what I considered really, really good friends down home that I thought . . . they are just gonna rally around. But after the funeral was over, so was their help and closeness. This has really stuck with me and even after numerous letters they still never contact me, so I gave up on them. And I have been SO ANGRY AT THEM.

In early grief, Ellen had attended one Compassionate Friends meeting, which she found helpful, but she could not bring herself to go back, and had "never understood why." What Ellen did understand, all too well, was that new relationships always present the potential for additional losses. Ellen's pastor and doctor, both of whom she confided in after Don's death, died a few years later. "It seems everyone of a professional level who could help me, I lost," she said. She decided she "didn't want to 'start over' with a new counselor 'cause I'm thinking, yeah, I'm gonna spill my guts to this person and then they're gonna be gone."

Many bereaved parents intuitively know when they are not strong enough to risk a new relationship. Sometimes this is interpreted by others as undesirable "distancing behavior," but it can be a necessary coping mechanism that allows parents' acute pain to heal and "scab over" a little until they feel ready to risk new relationships. This process of becoming strong enough again can be greatly enhanced by support from existing friends and/or family.

Irene: I Had to Stop Hiding

Irene, also a divorced mom like Ellen who raised her son alone, did not have a close, supportive family; in her case, friends and a counselor contributed to her healing. One close friend helped Irene through her son's funeral and "planted the seed of the healing that I needed to do. . . . She was my rock that I leaned on. . . . She knew I needed her and yet she didn't hover."

Two months after Bobby's death, Irene attended her first Compassionate Friends meeting and found other parents "further down the road" who gave her "a little bit of hope that yes, there is a tomorrow." She also received help when her doctor sent her to a grief counselor around the time of the first anniversary of her son's death. "I had several sessions with her and she focused me on what it was I was losing control of and helped me get over that first year and to get things a little bit under control, where I felt some control." Irene described the incremental coping process she used to help her regain control:

> I found that first year that I would sometimes be thinking if I can survive this five minutes, I'll worry about the next five minutes when this five minutes is up. And then time would extend, and I'd think if I can survive this next fifteen minutes I'll worry about the next fifteen minutes when this fifteen minutes is up. And then it becomes an hour. The time increments increase to the point that you say, if I can survive this day then I'll worry about tomorrow tomorrow morning. And I found myself doing a lot of that, because you just, you don't see the end of your pain.

[And what . . . was it that you did during those five minutes to survive?] I tried to not cry. I think the crying was the first thing I tried to stop because after a while you just, it was like I cannot cry anymore; it's too draining. It went beyond the point of being a catharsis to almost a little bit out of control, so you would think no, I'll try to not cry for five minutes. I'll try not to think about Bobby for five minutes. I'll try to think of gee, I need to write a check to pay a bill, or gee, I need to go to the grocery store, and then you would realize gee, ten minutes had gone by. It just gradually got better. But it was just, I think the crying was the first thing that I wanted to get to the point where I didn't do it all the time, because it drained me of strength and energy, and it was like there can't be another tear left in my body.

Irene used other coping methods as well. The year after Bobby's death, she began writing a journal to him, telling him all the things she wished she'd had just one last hour to tell him before he died. Looking back, Irene also recognized two turning points in her grief process. The first came when she used part of the insurance settlement from her son's accident to take a friend on a seven-week trip driving around the country.

I saw a lot of things that I had always wanted to see. And I always had Bobby with me, so when I was seeing all these things I wanted to see, I was also looking at them a second time for Bobby, because he never got to see them. And that trip basically got me back into the land of the living. . . . That trip was the turning point, and the real revelation . . . was standing at the Grand Canyon and realizing that I was just insignificant in the overall picture, and that millions of people had probably stood where I was standing, and a lot of them probably had been in pain. And I was able to in the grand scheme of things put my pain into the proper perspective on the order of things. And I thought—my pain—yes, I feel terrible; I hurt; I've lost my child, but on the grand scheme of things other people have suffered other things that my hurt pales in comparison, and that's the first time I knew that I was thinking in a healthy way. That I was able to just put things into perspective. But I really spent the trip running from Bobby—from the hurt—the farthest away I could get from where the pain was, because while I was seeing different cities and meeting different people and doing different things, I could put things back and cover them up for a while, til I had time to heal, or to scab over.

The second turning point came when an old friend Irene had worked for as a bookkeeper called and insisted she come work for him part-time during tax season. She had been typing court transcripts at home.

I was in my cocoon and I was safe, you see . . . but he kind of nudged me out of my nest. And it felt good. You know, I still wasn't a hundred percent, but I was starting to realize, yes, I maybe can function a little bit. . . . I thought, well, if he cares that much about me to worry about getting me back into the world, then I've got to cooperate, and I've got to find that strength within me to continue on that path. And it took a while, but I made it, and I had to consciously say to myself: you must get out. You must quit hiding.

Note that both Ellen and Irene had attended meetings of Compassionate Friends but they had very different responses to this type of support. Ellen demonstrates the devastating impact that lack of support from friends and additional losses can have on bereaved parents, even when family members are very supportive. Irene's experiences show that sometimes support comes unexpectedly, and just one hand extended in friendship can help lift a parent out of the abyss of grief and provide enough emotional strength to reengage with the world.

Experiences With Others At the Time of Death

When bereaved parents reflect on the circumstances surrounding their child's death, they evaluate their own behavior and that of others during that most unforgettable and critical time. Fran and Gail, representing opposite ends of the bereavement continuum, show how such appraisals can continue to impact how parents view their grief and evolving bereavement.

Fran: It Would Have Been Better If He'd Died Right Away

Fran's son David was born with a heart murmur that he eventually "grew out of"; however, twice as he was growing up they "almost lost him"—once at age 3 to meningitis and again at age 16 when a broken blood vessel in his neck required major surgery. By age 19, however, David's medical problems were behind him. He had graduated from high school and was also working at the local factory. Thus it came as a complete surprise when David, at age 19, left for a date with his girlfriend one night and was thrown out of the van they were riding in when it crashed. He sustained brainstem damage and died 4 months later.

Seven years after David's death, Fran continued to relive the trauma of watching her son lie in a coma in the hospital during those months.

> They, you know, kept him on the machines and stuff because he wasn't brain dead and you know brain waves started. . . . [So was he able to breathe on his own?] Yeah, after a while. It was probably four weeks—I don't know—before they took the respirator off. But his brain stem was so damaged, and they think that's what he died from, that either he had a grand mal seizure and his heart stopped and he stopped breathing, or his brainstem just quit working.

Fran talked of the additional trauma of being confronted by the hospital's unsympathetic social worker:

> She shouldn't even be in that profession at all. Because when she first saw us, she took us in this little room and she said, my name is ___ (I can't even remember what her name is now) and she said, I'll be your social worker, and I'll be talking to you every week about David. And we'll have meetings with the doctors and the therapists and all that. And she said, that "first of all," she said, "I'm gonna tell you

something." She said, "David is dead." And I said, "What?" And she said, "David is dead." She said, "the David that you know or the David that you knew will never be again." And I just wanted to absolutely kill her [nervous laugh]. I mean, it was just SO COLD.

David's condition stabilized, and in the fourth month he was transferred to a hospital in another state where Fran felt he would get the best care possible. She was shocked when the phone call came that he had died during the night ("we thought we were past the danger period"), and she still felt guilty about not being with him when he died. She also regretted that he was resuscitated at the crash site.

I would just rather have had him die that night. I think that time in the hospital did more to me than his death even. . . . I think what really upset me most about that was that they told me he couldn't feel pain, and I got into it with the doctor really bad over that, because I think he did feel pain. He had—they had cut his catheter off accidentally. And it had been off for several hours, and when we got there he was crying. And they assured us that crying was a reflex. And I think that angered me more than anything, that they were so unfeeling toward him that he didn't feel pain. You know, I think the doctors really need to look at that. You know, they said the same thing about babies, and now they're realizing that babies do feel pain. But ah, I think that really bothered me the most. . . . As a matter of fact, when I got into it with the doctor over him telling me David didn't feel pain, they sent me to see a psychiatrist [laughs] and I told him the same thing.

Fran's anger about these experiences had been slow to dissipate. The health professionals that she expected to help her had instead added to the trauma surrounding her son's death. When incidents like these happen, parents need even more time to regain control and self-esteem. Some will never be able to reconcile the part that others "who should know better" play in their grief. Gail had a similar negative experience with health professionals and like Fran had rebelled at their ineptitude. Over time, however, she found solace and healing in how she was able to stand up for herself and her son after his accident.

Gail: I Needed the Time He Gave Me

Gail's son Andy died following severe brain injuries from a car accident. Andy lived 8 days in the hospital, and 8 years later Gail felt that time was "the beginning of my taking care of myself." Struggling to control an uncontrollable situation, Gail did everything she could think of to keep her son alive. Doctors had not expected him to live through the night. "The next morning," she said, "I put him on a program."

Once a day my Buddhist friends came in and chanted with him. Once a day the priest came. . . . I had my Baptist friends doing all their prayer circles and all the stuff that they do. My sister visited once a day. So there was like a schedule from the first thing in the morning til at night. . . . And I took his picture and Scotch-taped it

to his chart, and insisted that when people came into his room, they introduce themselves to him, they tell him what time of the day it was, they tell him what they were
doing as they were doing it. . . . I would just always say to the neurologists: What
do you need next? What do you need to see next to make you feel like there's a
possibility here? And they'd tell me what they needed to see next and then I would
go tell Andy, this is what they need to see next. . . . And they just kept being amazed
that he was still alive.

   Within that 24-hour period when I first got there, there was a nurse that came
on shift. Actually it was probably sometime Saturday or Sunday. And she came into
me and she said, "I need to let you know that I've heard about you. And I'm not
going to participate in your charades. Your son is going to die. That's a fact. And
you might as well start accepting it." And I said, "I need you to know that I'm going
to your supervisor right now. I don't know where she's at. I don't care if she's here
or she's at home. But you are never ever to step foot in my son's room. I'm paying
$700 a day for that room. I have some say-so about who goes in and who doesn't."
   . . . They tried to put me on valium, which infuriated me. And I again told
them, "I might seem out of control sometimes. I might seem hysterical sometimes.
I might break down and cry sometimes. Those are my emotions. I am going to feel
them. If you don't like it, then do your best to stay away from me. Because I'm
going to experience whatever it is I experience. I'm going to be available for this
child." So they thought I was pretty weird. And I'm sure they thought I was pretty
difficult."

Gail believes Andy gave her those 8 days in the hospital to become able to
cope with his leaving.

The more time goes by, the more I'm really proud of how I was in that hospital. . . . I
was doing therapeutic touch the whole time . . . and I felt the fear leave Andy's
body. I felt him reach a place of peace and calm.

It was only after she was able to tell him that living was his decision and she
would be okay and somehow survive without him that another CAT scan showed
no brain activity and doctors told her he was brain dead. After praying to God to
send her a message from Andy about what he wanted her to do, she decided to
donate his kidneys and heart.

THE IMPACT OF OTHERS ON PARENTS' HEALING

Many bereaved parents are surprised that they suffer physically as well as emotionally after their child dies. Physical symptoms, such as sleeplessness, anxiety,
and depression prompt some parents to seek medical help. It is important for
bereaved parents to understand how stress can impact their bodies.[1] Parents' relationships with others can have a significant impact on both physical and emotional symptoms. Bev and Julie provide examples of how others added to their stress.

---

[1] The pamphlet "Physical Grief" (Williams, 1986) describes how stress can result in physical
changes in clear and concise language and offers helpful suggestions to manage these symptoms.

Bev: Society Just Doesn't Get It

When her 6-year-old son Edward died, Bev was a single mother working part-time and finishing her second year of college. She had divorced her son Edward's father 5 years previously, but he remained actively involved in helping her raise their son. Bev talked about how having her son changed her life.

> He was all I wanted, you know. I really didn't know that before I gave birth to him, but after I had him I found out. That was all I wanted in my life! . . . He was with me all of the time. I didn't, you know, leave him with a sitter or anything. You know, my mother would take care of him, or his dad.

She smiled as she remembered all of the various activities that she and Edward did together: reading, talking, art projects, traveling, skiing, and riding their bikes together. It was on a typical bike outing along a city bike path that tragedy struck. On their return trip back down the bike path, the wheel of Edward's bike struck a sewer grate and he and his bike were pitched off the bikeway into the path of oncoming traffic.

> I got myself to stop screaming and I walked up to him and he was still breathing. His head was bashed open, brain matter was exposed, and he was still right in that lane. I left his bike there but I picked him up and put him over in the grass. . . . I just kind of hovered over him [crying] . . . to tell him that I really loved him and that everything would be okay. . . . And then they got the helicopter . . . to come and med-flight him out. And then I lost it. . . . My ex-husband got there. He rode in the ambulance, but they strapped me down. . . . And then they just came in and they told me he was losing his pressure. I had to call my mom, get ahold of the rest of the family, and they showed up. . . . That's something you know that is permanently ingrained in my mind.

After her son's death, Bev was diagnosed with posttraumatic stress disorder, and 6 years later she continued to suffer debilitating migraine headaches, anxiety, depression, sleep disorder, and muscular aches related to stress.

> Now it has me so bad that it's really attacking my body. I'm in pain all the time. Not only the emotional pain of losing my boy but I have physical pain all of the time. I'm not able to function normally every day anymore. . . . The best way to put it, since Edward died, I died! Everything that it seems like I used to know, used to do, the way I used to live, the way I felt, was all gone. I just, I completely became an empty person, and there really was nothing that mattered to me at all. And I'm still struggling with that. . . . I don't feel I can ever get myself back again to who I was when I had my boy.

At age 36, Bev remained unable to work or function normally, and was living below the poverty level on disability payments. She received a small financial settlement from the driver of the car who hit her son but was still involved in legal action against the city in an effort to win an award because of the poor design, construction, and maintenance of the bikeway that caused her son's accident.

Lack of a support system was also complicating Bev's bereavement. She said she lost all of her old friends "gradually when I couldn't get back to their messages," and was alone most of the time.

> My experience is that society just does not get it. People seem to think that I'm young, attractive, I should have no problem. No one can imagine the wound and the pain and the effects. . . . And everybody thinks that the answer is to get a job, put this behind you, it's been too long. And that's entirely wrong. You do not forget about your kid.

Not only had Bev's mother "laid a tremendous guilt trip" on her for not being able to visit the cemetery after her son's death, she also blamed Bev for Edward's death.

> She said that I shouldn't have been out there. She said I took him away from her. . . . I've been treated inappropriately by my family all of my life, which is part of the situation I'm in. I have decided I don't want to be around them. They have hurt me enough all of my life. I am done with them.

As she talked about how her parents were always critical and judgmental of her, Bev added:

> It also made me know what kind of parent I wanted to be and that I would never treat my child as though I hated him. . . . And I don't know how I survived it—I really don't—but I knew that I would not do that to my boy and that he had my unconditional love no matter what happened in his life. So that really kills me too.

The pictures in her photo album showing their many travels and activities together attested to Edward's brief but happy life: "He was just so full of love." Bev found a way of healing herself from the wounds of her dysfunctional up-bringing by treating her son as she wished she'd been treated as a child. When he died, she lost "my best friend . . . my buddy." She also lost the healed self that he represented, and the wounds of her childhood were opened again when her mother blamed her for his death.

Bev's neurologist prescribed medication to ease her migraines and wanted her to undergo training in biofeedback to help ease her muscular tension. She was no longer taking antidepressants, and said she felt better off them; however, she also admitted that after her son's death she had abused drugs, and it was clear she wasn't sure she could keep from doing so in the future. "I ask God to keep me from being self-destructive," she said.

Bev's life situation, including lack of supportive others, compounded the impact of her trauma symptoms. Bev's tragic circumstances are multifaceted, but she is not unique in her need for support from others. All of the women interviewed in the "Mothers Now Childless" study had at some time experienced severe stress symptoms and unmet needs for support from others. The difference between the two interview groups was that those representing "survival" (Carol, Gail, Helen, Irene, and Julie) eventually found the type and amount of support that helped them transcend the trauma of their loss. Julie provides an example. Like Bev, Julie also experienced physical illness after her son was suddenly killed.

Julie: I Chose to Survive

Julie talked with pride about the accomplishments of her son Stuart, who at age 9 was already a leader at school, someone the other children looked up to. He had made several TV commercials, he loved to read, and he had an IQ in the top 3% of all children in the country. His life ended tragically one afternoon as he stood at the end of his driveway waiting to cross the street to visit a neighbor's son. His babysitter and neighbor watched in horror as a car sped down their street, ran Stuart down, and dragged his body 200 yards down the block. The woman driver had been at a party and had been drinking, Julie learned later, but she was unable to prove this because no testing was done at the scene. "The whole thing was covered up because she knew the chief of police. . . . She never even said she was sorry." The authorities she expected to see justice served failed Julie and her son, compounding her anger and grief.

Julie was no stranger to deceit. Two years before Stuart's death, she said, "his father left us for a friend of mine." Julie worked two jobs as a bookkeeper so that she and Stuart could remain in the house her son loved. "I found out that I could do it. . . . It was difficult, but I found out a spouse is replaceable."

Julie had had several subsequent traumas after Stuart's death. In her second year of bereavement she fell down her basement stairs, broke many of the bones in her face, and underwent reconstructive surgery. She showed the doctor, who was amazed at how well she was taking all this, Stuart's picture and said: "Look, I've survived the death of a child. Some people don't make a choice. I made that choice to survive. This is a piece of cake."

After Stuart's death, Julie's ex-husband began to demand she sell the house. Eventually she negotiated an agreement with him for his share of the equity. At the same time, Julie's lawsuit against the woman who killed her son dragged on for over 5 years. "With the case, I had to relive his accident with depositions."

> Stuart was killed while I was at work. I had just left for work at five minutes to four and he was killed a minute after four. I blamed his father, 'cause his father was supposed to take him that weekend but at the last minute canceled and I had to get a babysitter. . . . I blamed him because, again, he canceled out from seeing his son. . . . But then I also blamed myself. I blamed him and I blamed, you know, the woman who killed my son, but still I would blame, if the sun shined. Why couldn't it have rained that day? Then he wouldn't have gone outside. Because when I left he was watching a video, and he knew he had to ask permission. . . . Stuart, I made him

fanatic; if the kids came to the house, he would take them to the line at the end of the driveway [and tell them:] "you don't go past this."

After the court settlement, Stuart's father came forward and demanded a share of the award. Julie's attorneys had failed to get his signature denying all further claims when the house was sold, and she had to threaten to sue them before they agreed to pay him what he demanded out of their fees.

> I never wanted money. Then when I settled and my ex-husband came forward out of the clear blue because the lawyers screwed up on something, I had the check in my hands and I says to the lawyer: "I'll tear it up, so you don't get your cut, my ex doesn't get what he wants, and I never wanted this money to begin with. When she was found negligent she lost her license for a year, big deal." And they were like climbing over the tables at me because they knew I was going to do it. . . . I go to the attorney's office and he tells me this, and I thought I was gonna rip his lungs out. I was like, "What do you mean you screwed up? What do you mean he's stepping forward?" I said, "So, look, whatever he wants, you give him, out of your cut, your pay, or I'm going to sue you."

Four years after her son's death, Julie's father died. She made most of the funeral arrangements and delivered his eulogy. Julie said: "I got the strength from Stuart and Dad. . . . I says, 'let me know that Daddy's with you' . . . and I had both of them at the foot of my bed. I'll never forget. They were both there, and I mean, I was awake."

Seven years after Stuart's death, Julie once again had surgery, this time to remove cancer of the thyroid. "And when someone is trying to tell you that, well, based on your history, this is probably depression. I said, no, this is not depression, there's something physically wrong with me. And then thank goodness I switched gynecologists and they found it." Once again she told her surgeon why she was "taking this awfully well. . . . I said, 'look I've survived the death of a child.' He said, 'how do you survive the death of a child?' I said, 'I made that choice.' I said, 'some people don't make a choice.' I said, 'I made that choice to survive.'"

Making a decision to survive (discussed further in chap. 8) can be a key turning point for bereaved parents. Often it is relationships with others (positive or negative) that precipitate this decision. The support of others and appropriate interventions from caregivers can be essential for bereaved parents to develop the necessary physical and emotional strength to face the future without their child. The relationship between bereaved parents also can be a critical factor in their healing.

GENDER DIFFERENCES IN GRIEVING

Researchers and clinicians have begun to explore the differences between how bereaved mothers and fathers grieve (Bernstein, 1997; Blank, 1998; Detmer &

Lamberti, 1994; Dyregrov & Matthiesen, 1987; Gilbert, 1997; Levang, 1998; Littlefield & Rushton, 1986; Martin & Doka; 2000; Rando, 1993; Rosenblatt, 2000a, 2000b; Sanders, 1999; Schwab, 1990; Staudacher, 1991; Tedeschi & Hamilton, 1991). Mothers and fathers often do grieve differently and may be unable to give each other the kind and degree of support that is needed. Differences can manifest themselves in grieving styles, such as when one parent needs to talk and express emotions and the other needs to reflect and meditate or to take action.

In their book *Men Don't Cry . . . Women Do: Transcending Gender Stereo-types of Grief* (2000), Martin and Doka proposed using two different terms to classify grieving styles: "instrumental" and "intuitive." "Instrumental grievers," they said, "tend to have tempered affect to a loss. While intuitive grievers are more likely to experience their grief as waves of affect, instrumental grievers are more likely to describe it in physical or cognitive terms. While intuitive grievers often need to express their feelings and seek the support of others, instrumental grievers are more likely to cognitively process or immerse themselves in activity" (p. 5). In other words, the primary focus for experiencing, expressing, and adapting to grief can be either the heart or the head. Perhaps the most important point made by Martin and Doka, however, is that differences in grieving (gender-based or not) do not mean one way of grieving is better than another.

> There are many different styles of coping with loss. Each has distinct strengths and limitations. There are advantages in expressing affect and seeking support. But there are also complementary strengths in stoically continuing in the face of loss and in seeking amelioration of pain in cognitive and active approaches. In short, persons who draw from a broad range of adaptive strategies are, in fact, likely to do better. Persons with the widest range of responses, who effectively integrate all aspects of self, seem best able to respond to crisis. One can learn from both types of responses because, after all, different modes of adaptation are just that—differences, not deficiencies. (Martin & Doka, 2000, p. 7)

Bereaved parents often have diverse coping strategies; their developmental histories have been deeply influenced not only by gender but by personality traits, family of origin, and cultural cohort. One parent may have experienced a major loss in the past, whereas grief may be a totally new experience for the other. Husbands who view their role as protector of the family can begin to feel totally incompetent as they realize they cannot protect their wife and/or surviving family members from the pain of grief. Parents can attach totally different meanings to resuming sexual relations; one may have no physical desire for sex at all, whereas the other views sex as a way to offer love and comfort to the other. The trauma and stress symptoms experienced by the parents also can vary widely and can cause them to worry about each other's health. There can be differing expectations for support from friends and family and disagreements about how best to help surviving siblings. Parents can be so overwhelmed by grief that they cannot parent surviving siblings, at least for a time. Their fear of losing another child causes some to be overprotective of their surviving children. The loss can aggravate underlying differences in the parents' marital relationship, such as values, beliefs, assumptions, and expectations. Or the loss can bring parents even closer together as they find ways to comfort each other and share their experiences.

The unpredictability of the grief process often adds to marital stress. In early acute grief, parents learn they cannot predict when their next "grief attack" will come. A parent can be having a relatively peaceful day until the phone rings or a routine chore brings a sudden painful memory. Parents describe these flashbacks as "like having someone stab me in the heart with a knife." The intense and unpredictable emotions that accompany flashbacks can leave one parent temporarily incapacitated while the other remains unaware of what has happened.

Over time, many parents learn to dose their grief when possible, to allow themselves to take vacations from their grief, even if for only short periods. This adaptive coping technique often differs between parents, however. This was true for Jim and Virginia, whose 4-month-old daughter and second child died from sudden infant death syndrome. As they talked about their differences, Jim said: "Sometimes she wants to talk about it and I'm in the middle of a ball game and I don't want to talk about it because I just spent an hour there earlier and I don't want to go back down there right now." An important part of counseling bereaved parents is helping them to understand and allow differences in how they grieve (cf. Martin & Doka, 2000; Rosenblatt, 2000b).

Sharing the Same Loss Doesn't Mean Sharing the Same Grief

All of these potential differences demand increased communication, compromise, and compassionate understanding between parents at a time when both are overwhelmed by the amount of emotional energy their grief requires. Doris and Carol provide contrasting examples of the complex impact grief can have on marital relationships.

Doris and Tom: Learning to Accept Differences

About 6 weeks after her son Evan's death, when Doris "was finally out of shock and into hysterical," she called a crisis hotline and was put in touch with the local Compassionate Friends group. "He died in June. I went to the first [meeting] in August, skipped the next couple, and now I drive two hours to the meeting every chance I get. . . . I think the most important thing is to see somebody else survive." Her husband Tom has driven her to meetings, but does not attend.

> He tried for me a couple times. He's not, he's not a talker and ah, that makes me need Compassionate Friends more because he's the hardest person to talk to. Ah, he's not a talker, he never has been. You know, we knew that and stuff, it's nothing different. This isn't the first thing he never talked about. And it probably took him two years before he even said Evan's name. He's a workaholic. Ah, Evan died in the summer . . . and you know, looking back now, we think it was probably about twenty months before we really saw each other again. 'Cause he, at the time he was doin'

outdoor construction. . . . It was perfect for being gone all the time. . . . Ah, so he had an awful lot to occupy his mind and I had nothing. . . . It hurt and it still does that, you know, I couldn't be first on his list. And in a lot of ways—most ways—I am, but a lot of times it feels like I'm not, ah, because of the work. But he loves it. . . . Most of the time I don't complain, but he has a lot to keep his mind busy and I don't and I think I'm jealous of that sometimes. It's like he has a life and I don't, 'cause my job was taken away when Evan died, you know. . . . That's my purpose on earth, was to have that child and take care of him [crying] and I didn't do it right. [So you feel like somehow you should have been able to?] I should have been able to fix it, and I think that's probably what hurts my husband the most too—that he can't even talk about—you know, dads are supposed to take care of everybody.

Tom and Doris continue to grieve very differently. Doris described the wonderful eulogy that Tom wrote and delivered for his son at the funeral and added:

But that was the beginning and the end of it. . . . I have a problem crying around him ah, because a man answer is just to pat you on the head and tell you you'll be all right. And we finally talked much better, much better, after one day I just realized when he's just giving this man answer, I said, "That's just a bullshit man answer. Make it right. If it's gonna be all right, make it right." And for once he said, "you're right." It dawned on him what he was saying. And so we've gotten along much better since then. We never had any real problems, but our communication level's much greater. So when he's full of crap I tell him.

For a long time when people would say how many children do you have, he said none for a long time. Now he says our only child died. . . . I guess it kind of bothers him—it's like I wear it—like he said when our son was handicapped that I wore THAT as a badge. Now that I'm a bereaved mother, he says he thinks I wear that. I says, "Well I am. That's where I am right now." . . . It's like I need validation—I look for validation in things.

Doris continued to need the understanding and support of friends and family, particularly at holidays and on her son's birthday. Her needs for support at these times had been met only partially.

[Are there particular times that you've been able to identify when that really down period hits?] The birthdays, those times you're suppose to be celebrating life. . . . Evan was born in November and I was born in very early January. So we have Evan's birthday, Thanksgiving and Christmas and then my birthday, everything all at once, and by the second week of January, I'm just a zombie. . . . Christmas is just—it's nothing but a letdown anymore. It's for kids, and I don't have any. I mean the whole meaning of Christmas is for everybody, but the public spectacle we make out of it in this day and age is for children. . . . Mother's Day is easier now. But it's like I had to convince my husband I was still a mom. And once he figured that out, ah, and does something for me on Mother's Day, they're much easier. It makes me cry, but they're easier that someone acknowledges that. Evan died between Mother's Day and Father's Day, and I already had Tom's Father's Day present for him and I went ahead and gave it to him and I think that kind of blew his mind. But definitely his birthdays. . . . And instead of people calling or sending flowers or whatever, everybody thinks they need to leave me alone that day and then I end up so lonely I think everybody abandoned me. So, my sister . . . she lost her first baby too, and she sends me flowers on Evan's birthday. So that's a big plus.

Their different styles of grieving had become increasingly apparent to Doris and Tom. Doris needed to express and validate her grief; Tom needed to channel his grief into his work. Doris had to learn that Tom's reticence in talking didn't mean he wasn't grieving. Tom had to learn that acknowledging Doris's grief and assuring her she was still a mother could help her regain control of her life again. Doris concluded:

Things that I need to get out and talk and deal with, he's not there yet. But it bugs him right now. But that's fine. We're at the point where we can tell each other, "Don't you have somewhere to go, you're driving me nuts, you know." [You give each other that permission to do things differently?] Yes. We're—we're fine now."

Carol and Tony: Seeking Help and Helping Others

Carol and her husband Tony also grieved differently after the death of their son Scott, who had been born with muscular dystrophy. Carol described how she and her son had worked together to lessen the effects of Scott's degenerative disease:

He wanted to be a Cub Scout and they would not allow him to be, and they said to him, "How can you walk a balance beam?" He said, "I may not be able to walk that balance beam but did you ever see anybody go up steps backwards in leg braces?" He said, "I'll earn my badge that way." So, I mean he helped me survive this because what you could do today you could not do tomorrow, and he was the type of child that would say, "Mom, we'll find another way."
. . . He was just, there was so much laughter because Scott grew to be a big boy. He was nearly 6 foot, size 48 shoulders at age 15, and I had built up my strength so that I carried Scott room to room at that size. We would just laugh. He would say, "God, did you forget my Mom is so little? I've got to stop growing here!" That kind of thing, you know. But he was such a joy!

At age 15 the disease won out; Scott's lungs became paralyzed and he died in his parents' arms at a local hospital. Carol made the painful decision not to let doctors put him on life support, a decision that her husband supported at the time. Years later he admitted his private struggle to reconcile their decision. Carol talked about how differently they grieved and what eventually forced her to seek help.

When there is an illness, there is a closeness between that mother and child that's very hard for others to understand. We know what they're thinking, maybe before they do. We're an extension of their arms and legs and we not only lose our child, we lose our job. And you come crashing. And that need to be needed and that love, that special bond between the child, it can't even be explainable.
. . . You know, the fathers—they're out working—mothers are too, but the fathers are preparing, you might say continuously, for the child's future. My husband

was a giant of a father, a wonderful father. Ah, mothers are dealing on a daily basis, meeting the needs, and the separation is devastating in both cases; however, it *is* different.

. . . And, in our case, too, it was a day-and-night thing. As Scott got older I wouldn't disturb my husband because he had to get up at four-thirty in the morning; however, I knew it was very important to turn Scott every fifteen minutes at night. So, even our grieving in a sense; at first I would still wake up every fifteen minutes at night and go into the room and find the empty bed. You know, it was an automatic thing that I did. And to somehow help myself through that, I think I chose to begin to grieve Scott as a baby, and work up to what I could handle, then. And Tony was grieving Scott as an adult. And we were just, just everything was SO different.

. . . I was drawn to the cemetery, every day. And what I was finding is, what was helping me was a turn-off to my husband. You know, and then he'd talk to others, and they would say, "You should stop this." [Carol's going daily to the cemetery.]

During their second year of bereavement, when Carol became alarmed about her husband's continued acute grief, she "began to reach out for help." She learned there had been a bereaved parents group in their area that had disbanded, but she was given the phone numbers of three bereaved parents to call. The response from the first parent, who it turned out had attended Scott's christening as a baby, was, "Well dear, I'd like to help you. However, I do know that your child was adopted, and I think you should call an adoption agency." Carol hung up and called the next person.

He said to me, "How did your child die?" And I said "Complications of muscular dystrophy." And he, too, said that he wished that he could help me, however, their child died instantly in an accident, and perhaps I would get more help by calling the Muscular Dystrophy Association. And I was glad that I was not suicidal because the last call pushed me out the door and prompted me to do something. And the person said to me: "Our child completed suicide,[2] and there was no help for me, and I'm not going to help anyone else."

What she and her husband did was start their own group for bereaved parents, a group that has grown over the years and continues to reach out to help newly bereaved parents. Carol also volunteers extensively for schools, mental health boards, and other grief groups in her local area. The need to be needed, and the love she felt in her relationship with her son, are now channeled into her volunteer work to help others. Carol said:

Actually what I did is build a dream on sorrow so that no one else would feel so alone. . . . The only way for me to heal was to take this unacceptable reality . . . and turn it into some positive growth . . . in helping others. And that was my survival.

---

[2]Survivors of suicide prefer the terms "died by suicide" or "completed suicide" as less stigmatizing than "committed" suicide.

Joining in a reciprocal grieving process with other bereaved parents ("we're a lifeline to each other") allowed Carol and Tony to heal: "When you tell your story over and over again to someone who listens in a nonjudgmental way, you can see things differently." It also allowed their son to remain a part of their daily lives as they shared their experiences, strength, and hope with others. Carol and Tony found themselves modeling survival for other bereaved parents, just as Scott (a muscular dystrophy poster child) had modeled adaptation for so many families fighting disease and disabilities.

Gender-Based Research

The differences in parental grieving become apparent to most bereaved couples. The derivation and effects of these differences are less clear, and gender-based research continues.

Dyregrov and Matthiesen (1987) used five different instruments to measure the level of psychological health in mothers and fathers who had experienced the death of an infant between 1 and 4 years previously. Fifty-five couples were selected for the study. Their responses "demonstrated fairly strong differences between the partners' reactions, with mothers typically experiencing more intense and long-lasting reactions than fathers. Mothers also tended to perceive their family and friends as less supportive than fathers, while fathers were least satisfied with the support received from the hospital. Most parents felt the death had brought them closer together, although a considerable number reported feeling more distance to their partner" (Dyregrov & Matthiesen, 1987, p. 1).

Another study of 263 parents in Ontario, Canada, also noted more intense grieving by mothers than by fathers (Littlefield & Rushton, 1986). The study included 74 couples and 115 individuals. Sixty-seven percent of participants were women, 81% of whom were either married or living with a partner. Participants completed a 97-item amended version of the Grief Experience Inventory developed by Sanders et al. in 1977. Ninety-four percent of the deaths had occurred within the previous 5 years. However, time since death was not related to grief intensity, and computing the results while controlling for this variable did not alter them. The average grief intensity for mothers was higher than that for fathers, according to both male and female estimates. In other words, both parents rated mothers' grief as being more intense than fathers' grief. Respondents' ratings of their own grief correlated significantly with their total scores on the Grief Experience Inventory (Littlefield & Rushton, 1986, p. 799).

Dyregrov and Matthiesen (1987) proposed the following explanations for the gender differences reported by bereaved parents:

1   They may be caused by a difference in amount of attachment or "bonding" to the child,
2   They may reflect different reactivity to stress or different methods of coping in men and women.

3   They may arise because men underreport or fail to acknowledge emotions and reactions.

4   They may reflect the different social situation the two sexes experience following the loss.

They noted that a combination of these causes is possible and plausible. However, "the parents in the study wrote comments on their questionnaires that could be taken as support for the third explanation, that the observed sex differences were caused by men's underreporting or suppression of emotions" (p. 11). These men would be classified by Martin and Doka (2000) as "instrumental" grievers, as previously discussed.

Another study pointed out gender differences in the coping strategies of bereaved parents (Schwab, 1990). In this study, 25 married couples were interviewed and an instrument that measured 20 different coping strategies was administered. The participants were parents of children who died from a variety of causes, at age 0 (miscarriage) to 30. The time since the child's death ranged from 1 month to 8 years and 11 months. The study identified five major coping strategies used by parents: 1) seeking the release of tension, 2) avoiding painful thoughts and feelings, 3) using a cognitive framework to understand and deal with the experience of loss, 4) helping others, and 5) relying on religious beliefs. Other less-used strategies included seeking support through groups, seeking relief from pain, investing themselves in a new object of love, seeking professional help, staying alone, and visiting the cemetery. The following statistically significant gender differences were identified: Mothers were found to cry, read and write on loss and grief, help others, and stay alone to a greater degree than fathers. Reading and writing were coping strategies used primarily by mothers, whereas fathers relied more on keeping busy, on religious beliefs, and on talking about the loss (Schwab, 1990, pp. 407, 418–419).

Detmer and Lamberti (1994) emphasized that the gender differences sometimes noted in loss of a child are also seen by counselors assisting parents going through a divorce. They urged taking an androgynous perspective toward long-term adjustment to loss. That is, delineating and understanding the different responses, coping strategies, and culturally prescribed role behaviors exhibited by men and women can lead to better relations between the sexes and better adaptation to loss. Over time, some men and women may become able to choose coping strategies they feel are most appropriate for a particular situation. However, doing so will likely take them out of their comfort zone and require increased energy to learn such new approaches, which is particularly difficult during times of extreme stress and multiple internal and external changes.

When their child dies, bereaved parents need to understand and allow differences in coping styles. They must learn they cannot take responsibility for each other's grief process. As one bereaved parent put it: "It can be like learning how to ice skate. You can't keep your own balance and hold the other person up at the same time."

The differing ways in which mothers and fathers may grieve can accentuate each parent's feelings of being alone and unheard. Many bereaved parents seek out new "compassionate friends" who help meet their need for understanding and support. But seeking support from other bereaved parents can be very difficult to do for many parents, especially during early acute grief, which demands so much emotionally, mentally, physically, and spiritually from bereaved parents. Some parents may attend support group meetings once or twice and be so overwhelmed by both their own pain and that of the other parents that they cannot force themselves to go back. Many men who do attend a support group say they are there primarily to support their wives. "Those who continue are often surprised at how much they gain themselves from the experience" (Tedeschi & Hamilton, 1991, p. 27). It is important *not* to judge bereaved fathers as failing to process their grief when they resist group experiences and/or open displays of emotion. *There is no one right way to grieve and no one way for each gender to grieve* (cf. Martin & Doka, 2000). Rather, there are multiple patterns and a variety of useful coping skills that parents use to survive a child's death.

Some parents keep their pain very personal and private. Marcie, whose 15-year-old daughter was killed in a car accident, attached the following comments to her questionnaire. The unrelenting intensity of her pain continues. But she has taken a first step in trying to create some meaning, something positive, from her pain by sharing it in the hope of helping others.

Each day I still question whether I have earned the title "survivor." Here are some facts about my (our) bereavement that I had no opportunity to include in the questionnaire that may be relevant:

I cannot (even after $11^1/_3$ years) discuss my daughter's death or life without MUCH emotional distress. My husband feels exactly the same. Our friends and family are aware of this and comply. We have no pictures, personal effects, NOTHING displayed in our home to indicate that she ever existed. It is the ONLY way either of us can continue. We felt this way immediately after her death and have NEVER wavered from that position. Never a day has passed that I have not considered ending my life. I cannot say with certainty that at some point hence I will not do so. I do not discuss this with anyone, but have admitted it to my husband possibly twice in these $11^1/_3$ years. I have a Roseanne Barr/Lucille Ball type personality and continue to present this to the world. I frequently amaze myself that I am able to keep the facade intact when I feel completely desolate on the inside. It has almost become a perverted game-like ruse to see how many I can "fool" and how often with my zany, irreverent antics. For the most part, I appear to the world to be just as I was "before." How absurdly imbecilic they would have to be to believe that! I hope these sharings are of some help to you or someone."

What would happen in their marital relationship if Marcie and her husband disagreed about how to cope with their pain? What if Marcie's husband really needed to talk about his daughter and have reminders of her around the house and in his daily life? Those parents who have widely divergent grieving styles also have increased needs for compassionate communication and willingness to nego-tiate aspects of grief that may be affecting their marital life.

Although it is clear that marriages are greatly impacted by the death of a child, the general perception that divorce is more likely among bereaved parents is a myth. A recent national study commissioned by The Compassionate Friends, for example, found that "72% of parents who were married at the time of their child's death were still married to the same person. The remaining 28% of mar-riages included 16% in which one spouse had died and only 12% of marriages that ended in divorce." And within this 12%, "only one out of four of the parents felt that the impact of the death of their child contributed to their divorce." When bereaved parents do divorce, it is most likely they do so because they no longer wish to remain in a relationship that was troubled and unhealthy long before their child died.

SUMMARY

Bereaved parents' relationships with each other and with those around them are vitally important after their child dies. Parents vary in both the type and amount of support they need from others, and in their perceptions of what is supportive. When parents' needs are not met, some feel isolated, stigmatized, abandoned, and angry. Other parents see the kindness and concern of others as instrumental in their healing. The relationships they have with others can reinforce parents' fears that their child will be forgotten; conversely, others can join parents in creating lasting legacies and meaningful tributes in memory of their child.

Parents' reappraisal of the roles they and others played when their child died can reinforce their sense of helplessness or bring renewed self-esteem. Those around them can contribute greatly to bereaved parents' ability to withstand the trauma of early grief and enable them to deal with new losses and physical challenges. When their expectations are not met, some parents decide to end relationships with unsupportive friends or family members. Parents may also create new relation-ships as they seek out help and connect with others who try to understand them. The complexity of the marital relationship is greatly increased after the death of a child. Spouses often must learn to recognize and accept differences in their griev-ing styles and learn new ways to communicate and negotiate aspects of daily life affected by ongoing grief.

Feeling understood helps bereaved parents validate, normalize, and make sense of their experiences. Relationships are mirrors that reflect back to parents who they are becoming as they learn how to be bereaved parents. Healing comes as parents reflect back on their grief process and see they no longer have such an intense need to tell their story continually and to be understood; they now under-stand what living with loss means and they can choose to use this hard-won un-derstanding to help others.

Living forever with the loss of a child also requires spiritual understanding. As discussed in the next chapter, experiencing a spiritual crisis as a result of the death of a child is common among bereaved parents.

Chapter 6

Confronting a Spiritual Crisis: Where Is God When Bad Things Happen?

> I am a more sensitive person, a more effective pastor, a more sympathetic counselor because of [my son] Aaron's life and death than I would ever have been without it. And I would give up all of those gains in a second if I could have my son back. If I could choose, I would forego all the spiritual growth and depth which has come my way because of our experiences, and be what I was fifteen years ago, an average rabbi, an indifferent counselor, helping some people and unable to help others, and the father of a bright, happy boy. But I cannot choose. (Kushner, 1981, pp. 133–134)

Bereaved parents become painfully conscious of their own powerlessness—the inability to protect those they love most. Many parents turn to God, to the God of their own personal understanding, a higher power, one greater than themselves, for answers and solace. For many parents, faith is a lifeline to cling to; it offers hope and healing while they are crawling an inch at a time through the valley of death. But for many other bereaved parents, the death of their child precipitates a spiritual crisis, a wilderness experience of unanswerable questions and deep despair. Psychotherapist Ashley Prend (1997) aptly described this journey that has no shortcuts:

> The kind of spiritual/philosophical journey that grief initiates is common to every type of religion, spirituality, and faith. Being Catholic doesn't exempt you from doubt. There are no Buddhist, Jewish, or Moslem shortcuts. The kind of challenging journey from belief to doubt and back to belief again is truly an interfaith, non-denominational journey. It is a deeply private, individual process of making peace

with one's beliefs, one's uncertainties, one's sacred connections. No two of us will do this in precisely the same way. In other words, there is no single way to reach the Divine. (pp 108–109)

With grieving, just as you undergo a physical and psychological tearing down and building up, you also experience a parallel process of spiritual destruction and rebirth. If you can withstand the storm, if you can weather the destruction, and even embrace the confusion, it is possible to eventually emerge with a renewed, stronger faith. (p. 107)

THEOLOGICAL ISSUES PRESENTED BY THE DEATH OF A CHILD

In developing his pastoral Christian theology of a child's death, Christopher Currier (1982) addressed the theological issues that are central to the loss of a child: God's will, and what part God may or may not have played in relationship to the child's death (p. 8). The parents he ministered to experienced forms of guilt unique to parental bereavement. They felt they had failed in their role as parent to protect their children from death. Some held the belief that some sin from their past had somehow caused their children to die. And some felt that God was testing their faith by either allowing or making their children die (pp. 24–26).

Currier offered an argument that uses reframing to counter these parental guilts: "Since our experience teaches us we have the power to make decisions, then what does this teach us about God's will? How can God have a will and at the same time allow for human decision-making?" (p. 42). He answered these questions through biblical interpretation. Humanity has a participatory relationship with God, he maintained, as evidenced by our ability to make decisions. In Genesis God tells Adam and Eve they are "to cultivate" and "take care of" His creation (Genesis 2:15). In our relationship with God, we see that God is powerful in creating, while we are powerful in sustaining his creation (pp. 43–44). In our humanity, however, we beings do not always decide wisely. This is evident in the story of the crucifixion. As Currier elucidated: God, too, is a bereaved parent:

It was God's will . . . for Jesus to be followed and not that Jesus die on the cross. God wanted humanity in right and proper relationship both with other human beings and with Himself. This is the message of Christ. . . . Humanity chose crucifixion; God did not. (p. 44)

. . . While God was powerless to stop the crucifixion, He was powerful in not allowing human will to prevent what he set out to do in the personhood of Christ. (p. 45)

. . . The cross which Jesus died upon, a weapon of violent and painful death in biblical times, today is a symbol of love and life. God was not made impotent in the shadow of the cross but rather transformed His bereavement experience through resurrection so that the cross we see today in thousands of churches symbolizes hope and assurance. (p. 61)

Currier urged bereaved parents to view their experience in terms of what it teaches them about their expectations.

We need to consider how we learn our most valuable lessons in life. Does our learning come from sitting still or does it come in the living of life? (p. 51)

. . . We seem to have rooted within our collective consciousness a philosophy about life which says, "If I work hard and do a good job, then I will be a success." It is an expectation we seem to have. But more than an expectation, it is almost like a certainty, a guarantee as it were, that hard work *will always*, in every circumstance, equal success. If we . . . examine our experience with life looking for knowledge and understanding, then we come up against an untruth within our expectations, our guarantees about life. . . .

Experience teaches us our expectations—our guarantees [about life]—are unjustified. Hard work does not always equal or guarantee successfulness. There are times when hard work ends in failure. Therefore, if we follow what our experience teaches us about life, we have, on the one hand, expectations that hard work guarantees success and, on the other hand, experience which teaches us something quite different. Something has to give—change. Since we cannot change our experience, perhaps we need to change our feelings about our expectations and guarantees. Thus it seems our feelings that life is unfair and unjust come from what our expectations are about life. When what we expect to happen does not happen, the resulting feeling is that life is unfair and unjust. Perhaps what our experience is really teaching us is that our expectations—our need for guarantees about life—are unfair and unjust. (pp. 53–54)

Even Jesus was not immune from the human tendency to expect divine assurance. During his agonizing death on the cross, Jesus felt God had abandoned him ("My God, my God, why have you deserted me?"—Mark 15:34, quoting from Psalm 22). His mother Mary stood silently at his feet. Currier described what bereaved parents might learn from this:

Our experience [of a child's death] teaches us how significant silence and absence are. (p. 70)

Yet: . . . when we find ourselves experiencing feelings of silence and isolation, we need to learn how to wait silently in the midst of God's seeming absence so that we might be aware of His presence and open to what He will say to us. Our waiting must be one of expectation that God is going to do something. (p. 71)

. . . Because Job was willing to wait upon God, he was able to make sense out of God's apparent silence and absence (see Job 19:23–26). (p. 72)

. . . If we love our children, does not God, as our parent, love us? Likewise, when we as human parents experience feelings of suffering along with our children, does not God suffer with us? (p. 81)

Many bereaved parents take comfort in identifying with God as a bereaved parent. Others identify more closely with Job, whose friends came to comfort him with their own answers and ended up adding to his suffering by insisting that God was punishing Job for his sin. It was after Job prayed for these unhelpful friends that God gave Job "twice as much as he had before" (Job 42:10). Some parents find solace in recognizing that God "blessed the latter part of Job's life more than the first" (Job 42:12). But as noted in chapter 4, God blessed Job with only 10 more children—not 20, not twice as many as he had before (Job 42:13). The interpretation is that God did not need to give Job 20 new children because Job already had 10 children in heaven. Bereaved parents know that children are not replaceable; many, if not most, look forward to being reunited with their child in heaven.

The need to make sense of God's role in the death of their child can prompt parents to review their expectations about life. Currier quoted a bereaved father who, after watching his daughter die of leukemia, was ultimately able to make meaning of his experience, by reframing his thoughts about expectations:

> When I remember that Laura Lue was a gift, pure and simple, something I neither earned or deserved nor had a right to. And when I remember that the appropriate response to a gift, even when it is taken away, is gratitude, then I am better able to try and thank God that I was ever given her in the first place. (p. 85)

The preceding examples of Judeo-Christian searching for spiritual meaning during bereavement can be contrasted with other religions. For example, Rinpoche (1992) described a typical Buddhist approach:

> If our friend has lost a child or someone close to them who seemed too young to die so soon, we tell them: "Now your little boy has died, and it seems as if your whole world has been shattered. It seems, I know, so cruel and illogical. I cannot explain your son's death, but I do know that it must be the natural result of his *karma* [italics added], and I believe and know that his death must have purified some karmic debt that you and I cannot know about. Your grief is my grief. But take heart because now you and I can help him, through our practice and our good actions and our love; we can take his hand and walk by his side, even now, even when he's dead, and help him to find a new birth and a longer life next time." (p. 310)

Note that what he means by *karma* is not fate or predestination, but "the infallible law of cause and effect that governs the universe. The word karma literally means *action* [italics added], and karma is both the power latent within actions, and the results our actions bring" (p. 92). Buddhists believe that karma is the driving force behind rebirth or reincarnation; what happens to us in this life is the result of past life actions, and our actions in this life will result in the kind of existence we enjoy in the next life.

It is not the particular belief system that is of central importance in the preceding examples. Rather, it is crucial to understand that spirituality and religion can enhance and/or impede the healing of bereaved parents. Confronting a higher power and seeking to gain a personally meaningful understanding of their child's death and afterlife are critical aspects for most parents.

BEREAVEMENT THEODICIES

Based on their study of 145 parents of children who had died of cancer, Cook and Wimberly (1983) developed a typology of parental bereavement theodicies (systems of natural theology aimed at seeking to vindicate divine justice in allowing evil to exist). They identified five types of theodicies among the predominantly Christian parents they studied, who had been bereaved between 4 and 8 years at the time of the study. In describing how they had come to understand their child's death, parents gave the following types of explanations:

1   Those that blame or question the mercy of God. The child's death was attributed to a supreme being who was viewed as uncaring and unmerciful for allowing the child to suffer and die.
2   Those that view the death as a punishment incurred by survivors for wrongdoing. This type of theodicy was more common in the accounts of fathers.
3   Those that reveal their belief that the child's death occurred because it was intended by God to serve a good and useful purpose.
4   Those that regard suffering primarily as a state of mind, which is influenced by how one defines the situation.
5   Those that regard death in fatalistic, coincidental, or solely causal terms. In these cases, parents imputed little meaning to their child's death, regarding it instead as a matter of fate or nature.

The first three theodicies—blaming God, blaming self, and purposive death—were described far more frequently (Cook & Wimberley, 1983, pp. 227–228).

Three specific theodicies were found in parents' response to their child's death. First was reunion with the child in heaven. This theodicy relates the searching behavior accompanying mourning to the promise that religious commitment will enable the parent to be reunited with the deceased child. Second was interpreting the death as serving a noble purpose. This theodicy fills the need to impute special meaning to the loss, and provides impetus for action that may relieve feelings of normative confusion and helplessness. Third was interpreting the death as punishment for sin. This theodicy has a less beneficial influence on the adjustment of survivors because it blames them for wrongs now impossible to redress. However, this type of explanation may be perceived as legitimate by bereaved parents because it validates the sense of guilt frequently experienced by survivors regardless of their actual role in an individual's death (Cook & Wimberley, 1983, p. 230).

Thus, the results of Cook and Wimberley's study showed that "religious commitment is both cause and consequence of adjustment to bereavement" (p. 222).

SPIRITUAL BONDS AND MEANINGS IN THE LIVES OF BEREAVED PARENTS

In his study of parents who were members of a local chapter of The Compassionate Friends, Klass (1991) found religious devotion to be an important part of resolution of parental grief, yet only a part. Also significant to these parents was the solace they found in internalized inner representations of their dead child brought about through special memories of the child or by use of "linking objects" (Volkan, 1981; Wheeler, 1989–1999) that evoked the child's presence. There were many examples of the use of identification as well, with parents taking on what they perceived as the virtues and gifts of their child.

"For most of the parents in our study," Klass (1991) said, "it is the internalized inner representation of their child that connects them to the divine even as they feel cut off in other parts of their psyche. Klass quoted a father who talked of the months of praying during his daughter's illness.

> "Some of the children would get better and some would not. One night as she was going to sleep N. asked me, 'Daddy, how does God decide who gets the miracles?' I didn't know what to answer her. I still don't. I guess I still believe in miracles. How else do you account for the kids I saw get better with no explanation. But we didn't get one. So where am I now?" If he and his child were passed over in the distribution of miracles, his child was not passed over for heaven. He feels strongly that his daughter is in heaven with God and that he will rejoin her when he dies.
>
> . . . Thus, when the cultural symbols the parents brought into their bereavement cannot be deepened to include the experience of solace and to include the evil the parents have endured, these parents compartmentalize their religious life. In one part of their lifetime they feel themselves cut off from God. Yet in another part, they feel in touch with a child who is in heaven under the care of a protective God, or they feel soothed by ritualized memories which make the child present to them again and in doing so remove the isolation they feel in their world. In those parts of their life where the cultural symbols still provide a map of the invisible reality, the parents can function in the religious institutions as they did before. (Klass, 1991, pp. 204–205)

In his most recent report, Klass (1999) defined the complex, interdependent bonds and meanings that are in constant interplay in the spiritual lives of bereaved parents. Klass said this complex spiritual system, depicted in Fig. 6.1, is applicable to all of the world's religious traditions. If there is a change in any one of the spiritual bonds and meanings of the bereaved parent, then there is a corresponding change in each of the others.

> For example, the meaning of the child's death is found within the larger question of how the universe works. If the parent cannot make sense of the child's death, then the parent's understanding of how the universe works needs to be modified to accommodate the new reality. The place and power of the self in the universe and the meaning of the parent's life are often defined in terms of a long-standing sense of connectedness in the bond with the transcendent and in terms of community and family membership. The bond with the child is often felt as continuous with the parent's bond with the transcendent. If the parent feels cut off from God, the meaning of the parent's life, the quality of community bonds, the bond with the child, and the place and power of the self in the universe and in the community must be recast. When bereaved parents find a community in which their grief can be expressed and in which their bond with their dead child seems to be socially real, then the universe

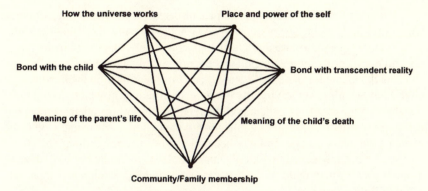

Figure 6.1 Klass's web of spiritual bonds and meanings in the lives of bereaved parents. From Klass (1999, p. 43), with permission.

may seem to work in a new and better way and their bond with transcendent reality may seem more sure. As they learn to use the bond with their dead child to live more creatively in their world, they may develop a new and stronger sense of their place and power in the universe. (Klass, 1999, p. 44)

THE SPIRITUAL DEATH AND RESURRECTION OF SOME BEREAVED PARENTS

When bereaved parents are unable to reconcile their spiritual beliefs with the irrevocable reality of their child's death, they can become stuck in the spiritual web that Klass describes so eloquently. As research demonstrates, parents who have established spiritual belief systems prior to losing their child may experience "cognitive dissonance" (Festinger, 1957)—an uncomfortable inconsistency between their beliefs about God and their attitudes and feelings following their child's death. Whether and how parents work through this dissonance can make the difference between remaining in a state of chronic mourning and surviving to reconcile their grief and reinvest in life despite living with their ongoing loss.

Some bereaved parents feel a need to blame someone for their child's death (themselves, others, God) because they cannot otherwise make any sense of the death of a child. This need to blame, even when none of the circumstances surrounding the child's death support it, is an example of attribution theory and seems to be an outcome of the rationality prevalent in many, mostly Western, cultures. But as psychotherapist and researcher Sukie Miller (1999) noted, this is not true for all cultures.

> In cultures in which life is a continuum and time is not something you run out of or use up, death does not signify the irreconcilable end of all life and all experience. Death is more an event, a space, a separation, followed usually by a resting period (for children the resting period is usually shorter than for an adult) and then new life. And this cycle is unending. (p. 83)

Miller provided compelling examples of bereaved parents in other cultures who consciously avoid the emotional fixation and/or freezing of self-blame. Miller believed that "one reason we don't heal more completely when a child dies has to do with our identification with God and the niggling thought that He *and* we are somehow to blame for the child's death. I call this identification the mirroring of God. I believe it occurs in virtually every modern family in which one or more members of the family assume a godlike relationship toward other members of the family—usually an adult or adults toward the children. Mirroring God is the phenomenon of us masquerading as beneficient gods to our children" (p. 38).

Miller acknowledged that all parents, regardless of ethnic or cultural background, ask why their child died, but her research highlights cultures that provide a very different response.

> In many places the family of a child who dies, and the child's friends, not only know why he died and where he is but can check up on how he's doing, ritually offer him gifts and blessings, and continue to play a role in his life after death. Imagine how it might be for us if we could follow our children's progress in some other world. Would it change how we miss them? Would it affect how we grieve? Would it help us heal? I think it would. (p. 14)

Other researchers noted the interconnection and powerful impact that culture/community and spiritual beliefs can have on the lives of bereaved parents. For example, Braun and Berg (1994) undertook a phenomenological study of 10 mothers who had experienced an unexpected death of their child and who were recruited from a local chapter of The Compassionate Friends. What they found affirmed the conclusions reached by Klass and Miller. "The ability to restore meaning after the death of a child was clearly linked to the prior existence of a meaning structure that could account for and 'place' the child's death" (Braun & Berg, 1994, p. 105). One of Braun and Berg's 10 participants fit this category. She provides an interesting example of attributing her child's death to God while continuing to believe that God's intentions are good.

> She expressed a strong conviction in divine benevolent purpose and accepted the death as being fair and orderly. . . . The challenge of the death did not pose a threat to her existing meaning structure. As she stated: "I'm a very religious person and I do believe that what God did was the best decision. He would have suffered all of his life. He would have had to have surgery after surgery after surgery. So He [God] took him right away instead of making him suffer more, because he suffered all his life already—4 months and he suffered the whole 4 months." (Braun & Berg, 1994, pp. 117, 119)

The other nine participants in Braun and Berg's study (1994) reinterpreted the meaning structures they had held prior to their child's death in order to give meaning to the death. There were three phases to this process of meaning reconstruction: discontinuity, disorientation, and adjustment, described briefly here.

Discontinuity: Meaning structures that held no place for the possibility of such an event as the death of a child included belief in being able to control life events, belief in the existence of order, and belief that other people also behave in ways that maintain order. The women who held these beliefs, which were inconsistent with the reality of their child's death, felt guilt at not being able to prevent it or attempted to attribute responsibility for what they could or should have done to prevent it to others. (p. 120)

Disorientation: When their meaning structures could not account for or explain the death of their children, several mothers "reported that they felt disconnected from the world. They viewed themselves as no longer existing in a world that made sense. . . . Another aspect of disorientation was a change in the view of the nature of life. A view of life as being secure changed to a view of life as being fragile. This changed view resulted in fear and distrust among many parents. . . . Concurrent with a collapse of assumptions about the security of life was a loss of hope for the future . . . and a changed perception of their power to control events. . . . In its most intense form, disorientation was manifested in the loss of a purpose in living." (pp. 121–123)

Adjustment: Prior meaning structures that did not account for the child's death (discontinuity) and were thus thrown into disorientation by the death were subject to reinterpretation to account for the child's death and restore a sense of meaning and purpose to the parents' lives. . . . Adjusted views were not necessarily permanent. The parents described themselves as moving back and forth between an adjusted view of the death and disorientation. . . . Relationships with other people were the reason for not committing suicide and were also what continued to provide meaning in their lives after the death. . . . Two factors that all of the informants reported as helping them adjust to their new reality were (a) talking about their child and the experience of the loss and (b) being understood. (pp. 124–125)

The iterative process of spiritual rebirth identified by Braun and Berg (1994) reflects the power of a parent's spiritual belief system to become both cause and consequence of adjustment to bereavement.

Just as Klass pointed out the development of a new self in many bereaved parents, Craig (1977) emphasized the need to understand the whole personality of bereaved parents. She noted that resolving spiritual questions and placing the child somewhere beyond the grave are crucial components in parents' search for meaning. Bereaved parents who "find an experiential communion with their invisible, yet known, beloved" child reach a "sense of wholeness." Further, she speculated that:

Perhaps it is because they believe their children are safely *there*—watched over by our Father which art in heaven—that the final decathexis occurs, and the haunting ghosts of bereavement find peace. Parents tell me that their children bring them back to God and make them aware, as their souls ache, that they are spiritual creatures. They often describe their bereavement as opening a new dimension of life and creating new life values. Death has brought to them, as to their children, a new beginning. (Craig, 1977, p. 53)

SPIRITUAL CRISIS AND SPIRITUAL GROWTH:
OPPOSITE ENDS OF THE BEREAVEMENT CONTINUUM

As we have seen, past research highlights the pivotal role that spirituality and/or religion can play after the death of a child. Four questions related to religion and spiritual beliefs were included in the participant questionnaire (see Appendix) completed by the 80 women in the "Mothers Now Childless" study. As shown in Table 6.1, a comparison of questionnaire responses by discriminant group indicated a significant difference between how the two groups viewed their faith, their church, and God's role in the death of their child.

More than half (55.6%) of the women in the group representing "perpetual bereavement" had experienced a spiritual crisis that remained unresolved. In contrast, almost half (46.8%) of those in the group representing "survival" had not experienced a spiritual crisis. They had been able to reconcile their child's death with their existing belief system. Another 29% of the "survival" group had experienced a spiritual crisis after their child died but had achieved some level of resolution.

It's important to remember that resolution, like survival, is not a place; it is a process that evolves. Parents may confront new spiritual questions as their loss evolves over time. It can help for them to realize that (a) spiritual growth is a lifelong process for most people, and (b) a child's death can suddenly bombard parents with spiritual questions they otherwise would have had a lifetime to work through and/or might never have had to confront at all.

Spiritual Crisis Can Contribute to Chronic Mourning

It is a myth that religion and spiritual beliefs always bring comfort during times of loss. Many bereaved parents do find solace in their faith, but it is also normal for parents to experience a spiritual crisis and question their beliefs. They may find it hard to pray or too painful to attend church. As the Rev. Dick Gilbert (1996) said, "I tell religious leaders that all of their inactive members are missing because of a loss of some kind." Sometimes parents don't return to church because of comments made to them about their child's death. Bereaved parents are extremely vulnerable, especially in early acute grief. As one mother whose daughter was stillborn put it: "It was like walking around without my skin on."

Negative Experiences With Others

Some of the women in the "Mothers Now Childless" study said they had "unpleasant experiences at church," often in the form of presumptive platitudes from people who were trying to comfort them: as one mother put it, "It was not God's will as a lot of people have said to me." Parents are often surprised by comments from others who presume to know what part God played in their child's death. Responding to such comments can be too painful and parents may choose not to

Table 6.1 Excerpted Responses to Participant Questionnaire by Discriminant Groups: The Spiritual Crisis of "Mothers Now Childless"

Response to Questionnaire	Perpetual Bereavement ($n = 18$) Frequency (%)	Survival ($n = 62$) Frequency (%)	χ^2 (80)
Reported experiencing a spiritual crisis following child's death:			6.39*
No crisis reported	5 (27.8)	29 (46.8)[b]	
Yes—Crisis has been resolved	3 (16.7)	18 (29.0)[b]	
Yes—Crisis remains unresolved	10 (55.6)[b]	15 (24.2)	
Changed religion after death:			1.15
No	7 (38.9)	33 (53.2)	
Yes	11 (61.1)	29 (46.8)	
Spiritual/religious beliefs helpful:[a]			3.86
No	6 (33.3)	11 (17.7)	
Both helpful & unhelpful	5 (27.8)	11 (17.7)	
Yes	7 (38.9)	40 (64.5)	
Importance of religion:			2.76
Not very important	6 (33.3)	17 (27.4)	
Somewhat important	4 (22.2)	9 (14.5)	
Important	5 (27.8)	13 (21.0)	
Very important	3 (16.7)	23 (37.1)	
Level of grief felt now:			15.96**
Grief dominates life	3 (16.7)[b]	0 (0)	
Feel grief daily	8 (44.4)[b]	24 (38.7)	
Feel grief weekly	3 (16.7)	16 (25.8)[b]	
Feel grief occasionally	3 (16.7)	22 (35.5)[b]	
No longer grieve	1 (5.6)	0 (0)[b]	
Believe survived child's death:			23.03**
No	9 (50.0)[b]	3 (4.8)	
Yes	7 (38.9)	53 (85.5)[b]	
Yes and no	2 (11.1)	6 (9.7)[b]	

[a]Discriminating variable used to determine group membership. [b] These results highlight and contrast the statistically significant differences between responses from the two groups.
* $p < .05$. ** $p < .01$.

attend church, at least for a while. As one mother said: "I find it difficult to attend church. The music is just too much for me. I get very emotional. I know that God didn't have anything to do with my son's death."

Some women described hurtful comments from members of the clergy that continued to impact them greatly. Bev, Fran, and Doris gave examples of this during their interviews. Bev described a talk with her pastor:

He's the one that did the funeral service for me, who I was active in the church with in the 70s—he said: "You know God really used you at one time, and he said, you need to go to church.' And to me, he was saying that if I don't go to church, I'm more or less damned, and I did not appreciate that! . . . I do believe in God and Jesus, but I don't feel very close to God, partly because of my anger over my son's death and partly because of my lifestyle. . . . I think that what I have come to . . . is that you can ask God for strength, you can tell God that you can't do it; He's got to do it. That's the point I have come to now, you know. I just say, I can't do it, you know, and I'm just gonna be a complete screw-up, and I don't know what to do, so you take care of it. [And He has?] So far.

Feeling judged by others, especially by clergy, adds to a bereaved parent's grief and can prevent parents from seeking help in exploring their spiritual questions. For others, like Fran, hurtful contacts with clergy can solidify a parent's belief about God's role in the death of their child.

I had one preacher come up there [to the hospital], and he wanted to pray with me every 3 hours, and talk to me about "now you need to get yourself right with God if you want David to get well." . . . That's not a time for hellfire and brimstone. It's, you know, a time for comfort. . . . I had one best friend and I've never really forgiven him for it. He told me that if I had been living the kind of life I should have been living, that David wouldn't have died [sigh]. . . . There's been times I hated God for taking David away from me. . . . I believe that you pay for what you do or don't do. I don't think God makes your children pay. You know, maybe I'm wrong. I may be totally wrong, but I don't think so.

Sometimes parents are hurt by clergy who fail to acknowledge their child's life and the enormity of their loss. This was true for Doris.

The worst anybody could have said came from the person you needed to believe in the most. . . . They can just put you down. The preacher from our little church stood at my son's casket and said a prayer for someone else's little girl because she was gonna miss him, and it just completely stunned me. He said nothing about me; nothing about Evan. You know, let's pray that in the future little so-and-so will get through missing her friend.

Questioning God's Role

Many of the women in the "Mothers Now Childless" study group representing "perpetual bereavement" felt bitter and angry at God. As one put this: "What God takes away innocent children? Not much about religion is meaningful since my son's death." But for some, faith and religion offered comfort and a ray of hope as they continued to grieve acutely. "I am very disillusioned about life. My life feels empty. My son has a stained glass memorial window at church. Without my faith I would be hopeless."

Two of the women in this group who were interviewed, Anita and Ellen, had experienced God's saving grace. Anita said: "Knowing there is a Heaven and Hell and God is our creator has kept me from committing suicide." Similarly, Ellen had relied on her spiritual beliefs to go on living: "I would think, boy, if that wasn't wrong (suicide) it would just be nice to just get on out of here. 'Cause I am just so tired."

Resolving a Spiritual Crisis Can Contribute to Healing

Redefining Faith

Nearly a third of the "Mothers Now Childless" in the group representing "survival" had experienced a spiritual crisis but had reached a level of resolution. For some, peace came as they reevaluated the nature of God.

> At first after my son was killed [in a car accident], I stopped having conversations with God. We are now close again. This has taken a long, long time. . . . I struggled for years with my crisis of faith. I had to redefine who is God.

Others found strength in a renewed belief in the resurrection and afterlife:

> I have gone through real times of turmoil. My brother was a priest and I worked for churches for years but found it hard to "believe" when it was my beloved daughter. Now, it supports my hope that I will be with my daughter again some day and that she is safe now.

As Klass noted (1999), for some "the place and power of self in the universe and in the community" had been recast as their spiritual growth evolved:

> I would have committed suicide without it. The chance that we may be together again helped through the most difficult times. . . . My Protestant childhood is significantly tempered by my later teachings. Our interactions with each other, our contribution to humanity and our ability to positively influence others defines my approach to life—spiritually, intellectually, and practically.

Redefinition of Religious Affiliation

Other women in the "survival" group had changed either their religious affiliation or how they practiced their religion as a result of working through a spiritual crisis. Carol described how she had reevaluated her religion after her son's death:

> I was on a [radio] talk show [discussing death of a child] with Father L. . . . The calls came in continuously as to God's will, and this is very difficult, especially for priests and a lot of clergy, to understand. It's like stripping God of his power. And I tried over and over again to say, "Father (and to the public) when something like

this happens, we bring our religion up real close. We take a good look at it. I'm a Catholic; probably always will be a Catholic. However, I won't be the Catholic that I used to be. We learned to fear God. My God has to be a loving God. . . . I can't even understand why my son had to have muscular dystrophy, let alone die. And I have to know that that loving God is giving people minds to find a cure for disease if there is none. That He's leaving it to man here on Earth. That He didn't choose my son to have muscular dystrophy and He didn't choose him to die at 15. He's cryin' right with me." And Father kept saying "but." No, there are no buts. I'm sorry and I won't back down [on this].

When clergy and church members do not allow bereaved parents to question their faith and church dogma, some change their religious affiliation. This can also happen when parents do not receive the kind and amount of support they need from their church. Gail said:

I was Catholic when Andy died. I didn't get much support or solace from that affiliation—I do (now) from Unity [a nondenominational Church]. The actual church service gives me a battery recharge each week. . . . You know I really do believe that whole thing that I'm a spiritual being in a human body. I'm not a human being trying to be spiritual; I am a spiritual being. And so, to me, Andy just shed his Earth suit, that's all he did.

Spiritual Turning Points

Some of the "Mothers Now Childless" in the group representing "survival" recognized a defining moment in their spiritual struggle that greatly impacted their ability to heal and reinvest in life. This was true for Julie. Around the first anniversary of her son's death, Julie attended a bereavement mass at her church:

I went alone and the priest was saying all the different stages of grief. And he got to, I think it was number eight, or number nine, and he says, "All of you who are out there saying the what if's and the if only's, that you could have done something to have prevented the death; there are two appointments that are made for you on this earth. One is when you're born. And when you're born the appointment is made of when you're going to die. So those of you that have been tormenting yourself with what is 'mea culpa' (and I was), there's nothing you could have done. It was already planned." And that snapped me out of it.

Julie called and volunteered to be treasurer of her Compassionate Friends group the very next day. When interviewed, she had been co-leader of the group for over 6 years. "I have a job here," she said, "and I'm doing my best in helping others through the valley of grief."

It is interesting to note how differently Carol and Julie were impacted by their church's doctrine of predestination. Both remained Catholics but with differing views of God's role in their child's death.

Choosing to Believe

Some of the women in the "survival" group had found comfort in their beliefs despite living with unanswered spiritual questions. These women remained in relationship with God and open to continued spiritual growth. One commented: "While I don't understand the death of my son and may never, I believe this is the path God has chosen for me. Maybe it's to give support to others—to be His little light to others."

For other women in the "survival group," their child's death became a catalyst for faith:

> Religion meant nothing to me at the time of my son's death. I now consider myself very spiritual and wish that I had been a member of a church and had some type of faith to get me through all the hard times. . . . Only after T.'s death did I look for something to believe in. I hate the term "new age" but it has helped me to make sense of what seems to have been "bad luck." Reincarnation theories have helped me tremendously.

It was clear that some had consciously chosen to believe in a loving God despite their child's death. One said: "I have a deeper understanding of God's care and His faithfulness to me. I could either reject a God who watched my daughter die or trust him. I decided to trust."

Sustained by Faith

Almost half in the women in the "survival" group did not report experiencing a spiritual crisis; rather, their faith and beliefs had been crucial in helping them survive their child's death. One mother believed: "Without my faith I would never have made it. I keep C.'s memory alive. I talk to God and C. on a daily basis. I feel she is with her father, my parents, her grandparents." Some were both sustained and strengthened by their faith: "I never would be healing without God's constant love and the grounding that faith gives me. I believe K. is in heaven and that gives me great comfort and that I'll be with her again one day. Her death has made my faith stronger."

Several women in the group representing "survival" were drawn back to their religion and became more committed to it:

> My beliefs and faith give me an inner peace and strength to get through life's difficult times. I had not been so active in my faith for many years but was drawn back when my son died. . . . My church was there for me when my son died and my priest was very helpful and comforting. I feel it rewarding to give back something [by volunteering at church].

Others felt their faith assured them their child was safe and they would be reunited again:

I believe my praying helped me so much. God did give me strength one day at a time. He gave me a dream. I saw my A. and Jesus as angels in the sky in flowing garments. That dream gave me assurance that my son was safe.

Messages From Heaven

Spirituality can be an important way that bereaved parents maintain a connection and build a new relationship with their deceased children. Both Gail and Julie talked of how comforted they were by messages they continue to receive from their sons. Gail volunteered that:

Andy comes to me in very strange ways, in very strange places to let me know that I'm not alone. There have been probably four times in the past eight years that I woke up in the middle of the night and felt him sitting on my bed holding me. . . . It doesn't happen when I want it, but it always happens when I need it.

Similarly, Julie continues to receive messages from her son:

Every time I was either going to the cemetery or coming out, that song [her son's favorite] would come on the radio. So that was like my sign from Stuart. And now whenever I ask him, "give Mommy a sign," I will hear that song. . . . They're around us. It's something else to grasp onto to get you through the day.

These experiences are examples of "after death communications" (ADC), which appear to happen much more frequently than previously thought. Several recent books provide examples of the differing ways parents can receive messages from their children (cf. Bernstein, 1997; Devers, 1997; Edwards, 1998; Guggenheim & Guggenheim, 1995; Lawson, 2000; Martin & Romanowski, 1994; VanPraagh, 2000; Wiitala, 1996). Some parents are reticent to share such experiences and fear others won't believe them or will judge them as mentally unstable. This was true for Julie:

I would tell my husband Dan about my visits [from Stuart]. One day Dan came back from a business trip and he said, "Julie, I've got something to tell you." I said, "What happened?" And he said, "You know what you always use to tell me [about visits from Stuart]—I never would believe you." He said, "Stuart visited me—when I was in S. D. . . . there I was, sharing a room with a client, and at the foot of my bed there was Stuart—exactly as you described it. I couldn't move, but I was awake. I know I was awake; it wasn't in a dream." And I was so happy that he didn't think I was crazy!

When parents are aware of and take comfort in contacts with their deceased children, such events can help integrate the child's death into the parents' present life-world. It is important to acknowledge this can and does happen to some (not all) bereaved parents. Simple queries such as "Have you felt ___'s presence since her death?" and "What was it like for you to experience this contact with your child's spirit?" help to normalize these experiences and facilitate the parent's ability to find or create meaning from them. Doing so can also keep parents open to discovering renewed connections with their child in the future, even when they no longer expect such events to happen. Here is a personal example.

In January 1999, 16 years after my daughter Leah's death, I was surprised and amazed by an "after death communication" from her, something that had never happened to me before. It happened to my father, her grandfather, who was with me at the time, as well. I had flown to Montana to visit both my parents. My father and I drove directly from the airport to the nursing home where my mother had lived for four years. Mother was surprisingly alert during this visit, listening as I shared current events from my life and work. On the table by her bed was a Christmas present I had given her the previous year—a small statue of a young angel with blonde hair who looked a lot like Leah. When a button underneath the base of the statue is pushed, the angel plays "Silent Night." At the end of my last visit, I had given the angel to mother to hold and told her that whenever she pressed the button both Leah and I would be thinking of her. But on this night in 1999, we did not talk about the angel and when mother tired, my father and I left and drove home in his new car. It was a typical cold but clear Montana night and very quiet in the mobile home park where my father lives. As he unloaded my luggage from the trunk of the car, we were both startled to hear "Silent Night" begin playing. The car radio wasn't on and we looked around to see if it could be coming from any of the neighboring houses but they were silent; the music was definitely coming from the trunk of the car. We both heard it clearly for several seconds and looked at each other totally perplexed until it stopped suddenly. It wasn't coming from anything I had brought in my luggage; and it wasn't part of the new car's extra features either. Later, after exhausting all of the logical possibilities, we both realized it had sounded just like the music of the angel statue. We couldn't explain it or prove it, but we'd both heard it and we both could think of only one meaning—that this was a musical message of reassurance from Leah. This was Leah's way of letting us know she was with us as we reconnected and coped with her grandmother's declining health. This was an uplifting, comforting, and totally unexpected event for me. And I believe it helped my parents greatly as well. Six months later my mother died a peaceful, conscious, and painless death with my father by her side. Today, the angel sits on my desk next to my computer. As I write this, she is my "linking object" to remind me of Leah's ongoing influence in this world, as well as the next.

The Importance of Spiritual Healing

As we have seen, spiritual struggling and questioning in one form or another is common for many, if not most, bereaved parents. Those who experience and resolve a spiritual crisis often provide hope to others (cf. Gayton, 1995; Holtkamp, 1995; Kushner, 1987; Sittser, 1996; Talbot, 2000b). But parents who have not resolved such a crisis remain vulnerable to yet another devastating loss, the death of their soul. This "dark night of the soul" was eloquently described by Marcie, one of the women in the "Mothers Now Childless" study who said she had not survived her daughter's death. She wrote the following poem and attached it to her completed questionnaire.

The Light
The light: unrelenting, blinding brightness, searing the soul, unbearable pain.
Turn away: first left, then right, down, up, behind—no way to escape the light.
Time intervenes, the painful brightness dims, almost imperceptibly at first.
The seared soul cools, hardens.
Turning away begins to give slight respite from the pain.
At last the vast devastation left by the light is realized.
Blindness: the soul has died.

This very real potential for spiritual death was confronted by Gerald Sittser, a professor of religion at Whitworth College in Spokane, Washington. In his book *A Grace Disguised: How the Soul Grows Through Loss* (1996), Sittser described his own lengthy process of spiritual healing. He watched his wife, 4-year-old daughter, and mother die before his eyes after a head-on collision. Their car was hit by a drunk driver who crossed over the center line going 85 miles an hour. This was his initiation into the world of bereavement. After this devastating tragedy, Sittser traversed his own spiritual crisis to reach some profound conclusions:

> We exacerbate our suffering needlessly when we allow one loss to lead to another. That causes gradual destruction of the soul. This destruction of the soul represents the tragedy of what I call the "second death," and it can be a worse tragedy than the first. The death that comes through loss of spouse, children, parents, health, job, marriage, childhood, or any other kind is not the worst kind of death there is. Worse still is the *death of the spirit*, the death that comes through guilt, regret, bitterness, hatred, immorality, and despair. The first kind of death happens *to* us; the second kind of death happens *in* us. It is a death we bring upon ourselves if we refuse to be transformed by the first death. (p. 87)

For bereaved parents, transformation can be part and parcel of resolving a spiritual crisis. Sittser's experience demonstrated to him that such transformation can make it possible for bereaved parents to "live in and be enlarged by loss, even as we continue to experience it."

SUMMARY

It is undisputed that bereaved parents can be spiritually wounded by the death of their child. Many parents consider their children a "gift from God" and expect God's help in raising them. When a child dies, most parents are challenged to reevaluate their beliefs about who God is and how God can allow evil to exist in the world. Some parents find peace by becoming able to fit the child's death into their existing belief system. Other parents undergo a spiritual crisis and spiritual reconstruction process.

Resolving a spiritual crisis is an iterative process characterized by discontinuity, disorientation, and adjustment as parents confront many interconnected questions. For example: What role did God play in their child's death? Did the parent's relationship with God play any part? Why are some children saved from death but not their child? Is God taking care of the child? Was the child predestined to die at a certain time? Did the child have some special destiny that could one day be revealed to the parents? Will parent and child be reunited someday? Will the child be reincarnated to live again? Does God have a plan at work that will ultimately result in some greater good? What can parents do with their anger at God, with unanswerable questions? How can parents reconnect with their child's spirit?

A child's death, in itself, is enough to bring about spiritual crisis. But it is also common for the crisis to be precipitated by insensitive and unhelpful comments from others. Some parents change churches; others change their religious affiliation; and still others cut themselves off from any relationship with God, at least for a while. Years after their child's death, unresolved spiritual questions remained prevalent for the majority of women in the "Mothers Now Childless" study group that represented "perpetual bereavement." The reverse was true for women in the "survival" group: the majority of these women had grown spiritually as a result of reevaluating, strengthening, and/or reformulating their spiritual beliefs.

In sum, the death of a child presents most parents with an awesome choice: to remain in relationship with the God of their understanding and continue to seek answers to their spiritual questions, or to give up on God and resign themselves to a spiritless life without purpose or peace. Perhaps the most important thing caregivers can do is to accompany bereaved parents on this painful spiritual journey. Caregivers can act as compassionate "companions" (Wolfelt, 1997) to grieving parents by encouraging questions, honoring their child's spirit, accepting the intense emotions of their struggle, helping parents clarify their beliefs, celebrating their expressions of faith, and describing their spiritual process as it evolves.

Chapter 7

Confronting an Existential Crisis:
Can Life Have Purpose Again?

[There are] three principal ways in which mankind can find meaning in life: by what we give to the world in terms of our creations; what we take from the world in terms of encounters and experiences; and third, the stand we take to our predicament in case we must face a fate which we cannot change. That is why life never ceases to hold a meaning, for even a person who is deprived of both creative and experiential values is still challenged by a meaning to fulfill, that is, by the meaning inherent in the right, in an upright way of suffering. (Frankl, 1969, p. 70)

Just as a child's death brings acute suffering and spiritual crisis, there is yet another loss that parents must confront: the loss of an anticipated future. Bereaved parents are left to create a future that cannot contain the physical presence of the child who died. The specific reasons for living associated with being a parent to this unique child are gone. Life goals often are severely impacted and parents struggle to find purpose for living. The emotional, cognitive, physical, social, and spiritual changes that result from the death of a child work together to confront bereaved parents with a heightened responsibility for creating a new existence. Parents must relearn the world (Attig, 1996) and their place in it as a bereaved parent. Years after their child's death, some bereaved parents still experience great difficulty in identifying new goals and a purpose for living.

THE ALTERED EXISTENCE OF BEREAVED PARENTS

Parents who move beyond the "why" questions related to their child's death come face to face with "what now" questions. What kind of life is possible now? What reasons are there to live, to create, to invest energy, to care enough about, to risk loving and being needed again? What is the reason for human existence? Why are we here? What can we contribute to make the world a better place even though our child no longer lives in it? What do we have left to give?

These questions tend to surface later in bereavement because in early grief parents often are overwhelmed by the emotional, physical, and social aspects of their loss. Acute grief requires day-by-day, and sometimes minute-by-minute, coping. Spiritual and existential questions arise as parents begin to think about and react to the reality of living forever without their child. Many factors can make confronting this existential crisis difficult and complicated. These factors are woven into each parent's unique life-world as the following examples demonstrate.

A Future Derived From Circumstances of the Death

Bereaved parents may lack needed resources and/or support, and they may continue to be impacted by ongoing, extenuating circumstances resulting from their child's death. This was true for Bev, whose lifestyle had been changed dramatically by her son's accident and death. She believed her ongoing lawsuit, then in appeal, represented her only hope for the future because a financial award would allow her to resume some of the activities that had been meaningful to her in the past.

Bev had worked from the age of 12, but had been living on disability payments since her son's accident. "My doctor says that I have a classic, textbook situation of posttraumatic stress disorder," she said. He testified in court about her ongoing trauma. "I have profound depression and anxiety and the anxiety is so intense that I really struggle with it and I've had periods where I have not been able to leave my house . . . because I feel SO terrible and have SO MUCH anxiety I don't want to see anybody. I don't want anybody to look at me. I feel like I'm crazy."

Asked what she would do if she won her lawsuit, Bev said: "I would get into art. I'd be traveling again. I'd be doing the things that I used to do again, and I really do want to adopt a child or children. That will make all of the difference in the world. . . . I just, I think they owe me at least that much, to get my life back and another child."

As Bev demonstrates, the circumstances of a child's death can provide a new, albeit unwanted, purpose, at least for a while. Some parents endure years of lengthy court trials and investigations. Seeking justice and/or working to prevent other deaths become some parents' new purposes for living.

A Future Created by Remembering the Child

Irene also lacked financial resources and emotional support. When interviewed, she was living alone, worked part-time, and had a very limited income. She had a heart condition that had required surgery two years prior to her son's death. Irene did not want others to forget her son, and this led to her decision to take a course at the local junior college in genealogy. She described the family project she initiated that would ensure others would remember her son.

> My sister and I are working on genealogy books for a Christmas gift for the five kids [cousins], because they really don't know about the family history. So we're trying to do like a generational thing. And this year we're gonna concentrate on my father and mother and my aunt who I was named for. We want the kids to know these people. I suggested doing this and so my sister's coming up Thanksgiving weekend and we're gonna try to put it together. . . . Next year I would like . . . to do a section on Bobby and a section on me, because I'm gonna have no other—you know there are no other descendants from me.
>
> It's gonna be fun, and it's probably gonna be a little bit painful when I start writing about Bobby because there were many painful things in his life. His alcoholism, you know; he did abuse drugs to some extent; there were lots of times he was not very nice and he stole things, you know; but I want him to be a flesh and blood human being. I want to write about him warts and all, 'cause I think it would be a disservice to him to write as though he never did anything wrong. These remembrance pages are going to be read by people generations from now, and I want them to know the entire picture because as people age they start to get involved in, gee, there is a family and yes, family is important. It seems like there's one person in every generation that gets interested in genealogy and the family, and it'd be a disservice to them if five generations from now they look at the thing about Bobby and go, "well, this guy was too good to be true." I want to write what Bobby was: he was beautiful; I mean he was handsome and beautiful inside. He was very troubled, had a lot of trouble—did not have a lot of willpower to a certain extent. But he was also funny. You know, the good and the bad. I think that's gonna be another healing process that I'm gonna go through, 'cause I'm sure it's gonna take some doing.
>
> And . . . I'm gonna ask the kids [his cousins] also to some day write their remembrances of him for future generations—so that future generations, even though Bobby never had any children, will know that there was another person who was very important in their lives and who he was and what happened and so forth. And because I've been involved in genealogy now, it has made me more aware of—not necessarily my own family—but it's made me aware that everyone out there in the entire world belongs to a family. And everybody loves; everybody grieves; everybody hurts; everybody has joy. It's another lesson that God is teaching me in this journey that I'm on to survive the death of my son.

Irene's genealogy project was helping her resolve some of her spiritual and existential questions and heal some of the pain she felt because she and her son would leave no descendants. As described further in chapter 9, many bereaved parents who pursue ways to keep their child's memory alive also discover new purposes and goals for their life.

A Future Created in Response to Helplessness

Most parents struggle to regain a sense of control over their lives after their child's death. Feeling at least some level of control is essential in order to function in this new world that reminds parents daily that they did not have the power to prevent their child's death. Doris and Carol who represent opposite ends of the bereavement continuum in the "Mothers Now Childless" study, provide contrasting examples. Doris described her awareness of feeling helpless to control her future.

> As I fill out the sections of your survey, it clearly shows that I feel *I* am not in control of my life, or my future. I do feel this way. I need you to know that most of this is due to my husband's career. At any time we can get transferred to another area. We have moved four times in our fifteen years of marriage. Our son only made one move with us. He was very young so we didn't have to worry about leaving friends or changing schools. I would hope our moving record would be different if he were still alive. We both have a strong, stable family background. And I hope we would have worked hard for that for our son. The not knowing what can happen next makes me feel out of control. I have quit every job I have ever had to go where my husband's company wants us. . . . I do not begrudge him this career. It is what he always wanted to do and he is happy. I am also VERY proud of him. I just wanted to say this so it would be considered when you read my survey results. I am still a stay-at-home mom. Though I am unemployed at this time. So, I would welcome the verbal interview. Grief, the grief process, and educating others are very important to me.

Learning about grief can help bereaved parents gain perspective about their loss and, as Doris demonstrates, can lead them to reach out to help others. When parents realize they can pass along what they have learned, they engage cognitively, which helps restore some level of control over emotions, as well as increasing self-esteem.

Carol reflected on how she had changed as a result of recognizing a need to regain control after her son's death.

> It was the fear of ever making decisions again [after taking responsibility for the decision not to resuscitate her son at the hospital]. . . . I had to be able to gain control again, and when I began to gain control, it changed me from going back to the person who was easily manipulated. . . . I've survived the hopelessness, the darkest days of desperation and now I can use this profound experience toward positive growth—toward helping others and facing whatever the future might hold.

Facing Fears About Aging

After a child dies, parents are confronted with the fact that child will not be with them as they age and face their own death. This cruel reality is especially wrenching when the child was an only child, when the parents' relationships with surviving children are strained, when family members live long distances apart, or when parents feel isolated and without a support system. Julie had found new purpose in living in the years since her son's death, but one fear remained.

> You know, why we outlive our children is a mystery to all of us. And I'm here for a reason and with the work that I was able to get involved in with The Compassionate

Friends in helping other parents, maybe that's why I'm still here. . . . I'm not afraid of death. It's just—my biggest fear is dying alone.

Subsequent losses within the family not only trigger bereaved parents' grief about their child, they also confront parents with their own aging and mortality. At the time she was interviewed, Fran was helping to care for her mother who was terminally ill with cancer.

I wonder when I get old, who's gonna take care of me? You know, what's gonna happen to me when I get to where I can't do for myself? . . . So it's like you really don't have a whole lot of people you can count on.

Facing Fears of Failure

Parents can feel that their child or children represent their major accomplishment in life and are the central focus of their world. Some parents experience a sense of failure when their child dies. Anita talked about how difficult it was to envision a future without her son and how her grief continued to severely impact her self-confidence and ability to pursue new goals:

Brad was my whole life. That was the one thing I wanted was to have a child. And he was just my whole life. . . . I can't imagine living x amount of years, however long it's gonna be, without him. I just can't. I can't envision myself functioning and actually living without him.

. . . I was going to be a certified teacher for early childhood development. And I thoroughly loved it. And when Brad passed away—it wasn't Brad that made me have this decision—I decided I couldn't go on. 'Cause I couldn't concentrate. I had no self-direction. I didn't work for three years after I lost him. All I did was eat and sleep, and hardly ate but I stayed in the house. I didn't function hardly at all. And finally Ray came to me—he said, "You know Anita, I'm working on my own now, and I'm starting to struggle. I need some help." 'Cause we had almost used our whole savings; we hadn't planned on that. And probably had he not come to me and said that to me I'd still be laying on the couch. But then I got up and found another job that's totally different. But I just knew I could not continue and get my master's or anything. So I gave that up. And I don't know, ah, I just feel that mentally—like I said earlier, I don't concentrate as well. I can't think, reason things out as well. So that's how I feel that I've gone backwards. . . . I've gone downhill. I don't have confidence in myself anymore. I don't feel like I can achieve. I feel like I make more failures than I do successes even today.

Some parents, like Anita, feel they have failed to complete their primary purpose for living after their child dies. This had been true for Gail also. She talked about how facing her fears had led eventually to increased self-confidence.

Surviving my son's death, has had to do with me going back and finding that inner child inside of myself and nurturing it and healing it and becoming the kind of parent that I wanted to myself. . . . I mean, just walking through all my fears. My fears professionally. My fears in my personal life. My fears physically. You know I've had to hit it at all levels—just going through that fear. Susan Jeffers (1987) wrote that book: *Feel the Fear and Do It Anyway,* and that's kind of become my mantra because so much of my life I held myself back in so many ways because I was afraid. . . . And what I've learned and now I'm experimenting with is that I can not feel safe and say ok, little girl, little Gail, you don't feel safe but still be present and [I can] calm my inner child down and say, you know, I can take care of you. Thank you for sending me the message that you don't feel safe. . . . Sometimes I don't even know why I don't feel safe, but it's always tripping up something that that little kid inside of me doesn't feel good about. And so you know, that's what I'm experimenting with right now—is that whole thing. It's like it weaves a tapestry of recovery and survival. See I don't feel like I'm surviving anymore. For me now that word doesn't fit. I've gone past surviving the death of my son. I'm living in light of the fact that I'm a bereaved parent.

Undertaking New Responsibilities

When a child's death leaves parents without goals and/or purposes they value, life becomes meaningless and mundane. Children provide a meaningful external focus; a child's death can turn parents inward again to seek self-direction. Becoming responsible for redefining their priorities and values is a very long, frustrating process for bereaved parents. Ellen and Helen, representing opposite ends of the "Mothers Now Childless" bereavement continuum, provide contrasting examples. When interviewed, Ellen was struggling to find new, meaningful purposes for living.

> You know, as far as I'm concerned my life is over. I'm forty-four years old and everything that I've had is all in the past—and the future, all it is is that day-to-day existence and I just, I don't know, but—I guess I do pretty good from day-to-day. I try to stay busy. . . . I call this life of mine an existence because Don was all that I had. . . . There's this void—this emptiness—I call it this big black hole in my stomach. . . . Don was my life. He's what I looked forward to in getting old, and him getting married and havin' a wife and makin' me a grandmother, and havin' my house filled with little kids runnin around. And there's nothing now, absolutely nothin'.
>
> [There's a question on the questionnaire about do you believe you've survived the experience, and you said yes, you're a survivor.] For what I don't know [laughs] but I'm still here. [You mean you don't understand why, what's enabled you to survive or why you should have survived?] Yeah. That too. It's like, what's the reason? Everybody says well there's a reason for everything, well, bull. You know. I don't know. Sometimes I feel like a fly or an ant or something; I'm just here. It's like there's no purpose, and I don't quite understand it. I keep thinking one of these days it's just gonna hit me like somebody slapped me in the face, and then I'm gonna think, that's why I'm here. That's why all this has happened. But it's just kind of strange that you get up every morning and you go to work. You work, you come home, you eat, you watch television and you go to bed. You get up and do the same

thing over and over and over. It's like you're not going anywhere. Everything's just at a standstill. And then somebody says, well, it'll get better. Your life will get better. And I think, no it won't. How can it? 'Cause everything that I had, that I looked forward to in getting old, was taken, and it's like my mind just stops right there. I can't see any further than that. I don't know. I can't imagine what else there would be. I want somebody to tell me what I'm s'pose' to be doin.

[Well it sounds like what you're saying is you need a new purpose in your life. You're never gonna replace Don. You don't want to replace Don. You don't want to forget Don. But maybe something out of this experience will help you to choose a new purpose that you feel is important.] Yeah. That's what I keep thinking. But I haven't run into it yet.

Helen talked about how she gradually made decisions to take on new responsibilities, to risk caring and valuing life again.

So then in 1990 on Mother's Day I decided I wanted this dog. I wanted another dog because I always had a little dog. . . . So here I am at three o'clock in the morning, I'm out here saying—"go potty, do what you're supposed to do"—and I'm thinking, why did I do this? Why did I want this responsibility? You couldn't get her away from me for nothing [now] [laughs]. It didn't take long. But that was my first [taking on a new responsibility].

[How long do you think you were in that period of "I just can't handle any responsibility?"] About seven years . . . [And when did you start the bereavement support group?] December of 1989. [So they were kind of together then weren't they—both of those decisions?] Yeah. Really. That's right . . . yeah, the responsibility started in again in 1989 to 1990. That's a good point—you brought that out. I didn't realize they were both about the same time. I probably, you know, felt that I should be doing something constructive.

. . . A lot of the people who come to the [support group] meeting or call, they'll want to know: "What's your purpose now? What do you feel? What are you still here for?" I say, I hope to find out too, someday. But in the meantime, this is what I'm doing. This is what I've got to do. And this doing what I'm doing now is so rewarding for me. And I know it's helping other people. I've gotten so many cards and letters and gifts and things. It blows me away to think that what I do comes from my heart, and they appreciate it so much. . . . Life is exciting again.

MOTIVATIONS FOR REINVESTING IN LIFE

There are many different ways that bereaved parents reinvest in life. Those ways are very personal and connected with each parent's unique loss and life circumstances. Again, there is no prescriptive approach to deduce from the preceding examples. We cannot promise bereaved parents that following a specific course of action will heal their pain and give them new reasons for living. But we can assure parents that identifying and exploring the spiritual and existential questions that accompany their loss can teach them the meaning of their experiences and uncover potential choices for their future.

The willingness to explore and confront existential questions after the death of a child can grow into a renewed commitment to living a purposeful life. As healing proceeds, parents can find that living matters to them again. They may need and want: (a) to feel needed again; (b) to make a difference in the world; (c) to offer others a positive model of dealing with devastating adversity; (d) to assert control and assume responsibility for personal fulfillment; (e) to honor their child's memory and their life as that child's parent; (f) to ensure something good comes from surviving their loss; and/or (g) to remain open to discovering God's will for their future.

THE IMPORTANCE OF EXISTENTIAL HEALING

As we have seen, the search for meaning is a central factor in the bereavement process of many bereaved parents. Meaning reconstruction helps to counter anhedonia and angst because it addresses the deeper psychological and spiritual realms of *values, beliefs, assumptions*, and *expectations*. These are the internal catalysts driving each person's decisions, actions, thoughts, and feelings. When life no longer makes sense to them, people in crisis can become open to reviewing and reevaluating these catalysts. It is at this level that personal change takes place and individuals begin to assume personal responsibility for their future. This was apparent in a study that asked people who had completed group therapy to identify those aspects most useful to them (Yalom, 1980).

Participants were given 60 cards with a different "curative factor" on each, representing 12 categories of "mechanisms of change in therapy." They were asked to force-sort the 60 cards from "most helpful" to "least helpful." The following five "existential factors" were included to represent an "existential category":

1 Recognizing that life is at times unfair and unjust.
2 Recognizing that ultimately there is no escape from some of life's pain and from death.
3 Recognizing that no matter how close I get to other people, I must still face life alone.
4 Facing the basic issues of my life and death, and thus living my life more honestly and being less caught up in trivialities.
5 Learning that I must take ultimate responsibility for the way I live my life no matter how much guidance and support I get from others. (Yalom, 1980, p. 265)

Yalom described the study's unexpected results:

The therapists in this study were not existentially oriented but instead led traditional, interactionally based groups, and the "existential factor" category was inserted almost as an afterthought. Hence, when the results were tabulated, it was with much surprise that we learned that many patients attributed considerable importance to these "throw-in" items which are not part of a traditional therapeutic program. The entire category of existential factors was ranked sixth in importance of the twelve categories (arrived at by summing and averaging the rank order of the individual items). One item—"5. Learning that I must take ultimate responsibility for the way I live my life no matter how much guidance and support I get from others"—was especially highly valued. Of the sixty items, it was ranked fifth most important by the patients. (pp. 265–266)

These findings were replicated in other studies. Yalom concluded:

These data all suggest that the successful psychotherapy patient becomes more aware of personal responsibility for life. It seems that one of the results of effective therapy is that one not only learns about relatedness and intimacy—that is, about what one can obtain from relating to others; but also that one discovers the limits of related-ness—that is, what one *cannot* get from others, in therapy and in life as well. (p. 266)

This awareness about personal responsibility for life can be one of the mean-ing constructions that bereaved parents eventually derive from their grief. But doing so involves a painful and lengthy process of self-reflection. There is no time table; it takes as long as it takes. And it is a process rife with anxiety, as "we are forced to look at things we would rather not see, to confront ourselves and to realize that we can no longer hide from ourselves or others. . . . Anxiety *throws* the person into possibility, into restless self-searching and into agitation to dis-cover and to pursue genuine purposes in living" (Moustakas, 1994, p. 38). Thus, struggling with existential questions can make a bereaved parent's grief process worse before it starts to get better. It takes tremendous courage to confront and work through these issues.

Donna Michaud Berger (1996), whose husband and three children were killed in a highway accident that left her critically burned, described her long and pain-ful healing process. At the lowest point she reached the limits of despair. Donna wrote:

I felt abandoned by God. I wanted out of the pain and misery. My only thought was that there is no God, and I sat on the bed for hours neither hearing nor seeing. I can't say what transpired during that time but when I came out of that semi-conscious state, I remember feeling deep remorse for denying God, a God who had always provided for me. It was at this lowest point that I realized that to live a life of faith is very difficult, but to live without it is impossible. For one brief moment in time I believed I felt what it was like to be truly dead with no hope of salvation. I knew then I would never again quesiton my faith in Jesus.

Ultimately, Donna's process led her to the support she needed to validate her thoughts, feelings, and perceptions and slowly she began to get involved in life again. She concluded:

> I learned that we each have our own unique purpose in life. There are lessons to be learned and tests to pass. We must face the challenges in our life, great and small, because they are the stepping stones of fulfillment of our purpose . . . I have also learned that I live *with* the people around me, not *through* them. Once I accepted this I was able to set my risen family free and start looking toward the future.

This does not mean Berger will ever forget her first family or condone their premature death. It means she will use her ongoing love and spiritual connections with them in positive ways. Berger eventually remarried, had three more children, and continues to facilitate support groups for bereaved parents and to share her hard-won wisdom with others.

The future for bereaved parents is always a future made in light of the limits to life's possibilities. As Yalom noted, "the more one's possibilities are limited, the closer one is brought to death. . . . The reality of limitation is a threat to one of our chief modes of coping with existential anxiety: the delusion of specialness—that, though others may be subject to limitations, one is exempt, special, and beyond natural law" (p. 318). Parents want desperately to believe that the ultimate loss, the death of a child, will never happen to them. Once it does, they must choose whether to survive and reinvest in life again. The next chapter continues the discussion of factors that can influence this crucial decision.

SUMMARY

We do not know whether all bereaved parents experience an existential crisis as their bereavement evolves. It seems likely most do—because a child's death tends to challenge deep, internal factors that drive parents' actions, decisions, thoughts, and feelings. A child's death calls into question a parent's beliefs, values, assumptions, and expectations about life. Constructions of self, relationships, and worldview that parents previously accepted uncritically may seem invalid, unrealistic, too rigid, or no longer applicable now that their child has died.

Resolving an existential crisis begins when bereaved parents ask themselves questions such as: What is still possible? What must we do because this child died, at this time and in this particular way? Parents discover new goals and reasons to live in response to these kinds of questions. For some parents, reinvestment decisions are made in response to the unique circumstances surrounding their child's death—such as when parents work to achieve justice and/or prevent future deaths. Some parents find new purposes in activities that preserve their child's memory. For some, a need to regain control of life can result in taking actions that later present new goals, such as helping others heal. Still other parents reinvest in their own development as they face fears brought to consciousness by the child's death, such as fear of aging, of dying alone, of risking and failing. Healing comes as parents undertake new responsibilities and come to realize they must choose to survive; only they can decide what new purposes will make their life meaningful again.

Questions remain and await further research: Can bereaved parents truly heal their pain and learn to live with their ongoing loss without confronting an existential crisis? Further, does anyone really transcend trauma and loss without reevaluating the basic premises that have guided their life choices?

Chapter 8

Deciding to Survive:
Reaching Bottom—Climbing Up

Life breaks us all sometimes, but some grow stronger at broken places.
(Ernest Hemingway, quoted by Ripple, 1986, p. 143)

Choices

When you have to be the one to tell the doctor
to unplug your dying child's respirator—
That's when you truly come to understand
that life is always about making choices.

You speak the necessary, devastating words
And you go on—
Into a different, unimaginable future.
Eventually you stop feeling like you are bleeding inside.

But the bruises remain—
Invisible and unfelt
Until you brush up against a memory
And suddenly feel the familiar pain take your breath away.

You learn to take comfort in knowing the bleeding will stop again;
Your breathing will return to normal
And you will go on—
Facing life's imperfect choices
And finding beauty among the brokenness.

       —Kay Talbot, June 21, 1991

In her comparative study of death of a child, spouse, or parent, Sanders (1999) concluded that those who grieve "make a decision, conscious or unconscious, to survive and begin a new life, or to remain in perpetual bereavement and, perhaps, die" (p. 44). Jeanne Blank (1998), a bereaved mother who researched the death of adult children, went further: "Those who lose a child experience such extreme anguish that suicide is a real possibility for them," she said. "In fact, it is so common to consider suicide that most of those who answered my questionnaire admitted they had thought of it as an option" (p. 79).

Other researchers have acknowledged that the acute psychological pain of grieving is one factor that can precipitate suicidal feelings. Shneidman (1996) declared that "suicide is the desire to reduce painful tension by stopping the unbearable flow of consciousness" (p. 17). When the shock and numbness that follow a child's death begin to wear off, bereaved parents become increasingly conscious that their child's death is not just a bad dream but is unrelentingly real. A desire for relief from the overwhelming pain of their new reality is one reason bereaved parents may consider suicide. However, the desire to be with their deceased child can be equally compelling. As Blank put it: "The important thing for bereaved parents and their caregivers to understand, I think, is that the parent is not only anxious to end the pain of his or her loss; the urge to be with the child is just as great as, perhaps even greater than, the need to end the pain" (p. 83). This was true for Evelyn Gillis (1986), who described her visits to the cemetery after the death of her daughter and only child:

> During this period my thoughts of suicide surfaced. At first it was just a strong urge to follow her. I could not accept on blind faith that she was safe and free from harm. I had loved and protected her in life and I wanted to love and protect her in death. Some spark of self-preservation brought me to a suicide counselor. She called me daily. Hour after hour she would listen to me talk about Lorena, how agonizing the pain was and how I could not bear it one more minute. She helped me to understand I really did not want to die. I just wanted the pain to stop, and suicide seemed the way to become free from this pain. It is because of her day-after-day patience and understanding that I am alive today. (p. 319)

Blank (1998) maintained that although thoughts of suicide are common for many bereaved parents regardless of the age of their child who died,

> there are subtle differences which bear on whether or not parents [of adult children who die] will actually carry it out. The most obvious difference lies in the family situation. Although some single parents lose an only child and some couples lose an only child, a young child who dies is more apt to have surviving siblings who demand the parents' day-to-day care. Obligations to other loved ones, in such cases, function strongly to overrule the parents' urge to end it all. Adult children who die, who did not live at home and were not as completely dependent on their parents as are young children, or who may even have established their own homes and families, are quite another matter. Independent adults who die do not present their grieving parents with the same deterrent to suicide as the young child. (p. 80)

Investigation of suicidal ideation and the risk of suicide among bereaved parents is an area needing further study. Some researchers have acknowledged this risk. Levav (1982) noted statistically significant and "remarkable" increased mortality among bereaved parents after the death of an adult child when compared with those of a matched control group over a period of 5 years. He postulated that "there are two mechanisms which might account for the deaths of bereaved parents: 1) engagement in life-endangering behavior (including suicide) and 2) the desolation effect [deaths precipitated by illnesses created or worsened by the stress of bereavement]" (pp. 27–28).

The stress of acute grief brings depression for many bereaved parents. Clinical depression is known to be associated with greater risk for suicide, and the situational depression of normal grieving can progress into clinical depression. Depression among bereaved parents was investigated by the Longitudinal Study of Families Following a Death from Childhood Cancer (Martinson, Davies, & McClowry, 1991). Forty mothers and 26 fathers were examined for depression 2 and 7 years after the death of a child from cancer. The researchers found the same results at 7 years postdeath as at 2 years: "The mothers and fathers were significantly less depressed than psychiatric outpatients of the same gender but significantly *more* depressed than same gender nonpatients. While parental depression did not significantly change statistically between the second and seventh years postdeath, there was a downward trend" (p. 263). Neither gender of the parents nor length of the child's illness significantly contributed to the variance in depression among the parents. These researchers concluded: "The results are of importance because the subjects basically represent a normal population of parents who experience the death of a child from cancer." In other words, even parents with no history of depression or other mental illness can suffer clinical depression after the death of a child.

SUICIDAL THOUGHTS AMONG "MOTHERS NOW CHILDLESS"

While conducting interviews for the "Mothers Now Childless" study, I was surprised that all 10 of these bereaved mothers volunteered they had had thoughts of suicide and not wanting to live after their child died. I had thought my own experience of considering suicide after my daughter died to be much less common. Fran and Irene, representing opposite ends of the bereavement continuum, talked about being suicidal. Fran's struggle had been a private one. "For quite some time I wasn't too sure whether I wanted to live or not," she said. "There was a time after he died that, you know, I had pills in my hand and I was ready to take them. And I don't know what stopped me. I guess God stopped me was the only thing. 'Cause my husband didn't know. I don't show everything; I keep a lot locked inside."

Looking back on the time when she felt suicidal, Irene realized she had remained open to other alternatives:

When I went through that period of being suicidal—in the back of my mind what I really wanted was to go insane. I really asked God to please let me just lose my mind because then they would put me in a nursing home or a mental institution and I could spend the rest of my life sitting in a rocking chair and forget the fact that my son was no longer alive and in this world. That to me was the best alternative to suicide. God didn't let that happen. I took the trip [around the United States] for seven weeks and got away from driving streets where I looked for Bobby every time I turned the corner. Got away where I knew he would never have been and it forced me to realize that the world was continually going about its business and paid no attention to the fact that I had a broken heart.

Both Fran and Irene credited God with keeping them alive through their darkest days of grief. This was true for Doris as well, but she also felt it was her fear of "not doing it right" that had kept her from following through on the plan she had had to kill herself.

I got past the point where I'd picked on the highway to where you're gonna drive your car off the cliff. I don't want to do that anymore. I didn't have the guts enough to do it at the time. A lot of people talk about it. I thought I was the only one, and then my group leader [at The Compassionate Friends] said he had a bridge picked out. So he said it would look like an accident so his wife would get the insurance and everything, and then I said, somebody else thought of this. [Can you say why you decided not to commit suicide?] I have no problem with dying, but I don't wanta be hurt. I was afraid that I couldn't do it right. You know, being dead, if Evan could do it, I can. But I don't want to be hurt. . . . That's probably the only reason.

At the time of the study, a few of the women in the group representing "perpetual bereavement" continued to confront a decision not to take their lives. Like Fran, Anita kept her ongoing ambivalence about living mostly to herself and relied on her belief in God to help her survive. "I think about it [suicide] occasionally," Anita said. "I'm not gonna say that I don't or that I've wiped it out completely. I'm living because I won't kill myself. I don't want to do that 'cause I don't want to screw up getting to heaven. So I'm surviving basically for that reason and for my family. . . . So that's why I feel that I haven't really survived losing him—'cause I welcome death and I don't worry about dying. I feel sorry for the people I'll leave behind but I'll be glad for myself."

For Marcie, suicide remained an option. On her questionnaire, she said she still questions each day whether she has "earned the title 'survivor.'" This remained a private struggle for Marcie:

For the most part, I appear to the world to be just as I was before. How absurdly imbecilec they would have to be to believe that! . . . I feel completely desolate on the inside. . . . Never a day has passed that I have not considered ending my life. I cannot say with certainty that at some point hence I will not do so. . . . As long as being alive is slightly better each day than not being alive, I'll continue. If a pattern consistently occurs of it being worse to be alive than to not be, I will opt to not live.

The study questionnaire did not directly ask the 80 participants if they had considered suicide, as Blank's 1998 study had, but there was a question about the kinds of decisions they had made since their child's death. In reviewing responses to this question it became apparent that many of the women had in fact contemplated suicide and made a conscious decision to survive.

CHOOSING SURVIVAL

As shown in Table 8.1, 38.9% of women in the "Mothers Now Childless" group representing "perpetual bereavement" made comments suggesting they had made a conscious decision to survive their child's death. This was evident in responses such as: "I have not fully survived, but I do exist. However, recently I find myself thinking about the future and not so much of the past. . . . Recently I made a major decision to try to do something constructive with whatever years I have left and move on."

The other 61.1% of this group did not make comments reflecting a conscious decision to survive. Rather, many made comments reflecting ongoing ambivalence, such as "For a long time I just survived from day to day, week to week. Maybe in a way that's what I still am doing. I really don't make plans for the future, not always sure if I have a future."

Table 8.1 Transformative Factors by Discriminant Groups: Decision to Survive

Questionnaire Narrative Responses	Perpetual Bereavement ($n = 18$) Frequency (%)	Survival ($n = 62$) Frequency (%)	χ^2 (80)
Reported making a conscious decision to survive:			6.96**
No	11 (61.1)[a]	17 (27.4)	
Yes	7 (38.9)	45 (72.6)[a]	
Level of grief felt now:			15.96**
Grief dominates life	3 (16.7)[a]	0 (0)	
Feel grief daily	8 (44.4)[a]	24 (38.7)	
Feel grief weekly	3 (16.7)	16 (25.8)[a]	
Feel grief occasionally	3 (16.7)	22 (35.5)[a]	
No longer grieve	1 (5.6)	0 (0)[a]	
Believe survived child's death:			23.03**
No	9 (50.0)[a]	3 (4.8)	
Yes	7 (38.9)	53 (85.5)[a]	
Yes and no	2 (11.1)	6 (9.7)[a]	

[a]As discussed, results highlight and contrast statistically significant differences between responses from the two groups.
* $p < .05$. ** $p < .01$.

The contrast apparent in the study group representing "survival" was striking. Almost three-quarters (72.6%) of this group made comments reflecting a conscious choice to survive and a commitment to reinvest in life, such as:

> To my way of thinking you have two choices—to stay in the pity bag or rise above it and go on, and I believe that was what my son was about—going out and making things happen.

> I survived by making a choice to survive. We know C. would not want us to live empty, unfulfilled lives.

> I decided to go back to grad school to focus on something rather than go crazy. I chose to live (vs. suicide or living unhealthily to speed the process)—to work at not being a statistic so that our marriage could survive.

The ongoing influence of their children and surviving family and/or spiritual beliefs appeared as major motivators for choosing survival. Acknowledging the common experience of suicidal thoughts as part of acute grief was also helpful. As Carol put this:

> The experience that I see—mine as well as many others in our [bereavement support] group—I know you're supposed to take that very seriously when someone says that [they're considering suicide] but I think it's just a dimension of you wanting to be with your child—especially in the searching and yearning part of the grief process.

FINDING THE WILL TO REINVEST IN LIFE

Sometimes the desire to live again follows a new threat to survival. Five years after her adult daughter died, Blank (1998) underwent surgery to remove a cancerous tumor. She wrote:

> I didn't cry or carry on. Maybe that surgeon thought I was brave, but in reality I just didn't care; it didn't matter much if I lived or died, because if I died, I would be with Cathy. That was what I really wanted. It matters to me now, however; in the intervening time I have decided I want to live. No, not decided; rather, the feeling that I want to live has come back to me. (p. 82)

Recognizing one no longer wishes to die can bring a desire to reinvest in life to conscious awareness. The decision to survive also can come as a response to suicidal fears. This was true for Gail. She talked about her early years of acute grief, about wanting to die, and how reaching out for help saved her from acting on those feelings. For the first 2 years after her son's death, Gail said, "I did everything I could to numb myself. . . . I drank a lot, worked a lot, and overate. . . . No matter what I did I couldn't get numb enough, which in the end turned out to be a blessing." She "hit bottom" when she realized she not only wanted to commit suicide but had a plan for doing so.

> It's like on the one hand being so detached from myself that I'm an observer and being this professional person, and on the other hand experiencing what I was experiencing. And one part of me when I knew I had a plan . . . it was like, ok, you definitely have a problem. . . . So I called a friend from high school . . . and just asked her to contract with me that for 3 months she would call me every day and make me promise her I wouldn't kill myself that day. If she'd do that for 3 months, in the meantime I was gonna do some other things. . . . She'd just talk to me and talk to me and talk to me until finally I'd say, ok, stop harping on me, I'll promise you for today [laughs].

During early bereavement, Gail found she could no longer bear to be around children and left the job where she had working with sexually abused children. She began attending Compassionate Friends meetings and continued for the next 2 years. She also tried various alternative healing strategies. She started getting massages, facials, and manicures for the first time in her life. She started running. She went to "every retreat I could find." She went through "rebirthing," a deep breathing technique:

> For me the rebirthing was really powerful because when you go through that process you can't be up here [pointing to her head], and I was so up here, and so in my head all my life. You know the longest journey is the 18 inches from your head to your heart. I had never made that journey. . . . All of this was really cathartic for me because it was really getting me in touch with all the stuff that Andy's death brought up, plus Andy's death. So it was everything. I mean I can't, for me I can't separate it out and it was part of me figuring out who I was in every aspect of my life. . . . All these alternative healing strategies . . . led my recovery and my healing process. It's real hard to separate any of them out from another because they're all so interwoven, and it continues.

Every year on the anniversary of her son's death and on his birthday, Gail plans something special to honor his memory, often with friends who she says have "listened endlessly." She shares photos of Andy and her memories of him, her fears of forgetting how he smelled and the sound of his voice, and her guilt over not being a perfect parent and not being able to save him. "I have learned that grief doesn't necessarily get 'better' as time passes," she says, "it just gets different." She experiences this sharing as a form of "letting go" of her grief. "I know I haven't learned all that grief has to teach me. I know I'm still on the journey."

Although she was "still resistant" to being around children, Gail said "the fear is diminishing yearly." She continues to feel a connection with her son, who comes to her "in very strange ways, in very strange places to let me know that I'm not alone." And she continues to meet and accept help from others who show her she is not alone.

Sometimes experiencing a desire to live again comes more suddenly and in the form of a cathartic release of pent-up emotions. This was true for Julie, who had also sought help, found out she was not alone, and became able to choose to live until it was her time to be reunited with her son. During the early months after Stuart died, Julie went to a psychotherapist, who ended up referring her to a local Compassionate Friends group.

Unless it's someone who has experienced the death of a child, they don't know what to do with you. And he had no idea what to do with me and he wanted to talk about my divorce. I said, "What do you want to talk about that nonsense for?" . . . I said, "Wait a minute. I want to talk about the pain I'm in." I said: "Here is a hole where my heart used to be." It was like someone had ripped it out with their bare hand. That's the intensity of my pain. But he didn't know what to do. He couldn't, so he would just listen to me. Three days a week I was going for three weeks, and then finally by the end of the second week he said, "I've heard of a support group and I think that's what you need," because he knew I was just getting more angry with him, because I'd be pissed off talking to him where he couldn't help me. So then finally, the end of the third week he gave me the name of Compassionate Friends.

And the first meeting I went to was horrible, as most of them are, but I found out that I wasn't alone. I was actually hunched over from my grief, and I was sitting there and I was able to straighten up in my chair and listen to other people whose stories were worse. I remember in the early days thinking of ways that I could do myself in, if I didn't eat, or if I got real sick. You know, just having the I-don't-care attitude. But I saw that I wasn't alone, and some people had worse stories than I did, and seeing someone, a mother that was pregnant who had also experienced the death of a child, but she was carrying a baby, and how jealous I was. I said, well, this could happen. So it gave me hope.

But then you go through the nights where—I was fortunate, I lived on an acre of land. And when I had the nonstop screaming, crying bouts that would last for hours—thought I was losing my mind, but remembered someone in one of my sharing sessions say this normally happens at six months. We had what was called phone friends. The first time that happened was one o'clock in the morning, and I couldn't stop. So I called one of my phone friends and I said, I can't stop. I was hysterical. And she said, Julie, this is happening to you a little bit sooner, go with it. And then eventually I stopped. Next time when it happened I knew it was gonna stop, because the first time it happened I knew it wasn't gonna stop. I thought this was it, I was losing my mind. And the second time it happened I was more in control, didn't last as long. But it was something I think that had to come out. Some people punch a wall; I screamed and cried.

During this time, Julie was contacted by a friend's pastor who asked her to come and talk with him.

He opened up the Bible and he says, "How does it feel to have this link with heaven 'cause your son's there?" And it was like, um? . . . He read me a passage from the

Bible and it said, "never again to be separated," that you'll be reunited, never again to be separated. It was like, it hit me like, this is good. I'm here, but this is temporary. This is like the [movie] *An American Tail* where he's separated from his parents. Eventually I will be reunited with Stuart. And I just drew on that song "Somewhere Out There" [from the movie], which I told you is my message [from Stuart]. So from this, Pastor M. like opened up my eyes to that, and made it seem like, okay, I have to survive until it's my time. . . . Here I went into Pastor M.'s office . . . and I was in a rage type of a period, but all of a sudden it was like, like just a release, like someone just opened up my head and like just allowed a release of emotion to come out, where it gave me something to hold onto. It gave me something to grasp onto. . . . I chose to survive.

HOW CAREGIVERS CAN HELP NORMALIZE THE DECISION TO SURVIVE

As the preceding examples demonstrate, when bereaved parents realize they are not alone in their anguished desire to die and rejoin their child, they become aware that such thoughts and feelings are a normal part of the grief process. It is normal for bereaved parents to feel alone, radically different from others, and without hope for a future without their child. But it is also normal for bereaved parents to be able to manage their overwhelming pain, confront their suicidal thoughts, and choose to build a different but meaningful future. The support of caregivers and of other bereaved parents in groups like The Compassionate Friends helps parents normalize their grief reactions and meet their psychological needs for understanding, nurturance, succorance, and affiliation. Meeting these needs helps lessen the psychological pain that can trigger hopelessness and suicidal thoughts.

In his brilliant elaboration of *The Suicidal Mind*, Shneidman (1996) declared that "the psychotherapist's main function is to be anodynic; to lessen pain" (p. 151). When caregivers willingly enter into a bereaved parent's pain and don't try to take that pain away, parents no longer feel alone. When pain is shared its power is lessened. This is not to say that caregivers take on another's pain; rather, we empathically hold it. We help carry the giant boulder of grief while the griever chips away at it. This is what Gail's friend did when she called her every day for 3 months and made Gail promise not to kill herself.

The second most important thing caregivers can do to support bereaved parents is try to understand their loss. When we acknowledge that a grieving parent is struggling not just to withstand acute pain but also to find reasons to go on living, that parent feels understood. Figure 8.1 acknowledges the need for bereaved parents to find the will to live again. From an existentialist perspective, the task of the therapist "is not to create will but to disencumber it" (Yalom, 1980, p. 332). It can be disencumbering for bereaved parents to have their pain acknowledged and to hear what helped other parents to survive. Table 8.2 lists some of those reasons.

"How will I ever be able to survive this pain? Will I ever want to live again?" These are normal questions after the death of a child. Deep inside you is the power you need to answer these questions – your "will power." It is the power that transforms awareness and knowledge into action.

Steps to developing and using your will power:

Even in the midst of grief, you can decide how you will *react* to your loss. You will know you are gaining control of your reactions as you begin to take positive steps (some examples: joining a bereavement group; seeking out information about grief; talking with a counselor, minister, or trusted friend about your loss; keeping a grief journal; creating memorials).

Recognize that you can change your world. The actions you choose to take in response to your child's death will impact your world of thoughts, feelings, attitudes, decisions, experiences, values, assumptions, expectations, and beliefs.

Believe that there is no danger in change. In grief, the danger lies in doing nothing—which can leave you in a state of perpetual pain and emptiness. The stress of unresolved grieving over a long period of time will impact everything about your life. As you confront your fears (such as fear of forgetting your child and who you were and are as that child's parent), you will come to embrace the reality that love never dies.

Commit yourself to change what you can. To get what you really want—a meaningful life and a continuing connection with your child—you must change. Doing "grief work" is a commitment to change. Giving up pain by feeling and releasing it does not mean you will forget your child. Just the opposite is true—the energy you once spent experiencing pain can be redirected to meaningful activities that honor your child and your relationship. Your role as parent changes to that of biographer as you reconstruct how your child lived and define the aspects of your child's spirit that live on through you and others. Your grief will "get different" and your pain will lessen gradually. You will no longer experience acute pain daily, but some pain will always remain. There will be occasional, temporary upsurges of grief, usually around holidays and anniversaries. You will always miss your child and be deeply saddened by your loss. Grief will teach you that it is an individual process that moves slower than any of us would want. Give yourself permission to accept that it takes as long as it takes!

Know that you have the power to manage your pain. You can make sense of this devastating experience by coming to understand how your child's death effects every aspect of your life. Learning more about your child and about your grief will give you the ability to control your life choices. One important decision you may make is to help and nurture others. When you choose to reach out to others, you will find meaning in life again and feel, in a special way, your own personal power. We call this personal power to make our own choices, will power.

Figure 8.1   Finding the will to survive the death of your child.

Sharing the experiences of bereaved parents who have decided to survive the death of their child can offer hope to those in acute grief. As shown in Table 8.2, there are many reasons bereaved parents choose to survive. Such a list can help a bereaved parent identify what they are struggling with in their grief process and what might be helpful for them to think about and discuss.

Clinicians, of course, carefully consider and adapt therapeutic discussions and interventions to match the unique needs of individual clients. In those cases where clients have preexisting mental illnesses or disorders (diagnosed or undiagnosed), the pain of grief must be lessened before other psychological issues are addressed. The following therapeutic goals are paramount in working with bereaved parents:

1 To protect clients from self-destructive impulses, including temporary hospitalization if necessary.
2 To make pain management the first goal of therapy.
3 To listen to each client's story with an attitude of openness and a willingness to learn and understand what the loss is like for that person.
4 To encourage clients to seek appropriate medical monitoring by a trusted physician, including the use of psychotropic medications when indicated.
5 To help clients identify their unique psychological needs that are not being met.
6 To help clients explore options and resources to meet those needs that are most clearly tied to their psychological pain.

Table 8.2 Some Reasons Bereaved Parents Decide to Survive

Reasons given for *not* committing suicide:

Fear of not doing it right, of remaining alive but physically incapacitated and a burden on others
Not wanting to sin, to break God's commandment
Fear of not being reunited with the child who died because of taking one's own life
Not wanting to hurt other loved ones who would be left behind
Not wanting to disappoint the child who died
Believing one must live out one's predestined life no matter how painful
Coming to realize that surviving the loss and finding some meaning and joy in life again are possible

Reasons given for reinvesting in life:

To ensure the child will be remembered
To honor the child's life and create a meaningful legacy
To help others survive who also grieve for the child
To help educate society about grief and loss so other parents won't feel so alone
To accept and bear one's destiny with courage
To turn suffering and anguish into something positive and meaningful

The fact that many bereaved parents consider suicide is certainly sobering, but the good news is that clinicians, as well as caregiving friends and family, can and do help bereaved parents survive. In some cases, acute grief is the precipitating factor that brings a client to therapy. The pain of grief can create a cracking open of the psyche, a kind of vulnerability conducive to personal change and positive growth that would never have been possible before. Doris Smeltzer (personal communication, August 30, 2001) eloquently described such a process. Her beloved 19-year-old daughter Andrea died in her sleep after a 13-month struggle with bulimia, when an electrolyte imbalance caused her heart to stop. Doris wrote:

> The second year (of grief) was darker than anything I could imagine. I felt that I was in a never-ending tunnel that tightened at times smaller than my body size. I would sit in the blackness, just running my hands along the craggy surroundings, hoping to find an opening large enough for me to fit through—frightened that I could not; afraid that I would. I rounded a corner that second summer and miraculously acquired a dim light that I now carry with me. I have made a few turns that have led me back through a bit of the tunnel I've already traversed, but the light allows me to see the jagged edges that tripped me up before, the deep crevices in which I languished. I can now see my way around and out of these hazards.
>
> I have thought long and hard about what made the difference. How did I acquire the light? I went on antidepressants for a few months. I had been spiraling downwards and they helped lift me to the edge of that spiraled crevice. I read a number of articles and books: one about a woman who had lost both her teenagers within months of each other; one about a man who lost his wife, mother and young child in an automobile accident. These helped me see, in a new way, that my pain was not unique to me and that it could, truly, be worse. A dear friend, whom I had made just since Andrea's passing, died. She had survived an eating disorder, had gone on to earn a Ph.D., was a champion in our attempts to educate the world on these disorders, and was eight and a half months pregnant with her first child when she died in mid-sentence when her heart suddenly burst. She suffered from a previously undiagnosed heart defect. On the day I learned of how she passed, it was as if I could hear Andrea's voice saying, "Do you see, now, Mom? There was no guarantee that had I survived my disorder, I would not have left, prior to you, sometime later."
>
> I spoke with a counselor who, in one fortunate meeting, helped me see what my dear husband and other daughter had been attempting to teach me for many months. On this occasion, though, I was ready to hear the words—that when we look back at the "should haves" and "if onlys" we tend to see them in a stagnant, one-dimensional realm. We forget how dynamic the situation was—the many factors involved in our decisions and in others' reactions—how truly complicated and intricate was the reality of "then." I could not see the truth of that until the day that I was ready.
>
> All of these epiphanies happened in just a few short months and have played instrumental roles in my corner-rounding experience. I am better than I was. I trust the process more. I believe that Andrea's life was complete here. Because I have not joined her, my life is not. My soul still has lessons to learn.

While in the midst of anguish and depression, Doris reached out for help and gained new perspectives that greatly impacted her decision to survive her daughter's death.

When faced with survival decisions, "one cannot *not* decide" (Yalom, 1980, p. 333). Not deciding is in fact a decision, albeit a passive one. When we help parents to understand that it is common and necessary to consciously confront a wish to die and/or a wish to not go on living after the death of their child, we remind them of their own power and resources. This brings hope and the ability to regain control of life again, even though it will be a much different life than could ever have been imagined. As one mother said: "Since T.'s death I have become a person that I respect and love. I have the strength and courage to move ahead and feel very fortunate to have a second life. I often feel my son died so I could live. I would never be the person I am today if it had not been for him." After "the dark night of the soul," dawn does come for most bereaved parents and with it gradual renewal and new joys, even as they continue to miss their child just as much.

SUMMARY

Although not all bereaved parents become suicidal, not wanting to live after a child dies is a normal and common experience. Suicidal thoughts can develop from a desire to end the anguishing pain of grief, from untreated depression and feelings of hopelessness, from wanting so desperately to be with their child again. Psychiatrist Gordon Livingston (1999) described this desire during the year after his 6-year-old son Lucas died.

> Sometimes at night I think about driving to the airport, getting into the airplane, and flying west at one thousand feet in the darkness, until I meet the mountains. It would happen near Frederick, where Clare and I were married, lending the end a certain symmetry. I could not, of course, inflict that upon my family, but the idea that I might thereby join Lucas fills me with anticipation. I have had patients who have lost children and told me of a wish to follow them. Now I understand. (p. 140)

As bereavement proceeds, many bereaved parents find themselves remaining ambivalent about life; some may hide their true feelings from their family and friends. The knowledge that their feelings are not abnormal and that they are not alone and hopeless can sustain parents during especially difficult times, as can their faith in God and hope for reuniting with their child again in Heaven someday. "Nietzsche said that only after one has fully considered suicide does one take one's life seriously" (quoted in Yalom, 1980, p. 333). Even during deepest grief, when parents are unable to care about or take their own life seriously, they still continue to care deeply about their child's life. Often, it is a desire *not* to let pain be their child's only legacy that compels parents to carry on. As discussed in the next chapter, finding ways to remember and honor their child can present parents with new reasons to live. Resolving to live because of and in honor of the impact their child had on them helps bereaved parents move beyond pain and toward peace.

Chapter 9

Remembering With Love: Bereaved Parent as Biographer

The morning glory blooms but for an hour
and yet it differs not at heart
from the giant Pine
that lives for a thousand years.
—Teitoku Matsunaga, 16th century Japanese poet
    (quoted by Zunin & Zunin, 1991, p. 87)

When bereaved parents consciously choose to survive after the death of their child, most want both a meaningful life again *and* a continuing connection with that child (cf. Fox, 2001). This often is accomplished by redirecting energy once spent experiencing the pain of separation into activities that remember and honor the child and the parenting relationship. The role of parent changes to that of biographer as parents reconstruct how their child lived and define aspects of their child's spirit that live on through them and others. Tony Walter (1996) pointed out that "in the classic (bereavement) texts there is [both] a major theme emphasizing detachment [from the deceased], achieved through the working through of feelings, and a minor theme emphasizing the continued presence of the dead and a continuous conversation with and about them" (p. 8). Western societies focus on the major theme of detachment, and this is one reason why bereaved parents often find that others fail to recognize and support their need for an ongoing relationship with their child. Walter urged that *both* themes can be effective grief processes. "Bereavement," he said, "is part of the never-ending and reflexive conversation with self and others through which the late-modern person makes sense of their existence. In other words, bereavement is part of the process of (auto)biography, and the biographical imperative—the need to make sense of self and others in a continuing narrative—is the motor that drives bereavement behavior" (p. 20). This "biographical imperative" is especially true for the bereaved parent because the child represents part of the parent's self; the child has played crucial roles in defining the parent's identity.

Just as parents must learn how to parent, they also must learn how to be a bereaved parent. It follows that the deceased child continues to play an essential role in helping parents define who they are now that the child has died and who they are becoming as they face life deeply wounded and without the physical presence of that child.

Redefining the self as a bereaved parent often involves the psychological processes of introjection and/or identification with the child (Klass, 1988, 1993, 1999). Klass (1988) concluded that "the resolution of parental grief is found in the development of a new self. The new self, with its new social interactions and its new sources of solace, learns to live in a world made forever poorer by the death of the child." The majority of bereaved parents in Klass's study who had reconciled their loss found solace by *introjection*, by keeping intact a sense of the child and their emotional bond with the child through linking objects, religious devotion, and/or rituals that evoke the child's memory. Other parents internalized their child by *identification*, by "integrating the inner representation of the child with the self-representation in such a way that the two cannot be distinguished" (pp. 179–180). Both of these psychological processes support Walter's theory of bereavement as biography.

The relationship with the deceased child continues to be a focus for out-come-related research involving bereaved parents. For example, Rubin (1984, 1992, 1993, 1996) proposed using a two-track model of bereavement that considers both bereaved parents' functionality and their relationship with the representations of their deceased child. In this model, resolution is evidenced by both adaptive functioning and an ongoing, comfortable bond with the deceased child. "The connections to the representations of the deceased and to the memories of the relationship to the deceased continue on across the life cycle," Rubin (1996, p. 220) noted. "It is how the involvement is maintained and at what or whose cost, that becomes the important question" (Rubin, 1996, p. 224). In other words, some degree of balance is needed so parents can both maintain the relationship with the deceased child and continue reciprocal relationships with surviving siblings and others. "The relationship to the deceased should be both fluid and manage to coexist as an adjunct to the ongoing relationships with the living" (Rubin, 1996, p. 221). The following sections discuss some of the ways that bereaved parents build new, ongoing relationships with their deceased child and how doing so can impact other relationships and aspects of their lives.

MEMORIALS AND THE "BIOGRAPHICAL IMPERATIVE"

Bereaved parents create memorials to honor their children in diverse ways, as shown in Table 9.1. Such activities and new ways of being in the world are external applications of parents' internal, psychological processes of introjection and/ or identification with their deceased child. Parents may or may not consciously recognize they are doing this, however. Ann Finkbeiner (1996), a journalist and bereaved mother, interviewed 30 parents who had been bereaved 5 years or more. She, too, found that parents continue their relationship with their children in diverse but personally meaningful ways.

"I think," she said, "the parents insert the children into their lives and continue living, one person now, [both] parent-and-child. This is difficult to describe. It's as if the child's life was a forward momentum that death interrupted, like a sudden stop in the middle of a song or a dance or a long pass, and the interruption is intolerable. If the parent doesn't let go, the child's trajectory continues via the parent. This trajectory is neither the child's original path nor the parent's; it's somewhere between" (p. 256). This new "joint trajectory" was something Finkbeiner noticed in all 30 parents.

> During the interviews, some parents became terrifically happy talking about something that often seemed peripheral to the subject of the interview. Eventually I learned to look for the connection between whatever they were happy about, and the child. Leight, for instance, missed doing things with Johnny and talking to him, so Leight volunteers in a hospice program and sits and talks with people who are dying. Chris worried that he hadn't listened enough to Mary; between his other daughter and the Seasons suicide bereavement group, he spends a lot of time listening, especially to people "during their times of difficulty." Anne's son, Robert, loved adventures and was just on the brink of flourishing; Anne has since quit her job, worked in China, came back and got another job, quit that, and is now working in South Africa. All the parents profiled said that these were things they wouldn't otherwise have done; none were aware of the connection. (p. 257)

The memorial activities listed in Table 9.1 demonstrate a conscious decision to act in memory of the child, to preserve the bond with the child, to create a legacy. Yet, as Finkbeiner found, parents may not be aware of how the actions they undertake serve to provide new meaning in life in ways that reflect their child's ongoing influence. The following personal example demonstrates how one such action unexpectedly took on new meaning and became a conscious connection with my daughter.

In 1992 my mother's health began failing and I realized that at some point in the future she might need nursing-home care. It was difficult to try to be of help to my parents living so far away from them, but I did what I could. In December 1993, an article and photo appeared in my local newspaper about a woman who visited nursing-home residents with her dog. Immediately I thought of my chocolate Labrador, Hershey, and how much she loved being with people. What better way for me to learn more about nursing homes? So in January 1994, Hershey and I began doing "animal-assisted therapy" twice a month at a local nursing home. By then, my mother had suffered additional small strokes and needed nursing

Table 9.1 Examples of Ways that Bereaved Parents Remember and Honor Their Children

Monetary memorials:
  Establish special scholarships or camperships
  Fund a community outreach program or sponsor an event in the child's name
  Buy gifts for needy families on holidays
  Contribute to community, church, hospital, and/or other organizational causes, such as bereavement support groups, medical research, and worthy charities

Symbolic memorials:
  Plant trees, flowers, or special gardens
  Commission a statue or fountain, memorial bricks, or a park bench with a name plaque
  Create a special trophy or award for a sporting event
  Donate a stained-glass window, tapestry, hymnals, etc., to a church
  Select and donate special books to libraries and schools
  Design a special headstone for the child's grave
  Create a children's memorial wall in a park or cemetery
  Design, sew and/or wear special jewelry, clothing, a quilt square, etc., in memory of the child
  Pass on some of the child's possessions to family, friends, and/or needy individuals and organizations

Ritual memorials:
  Attend special masses or memorial services at church
  Decorate the child's grave on holidays and special days
  Make an altar and light candles and/or say special prayers for the child
  Hold a remembrance-day gathering for friends and family who knew the child and include special events, such as a balloon or butterfly release
  Play special music that creates a connection with the child
  Say a prayer, read a poem, and/or light a candle in memory of the child before a meal or at other special times

Developmental memorials:
  Write the child's eulogy, obituary, and/or biography
  Create photo albums and/or paint pictures and put together collages or videos about the child's life
  Keep a journal of bereavement experiences
  Attend bereavement conferences, workshops, or groups and/or participate in bereavement studies
  Read books and other publications about bereavement
  Establish a bereavement support group, newsletter, or other community outreach programs
  Speak in public about the child and/or bereavement
  Serve others in special ways such as being the newsletter editor, facilitator, or telephone contact for a bereavement support group
  Volunteer for hospice or work for other charitable organizations
  Write poetry, pamphlets, or articles about the child and/or bereavement
  Conduct research, teach, or counsel others about bereavement
  Reach out to help other bereaved parents and/or nurture and help other children
  Choose to "become a better person" and live each day in ways that honor the child's memory

care. In September of that year I went to Montana to help move her into a nursing home. The knowledge I had gained from my nursing-home visits with Hershey helped me greatly during this difficult time.

Back home, Hershey and I continued our visits. If I couldn't visit my own mother in her nursing home, at least I could visit someone else's mother. No matter how tired I was when Hershey and I arrived, I always left there energized and emotionally uplifted.

Then one day in late 1994 as I was looking through my daughter Leah's memory album, I suddenly became aware of yet another reason these visits were so meaningful. I reread the letter Leah had written from camp during the last week of her life. These words she wrote took on new meaning: "I have a cough and I can't go swimming but that doesn't spoil my fun one bit. I read and drink water out of cups. And I talk to people who need company." This was what Hershey and I did at the nursing home. We visited people who needed company! That realization was a defining moment. Here was something I was doing in my daily life that provided a meaningful connection with both my living mother and my dead daughter. Every visit after that brought the joy of feeling their spiritual presence and knowing I was continuing Leah's legacy of talking to people who need company.

This personal experience echoes what Finkbeiner (1996) found among the parents she interviewed. When they talked about something that made them "terribly happy," it turned out to have some connection with their child, even though they weren't consciously aware of that connection. It follows that as caregivers we take an appropriate, proactive role when we encourage bereaved parents to pursue the "biographical imperative" and celebrate those memorial activities that preserve the bond with their child in meaningful, life-enhancing ways.

As Rubin (1996) pointed out, it is also vitally important that parents consider the impact of such activities on other relationships in their lives. There can be disagreement between parents and/or surviving siblings and family members as to how much the deceased child should remain a part of daily life. Like the Haser family that Rubin (1996) described, some bereaved parents can put so much energy into focusing on their deceased child, that they have little left to give to surviving siblings and/or others. Rubin described this potential dilemma:

> On the one hand, if we remain rooted to the past and totally preoccupied with the loss, we risk losing the opportunities and relationships of the present. On the other hand, if we distance ourselves too much from what was but is no longer available, we remove ourselves from our origins and root relationships. To deny the importance of our core relationships either at conscious or unconscious levels is to risk losing the ability to feel secure in the very inner fiber of our being. For if we cannot depend on the ongoing experiences of having been loved and cared for in the past, via our memories and experiences with significant figures, the basic security that is provided by our early attachments is compromised. (Rubin, 1996, p. 229)

A child's death brings physical detachment, but maintaining the inner bond with that child protects the psyche and promotes conscious living as the loss evolves over a lifetime. This is not to say that achieving a healthy balance between re-membering the deceased child and remaining invested in relationships with the living is easy. Doing so is a demanding, sometimes disjointed process, subject to periods of stalls and tentative re-starts. Margaret Stroebe (1997) used the word *oscillation* to describe adaptive coping to bereavement. Oscillation seems an es-pecially appropriate word to describe the fluctuations between one's relationships with both the dead and the living. When there is no oscillation, no fluid move-ment, dysfunction results. Thus, the two tracks of Rubin's model—functionality, and relationship with the deceased—are separate but also symbiotic; each influ-ences the other. The women in the "Mothers Now Childless" study provide ex-amples of this interdependency.

REMEMBERING AN ONLY CHILD

The bereavement questionnaire that the 80 participants in the "Mothers Now Child-less" study completed had several questions related to the interplay between the child's life, the parent's identity, and investments in relationships. What had these women learned from being a mother? Had they found ways to memorialize their child? Did they have significant relationships with other children? Responses by discriminant group are shown in Table 9.2.

Many of the women wrote extensive descriptive comments on their ques-tionnaires. Some attached copies of their child's obituary, memorial service bulle-tin, photos, poems, and/or other publications about their child and/or their activi-ties in honor of their child. For some, like Julie, remembering provided motivation to survive:

> In the beginning I didn't think it was possible to survive it, but, I made up my mind that the only way people would remember him is through me, and that was basically how I was able to get the strength to want to go on. . . . I feel that I'm the only person that will keep Stuart's memory alive, because my ex-husband told me the third week after, he was going to go on with his life and pretend he never had a son. And my crusade then became to keep his memory alive. . . . Whether it's tending his grave, or making a memorial, or just mentioning him, even if it's offensive to someone. It's something that I have to do. . . . People who don't know him do know him because I talk about him all the time.

LEARNING FROM MOTHERHOOD

As shown in Table 9.2, 78 of the 80 participants said yes, they had learned from being a mother. Their comments about what they had learned were diverse. Sev-eral said being a mother taught them to love unconditionally and gave them the ability to teach, to accept differences and disappointments, to be responsible and

Table 9.2   Comparison of Responses to Participant Questionnaire by Discriminant Groups: Relationship with Child/Children

Response to Questionnaire	Perpetual Bereavement ($n = 18$) Frequency (%)	Survival ($n = 62$) Frequency (%)	χ^2 (80)
Level of grief felt now:			15.96**
Grief dominates life	3 (16.7)[a]	0 (0)	
Feel grief daily	8 (44.4)[a]	24 (38.7)	
Feel grief weekly	3 (16.7)	16 (25.8)[a]	
Feel grief occasionally	3 (16.7)	22 (35.5)[a]	
No longer grieve	1 (5.6)	0 (0)[a]	
Learned from motherhood:			.89
No	1 (5.6)	1 (1.6)	
Yes	17 (94.4)	61 (98.4)	
Memorials for child:			.02
No	1 (5.6)	3 (4.8)	
Yes	17 (94.4)	59 (95.2)	
Current relationships with children:			7.80*
No	9 (50.0)[a]	17 (27.4)	
Yes and no	2 (11.1)	1 (1.6)	
Yes	7 (38.9)	44 (71.0)[a]	
Believe survived child's death:			23.03**
No	9 (50.0)[a]	3 (4.8)	
Yes	7 (38.9)	53 (85.5)[a]	
Yes and no	2 (11.1)	6 (9.7)[a]	

[a]These results highlight and contrast statistically significant differences between responses from the two groups. For example, 50% of those in the group representing "perpetual bereavement" did not have current meaningful relationships with other children. This contrasted to 71% of those in the group representing "survival" who said they did have relationships with other children.
* $p < .05$. ** $p < .01$.

patient, to nurture without smothering, to have fun, to "love yourself through your child." One said she'd found it easier to understand her own mother and came to appreciate the awesome cycle of life. Other participants focused on what they'd learned from becoming a bereaved mother. "Motherhood can be the happiest and the most painful experience of life," one noted. Another said, "I hope I was a good mother; we fussed sometimes." Several learned to appreciate each day they'd had with their children. And others pointed out that "motherhood continues to live even after a child's death." One said her ongoing connection with her son "allows me to be more intimately attached to others." Another mother concluded, "You can't control a child's destiny—just honor their soul."

Only one woman in the study, Marcie, said she had *not* learned from her motherhood experiences. A second woman, Jody, left the question blank. Their reasons help us understand the interdependency between a parent's relationship with their deceased child and their ability to function as that child's bereaved parent.

Marcie: Remembering Is Too Painful

When asked if she was aware of having learned from her experience of being a mother, Marcie wrote: "No—the pain is too severe and blinding to allow me to be cognizant of any learning experiences from motherhood." In response to question 24, which asked if she had found ways to memorialize her child, she checked *Yes* and wrote "writing (sample enclosed)." She attached her poem "The Light" (see chap. 6) and a short memoir she had written about her father, who died "less than three years" before her daughter.

"All my life I felt complete, unconditional love—as though I was his most treasured possession," she wrote. Marcie described the close and loving relationship between her daughter and her father. "He was an ever present part of her life, as she was his." Marcie's father died at age 71. "I thought I would surely succumb to the searing pain of losing him. There was no way I could know that less than three years later, I would bless the day he died that peaceful death rather than have him live through the devastating pain of losing his first grandchild, his precious granddaughter, my only child, at the age of fifteen."

Marcie's daughter died an hour after sustaining a broken neck in a car crash. Of the 80 study participants, Marcie was the only one who indicated she could not bear to talk about her daughter's life or death to others and did not have any momentos of her daughter in her home. Presumably other women contacted who may have felt this way chose not to participate in the study.

Prior to her daughter's death, Marcie said she had "attended church semi-regularly. After her death the music and ceremony became more than I could bear emotionally so I discontinued efforts to attend. What faith I had has been severely damaged." In response to question 29, which asked whether participating in the study had been helpful or unhelpful to her, Marcie wrote "undecided," but she asked for a copy of the study summary.

Marcie experienced two emotionally devastating losses in a short period of time that complicated her grief and brought spiritual crisis. She remained in deep despair at the time of the study. Yet her willingness to share her feelings and experiences in the hope of helping other bereaved parents and her decision to write about her losses in memory of her daughter and father are positive signs that she is continuing the grief process in her own time and in personally meaningful ways. Marcie demonstrates the kind of stalls and restarts that can characterize coping after a child's death. It is important to recognize and honor that process. Here is an excerpt from a letter I wrote to Marcie in response to her questionnaire and attachments:

> Thank you so much for participating in my study of bereaved mothers. I will be sending you a copy of the study summary as soon as it is available—probably late in the year.

I wanted to thank you for the composition you sent and for your honesty in sharing with me your continuing struggle to survive your daughter's death. For many years I also found it nearly impossible to share with others my grief over losing my daughter Leah, my only child. To me it was as if talking about her life and how much she meant to me would mean losing her all over again. I now see that I hung on to my memories and my feelings and guarded them jealously for that reason. Gradually and through a series of circumstances too complex to describe here, I came to understand that sharing my grief about losing Leah has exactly the opposite effect for me. The process of talking about her to select others who know how to listen has helped me to better understand just what she means to me. Her influence on my life has increased rather than diminished, and I have been able to experience joy in living once again.

My values and beliefs about what is important in life have also changed dramatically during the twelve years since my daughter's death. I have come to believe that over time the experience of being without our children can change. The pain can soften and be outweighed by a gratefulness for the good memories, and there can be a recognition of the value of the lessons learned from coping with such a devastating loss. There is, I believe, never a "recovery" and never an end to this experience of bereavement. Rather, there is recognition that we continue "becoming" the people we are meant to become, shaped by the depth, breadth, and intensity of those happenings which are truly important in our lives here on Earth, and instrumental in some yet unknown way to the life that awaits each of us beyond.

I am enclosing a booklet I found helpful in my own grief journey. I wish you peace and new joys in your own continued "becoming."

Jody was the other participant who did not describe learning from being a mother. She left the question blank. But she did describe how activities in honor of her daughter were helping her to invest in relationships with the living, despite the pain of feeling cheated.

Jody: Feeling Cheated But Going On

Jody had experienced significant losses during the 2 years before and the 2 years after her daughter's death. She also had had a spiritual crisis and changed her religious affiliation. "For a long time I was angry and didn't practice any religion," she wrote. At the time of the study she indicated her religious affiliation was "important" to her. "I believe in God and I'm here for a reason and things happen for reasons unknown to us." She described her spiritual beliefs as being both helpful and unhelpful to her in dealing with her daughter's death. Under "unhelpful beliefs" she wrote: "I don't believe children should die first. I don't like it and I feel I was cheated." Under "helpful beliefs" she wrote: "I believe we'll be together with God some day."

Jody noted several ways she had found to memorialize her daughter, who died at age 7. She kept a journal, contributed money for research of her daughter's disease, spoke at Compassionate Friends groups, and compiled a book of memories of her daughter by asking family and friends to contribute. Five years after her daughter's death, Jody began volunteering regularly as a mentor, teacher, and speaker for various organizations. She also was active with various church programs and youth groups. She said she had survived: "I am still living and going on."

CURRENT RELATIONSHIPS WITH OTHER CHILDREN

As shown in Table 9.2, the vast majority of both groups of women in the "Mothers Now Childless" study had created memorials for their child and learned from their experiences of being a mother. But there was a statistically significant difference between the two groups regarding current relationships with other children. Question 26 asked: "Do relationships with other children play a significant part in your life today? Over 70% in the group representing "survival" said yes, whereas half of the group representing "perpetual bereavement" said no.

Having a significant relationship with another child or children can be one way a bereaved parent reinvests in life. In their 1980 study of perinatal death, Peppers and Knapp (1980) found that:

> For most women, relief comes with the birth of a subsequent child. For mothers who want and value children, having a healthy subsequent child goes a long way in resolving their grief for the previous loss. In fact, many mothers told us that it was only after another birth that they knew that they had "made it." Their lives could then be put back together. (p. 45)

There is relatively little research that focuses on the relationship between bereaved parents and their surviving children and/or the decision to have additional children. There are remarks throughout the literature, however, that suggest having surviving children to care for can give bereaved parents motivation for surviving their loss, just as working to ensure others would remember her only child gave Julie strength to carry on.

If having significant relationships with other children contributes to healing some of the pain of bereaved parents, what is it about such relationships that produces this effect? Is the ability to establish new relationships with other children only possible after the painful emotions of acute grief have diminished? This was true for me. Ten years after my daughter's death and after working through my own spiritual crisis and becoming a member of a church again, I was asked to teach Sunday school. I chose to teach the second and third grade class, children who were the same age Leah had been when she died. I found doing so both healing and meaningful. It allowed me to use my nurturing and parenting skills again and brought back the joy of watching children learn and grow.

REMEMBERING, REINVESTING, AND RESOLUTION

Participants in the "Mothers Now Childless" study who said yes, they had found ways to memorialize their child, yes, they had learned from motherhood, and yes, they had developed a significant relationship with other children since their child's death, demonstrate a connection between remembering, reinvesting, and resolution. Here are three examples of women who give words to what Walter (1996) termed "the biographical imperative—the need to make sense of self and others in a continuing narrative" (p. 20).

Karen: Remembering the Past While Creating The Future

Karen's 15-year-old son died after being "struck by a hit-and-run drunk driver while bicycling home." She described what she had learned from motherhood:

> Although my son was just reaching early manhood when he died, I can see that in his short life he was the kind of person I wanted him to be and I'm very proud of that. In raising him, I learned more about my abilities to teach, accept differences, disappointments, etc. I was rewarded by a living son who touched many around him with his character. I would not have missed this motherhood experience even if I knew the outcome beforehand.

Karen's son's name is included "on the children's memorial wall in a local park (I served on the steering committee which established the park). We established a campership fund in his name that sends needy children to the Y camp each summer." Karen has also developed relationships with other children. "I am particularly close to two nieces, two nephews and my God-daughter. I enjoy being a part of their lives and watching them grow and mature. We share special holidays together and talk/write frequently. I also maintain contact with three of my sons' friends, two of whom still send Christmas cards and watch the Super Bowl with me every year. These two young men give me a sense of what my son might be like if he were still alive; we share fond memories of him." Karen began volunteering with a youth foundation 9 years after her son's death. She concluded: "I will never forget my son but I believe I have survived his death in that I am living and enjoying a full life which I think he would want me to do. My career, travel, family and friends, socializing and home and investment management for my future are examples of survival."

Karen's life as a bereaved parent perpetuates her son's legacy as she reaches out to "touch others." Continuing a relationship with her son's friends helps to create his biography through shared remembrances.

Sally: My Work Is My Son's Work Too

Sally's 17-year-old son was killed in a weather-related auto accident. At the time of the study she was completing a college degree in pastoral counseling, having returned to school 9 months after his death. She listed what she'd learned from being a bereaved mother:

1) that having "learned" does not take away the pain or provide an adequate reason for the death; 2) that love is stronger than death—there is a communion of spirits that is real and reaches across death; 3) that the failure to reach out can cause great suffering; 4) that God is real and more than an idea; 5) that fear keeps us from doing so much good in terms of being gifts to others; 6) the limitations of a psychology that ignores spirituality; 7) the importance of humility.

She had found a variety of ways to memorialize her son: "poetry, scholarships, public speaking, library books, telling my story to groups and using my son's art in lectures, liturgies. My thesis, my counseling work, the way I choose to live my life." Sally also had relationships with other children: "My friend's daughter (my God-daughter). The children of some of my friends—they knew my son; they remind me of him; and I enjoy them in their own right. Some come to me with their problems; some reach out to comfort me. I feel like this softens the sense of being 'a bad mother' because my child died."

Sally's religious affiliation had changed since her son's death: "My faith has deepened," she wrote, "but it has not been an easy road. It has deepened because of profound experiences of connections with God and with my son." Two years after his death she became a bereavement support group facilitator: "I feel this is part of my son's work as well as mine and it is work I genuinely learn from and enjoy." Sally's son lives on in the work she does to help others and although they are physically apart, he remains connected to her daily life.

Gina: A New Bond of Shared Understanding

Gina's 17-year-old son was killed instantly when he lost control of his car while driving 5 friends home from a football game and was ejected. No one else was seriously hurt. Like Sally, Gina listed what she had learned from being a bereaved mother:

1) there is no love that compares to the love between a mother and her child; 2) there is no greater pain than to lose your child; 3) the "world" treats you differently when you are childless; 4) I will always ache to have a child of my own. I still miss all aspects of being a mother.

Gina described how she'd worked through a spiritual crisis after her son's death:

For a long time I was angry at God for giving me only one child (I come from a large family; I'm the only one who had only one child) and taking my child back. It took a long time and a lot of work to come to terms with the thought that God doesn't have the power to protect us nor to take life away.

Gina said her ongoing relationships with her nieces and nephews are very important to her.

My two sisters and I were all pregnant at the same time. Our kids grew up playing, fighting, competing with each other. They are very close to me. They feel his loss almost as much and we all realize that the others understand. There is a strange bond between myself and my nieces and nephews. They try to "fill in." My niece told her three kids it was ok to call me "Grandma."

Gina's son had a savings account and she used it to create a memorial that symbolizes their ongoing connection: "I used it to have a diamond necklace made with his name on it. My husband bought me a diamond-covered heart that hangs just below it. I never take either off."

In a note attached to her questionnaire, Gina apologized for taking 2 months to complete it. "I would answer a few questions and then walk away. I found myself avoiding it. My life is happy now and it was tough to mentally go back to 'day one.'" Gina's bond with her nieces and nephews helps her live in a world that treats her differently now that her only child has died. She sees that she has not resolved all of the pain of missing her son, but she sees, too, that she is happy again and that he remains part of this new happiness as well.

SUMMARY

The need to make sense of self and others in a continuing narrative—the "biographical imperative" defined by Walter (1996)—is part of the lifelong process of human development. Throughout life there is an ongoing tension between individuation and interdependency, between how we see ourselves as unique from others and how we see ourselves as a part of others. When a child dies, a parent's world no longer makes sense; a part of the parent has died too. There is a heightened need for psychic synthesis—for integrating the good memories and positive qualities of the child with the painful emotions that accompany the daily reality of that child's physical absence. When bereaved parents use introjection and identification to maintain a positive relationship with their deceased child, their ability to function improves. As functioning improves, parents become able to reengage with the world, and often the ways they do so reflect the continuing influence of their child. A new kind of descendency results, as parent and child create a future together that honors the past. Resolution becomes evolution. But resolution does not mean parents no longer feel pain. Rather, parents become able to carry their pain forward with them in a personally unique process of "oscillation" (Stroebe, 1997). Often reaching out to help others becomes part of this process, as chapter 10 demonstrates.

Reaching Out to Help Others: Wounded Healers

The only way for me to heal was to take this unacceptable reality and turn it into some positive growth in helping others. It [starting a support group for bereaved parents] gave me a future again. I needed to be needed. I once heard Pope John Paul II say: "When you meet the needs of others, it gives you a new meaning to life, which gives rise to hope." [Carol]

For many bereaved parents the "turning-point decision" to survive (Sanders, 1999; see chap. 3) and the ability to feel alive again come as they reach out to help others. Reaching out can mean deciding to volunteer in helping organizations for some, working in "helping" professions for others. And many bereaved parents reach out to help friends, family members, and/or coworkers who experience a loss. Reinvesting in relationships and using what has been learned from surviving their child's death to help others validates these parents' experiences, helps them to build a new relationship with their child and to perpetuate their child's legacy, increases their sense of self-worth, makes them feel needed, provides new purpose and direction to life, and can help combat depression. As other researchers and therapists have noted (Bettelheim, 1952; Frankl, 1978; Higgins, 1994; Jozefowski, 1999; Schneider, 1994; Young-Eisendrath, 1996; Videka-Sherman, 1982), some parents discover new hope for the world as they come to realize that if they can survive such acute suffering and change in positive ways, it is also possible for others to transcend tragedy.

FROM VICTIMS TO HEALERS

Bereaved parents who are further along in their healing and able to help others provide a model of transcending trauma and living with loss in positive, nurturing ways. Valent (1998) emphasized the importance of the ability to take care of others. "Rescue, care, nurture, and preservation carry deep pleasures and joys," he said. "Parents; those in the medical profession; and rescuers such as police, firefighters, and charities have particular ideals, and all place high value on the worth of preservation and facilitation of others' lives. . . . Successful rescuing is incorporated in one's identity as a good firefighter, doctor, or mother; a life giver; or empathic nurturer" (p. 131). Helping others can provide bereaved parents with a new purpose in life and restore the sense of caregiving competence that often is diminished by the inability to keep their child alive. Parents often feel that their child continues to influence and inspire others through them. There are many examples of bereaved parents who have pursued new causes, careers, and/or creative projects after their child's death. Because each child is unique both in life and in death, many parents discover at least one meaningful purpose they alone can pursue: something that requires them to use what they have learned from being that particular child's parent and then that particular's child's bereaved parent.

Some worthy causes created by and because of a child's influence are well-known: Mothers Against Drunk Driving, the National Center for Missing and Exploited Children, and the Make-A-Wish Foundation, for example. Glen and Linda Nielsen are bereaved parents who reach out to help other parents now childless. In memory of their daughter, they established a biannual national conference, "In Loving Memory," to help parents honor their children and heal. Their daughter and only child, Lisa Marie Champlin, died at age 22½ after living with brain cancer for 5½ years. Glen has written about his experiences in "A Step Father's Journey" which is posted on the In Loving Memory website (see Resources). "I have come to understand," he wrote, "that most real healing I do results from some expression of my love for Lisa. When I feel that I am doing something in her honor, I end up feeling good about it and am involved in life, not just going through the motions."

The outreach parents pursue does not have to require public activism, however. It can be as simple as making the difference in one other person's life: a difference made because a bereaved parent reaches out to help in ways that only she or he can offer. And through this helping that is done because their unique child lived and died, parents find reasons to live in the present and hope for the future. This doesn't mean they wouldn't give up meaningful endeavors and personal growth if doing so would bring their child back. It does mean that facing the reality that death is forever eventually requires parents to consider what is still possible and worthwhile doing. The women in the "Mothers Now Childless" study provide examples of the variety of answers to this painful question.

"MOTHERS NOW CHILDLESS" WHO HELP OTHERS

As shown in Table 10.1, a total of 83.4% in the group representing "perpetual bereavement" did *not* volunteer to help others at the time of the study. This contrasted with a total of 77.4% of those representing "survival" who *did* volunteer to

Table 10.1   Comparison of Responses to Participant Questionnaire by Discriminant Groups: Volunteering and Working to Help Others

Response to Questionnaire	Perpetual Bereavement ($n = 18$) Frequency (%)	Survival ($n = 62$) Frequency (%)	χ^2 (80)
Volunteer work:[a]			22.94**
Does not currently volunteer	14 (77.8)[b]	12 (19.4)	
Volunteered before death, not now	1 (5.6)[b]	2 (3.2)	
Started volunteering after death	2 (11.1)	29 (46.8)[b]	
Volunteered before and after death	1 (5.6)	19 (30.6)[b]	
Volunteer organizations:			33.69
Charities	0 (0)	6 (9.7)	
Church	1 (5.6)	12 (19.4)	
Bereavement support	2 (11.1)	13 (21.0)	
Schools/public education	0 (0)	5 (8.1)	
Community service/hospitals	0 (0)	12 (19.4)	
Does not currently volunteer	15 (83.3)	14 (22.4)	
Find volunteering meaningful:			0.06
No	0 (0)	1 (1.6)	
Yes	3 (16.7)	46 (74.2)	
No response/not applicable	15 (83.3)	15 (24.2)	
Reaches out to help others by volunteering or working in a helping profession:			8.66**
No	11 (61.1)[b]	15 (24.2)	
Yes	7 (38.9)	47 (75.8)[b]	
Employment:			2.62
Not currently employed	2 (11.1)	16 (25.8)	
Started work after death	3 (16.7)	14 (22.6)	
Worked before and after death	13 (72.2)	32 (51.6)	
Occupation:			7.16
Clerical	6 (33.3)	9 (14.5)	
Service/sales	4 (22.2)	12 (19.4)	
Technical/arts	0 (0)	2 (3.2)	
Professional	2 (11.1)	16 (25.8)	
Managerial	4 (22.2)	7 (11.3)	
Not currently employed	2 (11.1)	16 (25.8)	
Find work meaningful:			0.44
No	4 (22.2)	8 (12.9)	
Yes	12 (66.7)	38 (61.3)	
No response/not applicable	2 (11.1)	16 (25.8)	
Believe survived child's death:			23.03**
No	9 (50.0)[b]	3 (4.8)	
Yes	7 (38.9)	53 (85.5)[b]	
Yes and no	2 (11.1)	6 (9.7)	

[a]Discriminating variable used to determine group membership. [b]As discussed, these results highlight and contrast statistically significant differences between responses from the two groups.
* $p < .05$. ** $p < .01$.

help others. The disparity between the two study groups remained when considering both those who helped others by volunteering and those who worked in helping professions. The experiences of women in both groups helps us better understand how helping others can influence bereaved parents' lives.

Helping Others While Struggling to Survive

Of the seven women in the group representing "perpetual bereavement" who either volunteered or worked in a helping profession, four said they had *not* survived the death of their child. The following synopses help to explain why they felt this way at the time of the study.

Bonnie: "No Past; No Future"

Bonnie's son died at age 20 during an "alcohol-related swimming accident." Prior to his death she was a museum historian. She had been a single, divorced mom raising her son alone since he was 4 years old. Bonnie described her belief system as:

> a kind of cosmic understanding of the cycle of birth and death which was shattered with my son's death. I need to find meaning in a world where all personal understanding was betrayed. With my son's death, I found the loss of connection painful. I decided I wanted to work more closely with people for the remainder of my professional life.

She "decided to contribute to life by social work." Six years after her son's death she became a residential counselor/case manager for a long-term substance abuse program. She felt she had learned from being a mother and commented that "the connection with my son allows me to offer a more intimate attachment to others."

Bonnie did not feel she had survived her loss, however. "The pain is still there daily," she said, "but it has dulled to a tolerable degree. I find it doesn't exactly get better but rather it becomes different." She said she "almost never" discussed her grief with others. Completing the study questionnaire was difficult for Bonnie: "I almost returned this study without completing it. The recent death of my mother has been painful. I fell free-fall: no past; no future."

In changing professions, Bonnie did what psychotherapist Ashley Prend (1996) calls "going to the source of the pain." In the hope of preventing other deaths, Bonnie works to help others recover from alcohol and drug addiction. She demonstrates the courage it takes to reach out to help others during acute grief. Yet we can speculate that doing so may help over time to ameliorate some of Bonnie's feelings of being alone in the world since the death of her mother.

Molly: "Needing to Be Needed"

Molly's 21-year-old daughter died 3 hours after an automobile accident. She had raised her daughter alone. "It was the most important role of my life," she said. "I learned so much from being a mother—more joy, love, pride, and compassion than I ever imagined possible." After her daughter died, Molly said she lost her faith in God. Molly's family and friends, however, were "very helpful. [They] gave support and encouragement to carry on, without telling me how I should or should not feel. [They were] always there to listen to me." Molly continued to find her work as a medical practice administrator, which she began 10 years before her daughter died, meaningful. "My job and fellow employees have played a large role in retaining my sanity."

Three years after her daughter's death, Molly's parents died, within a month of each other. At the time of contact (6 years after her daughter's death), Molly said she was "struggling to fight bouts of self pity and depression—thoughts of how to overcome them. I write poems and I had started writing a book but found the book too painful to continue. I give Christmas gifts to needy children." She added that she'd "recently (made) a major decision to try to do something constructive with whatever years I have left and move on. I have not fully survived, but I do exist. However, recently I find myself thinking about the future and not so much of the past."

Molly found completing the study questionnaire "helpful" because "perhaps in some small way I can help another bereaved parent and that is important to me. It is a nice feeling to be needed again." Support from family, friends, and coworkers helped Molly withstand the pain of acute grief, and she was beginning to confront her depression as she recognized her desire to feel needed by others again.

Martha: "A Decision I Make each Morning"

It had been 13 years since Martha's 17-year-old son had died of "unknown causes in his sleep." She said "the coroner likened it to a crib death." Unlike Molly, Martha found her family and friends "very unhelpful" after her son's death. "[They] never mention his name and when I do, quickly change the subject." Eleven years after her son's death, her husband "lost his job after 23 years of service." His new job required them to relocate "from an area we had both lived in all our lives. . . . I have no family or close friend that I can share with."

Martha said her job as a secretary was meaningful to her "most days. I work in personnel and enjoy dealing with and helping our employees." She added: "I have a difficult time sympathizing with peoples' minor problems—minor compared to my major problem. Once a very organized individual, I am now very disorganized. I have lost my passion for a lot of things, such as family gatherings, taking pictures, etc." At the time of the study, Martha said: "I don't feel that I have survived. I am surviving. It's a decision I make each morning when I get up. To know that my son is with his Father in heaven is probably the one thing that has kept me 'sane.'" Martha points out a common challenge for bereaved parents who work with others who have not lost a child: She sees her loss as major and the problems of others as minor. Helping others requires the ability to see their problems from their perspective, and this is very difficult for parents who have not had their own needs for support and understanding met. This was true for Betty as well.

Betty: "They Never Bother With Me"

Betty's son died 3 months after he was diagnosed with a brain tumor at the age of 18. She also had lost her parents and other family members and friends, some before and others after her son's death. She said her few remaining friends were "very unhelpful. They never bother with me since my son's death. No phone calls— no cards— I don't hear from any of them."

Five months after her son's death, Betty began doing housekeeping for a nursing home. She wrote: "I like doing things for other people. I like working with the elderly folks." But in response to the question about how she had changed in the 9 years since her son's death she wrote: "I stay to myself most of the time. I don't do a lot of things I use to do. I don't celebrate holidays anymore. I don't like to be around people."

Betty had changed her religion and commented that she didn't blame God for her son's death. "It was not God's will as a lot of people have said to me." She said it was "difficult to attend church. The music is just too much for me. I get very emotional." Lack of support and hurtful comments from others had influenced Betty's ability to trust and enjoy being with others, even though she did like helping the elderly at the nursing home where she worked. Betty said she had not survived her son's death and rarely discussed her grief with others. "Answering these questions has been painful," she wrote. "I don't think I have really accepted my son's death."

Helping Others Does Not Guarantee Healing

The preceding examples demonstrate that "reaching out to help others" does not, of itself, guarantee healing. Healing, or the absence of it, must be understood within the context of each parent's life-world. Other factors, such as additional losses, lack of support from family and friends, unresolved spiritual questions, and changes in job status or living conditions, can prevent or delay healing. Helping others did not seem to lessen the impact of such factors for the four women just described, but it may have helped them to bear the pain added by these circumstances. It seems clear that outreach is not a cure-all for healing grief, but it can be a catalyst that makes pain bearable and a future possible.

The Potential for Reciprocal Healing

Women in the "Mothers Now Childless" group representing "survival" provide examples of the ways in which helping others can contribute to a bereaved parent's own healing.

Cathy: "My Life's Work Must Have Special Meaning"

Cathy's 17-year-old daughter, Sally, was riding with friends one afternoon, the day after the senior awards ceremony at her high school. Their car ran off the road and flipped. Sally was thrown out of the car and died an hour later. The driver was slightly injured; the others girls were okay. Sally's funeral was held the day before graduation. That same week, Cathy graduated from college. "I not only lost my identity as a mom but also as a student," she wrote.

A year later, Cathy became a full-time volunteer coordinator for a nonprofit, residential treatment facility for abused teenage girls. She "recruits, screens, trains, places, supervises, and rewards volunteers for this agency. My primary focus is to get Big Sisters (sponsors) for our girls." She did not work outside her home before Sally's death.

> This work is extremely rewarding for me. I now have 50 girls who need me and benefit from my work. I see my daughter every day when I look at our clients. Some of my longing to be a mom again is helped. In my work I am regarded as a favorite aunt. The girls at the facility depend on me for good things. I have to be careful so I don't get too close with any of them. It is wonderful to be needed by them. I often see my Sally in them. I do not have any close relationships with children outside of my work.

When asked what decisions she had made since her daughter's death 11 years prior, Cathy wrote:

> I am a survivor. I know how fragile life really is. The rest of my life's work must have special meaning. Whatever I can do to help others is offered up in memory of my daughter. I do not have any family at all other than my husband. I am an only child—I must make and keep close friends. I used to think that Sally was an extension of me. She was the better, new, improved me. After her death, it was hard for me to believe that this was not true. I finally realized that I was a separate identity (I was only 19 when Sally was born).

Cathy had learned much from being a mother: "I learned I was a good teacher, role model, etc. I didn't think I was at the time. I learned fast how to be a mom. Sally was the first baby I ever held in my arms. I learned I had good common sense and I learned to trust my instincts and intuition."

Cathy said she had worked through a spiritual crisis and changed in many ways since her daughter died. "I am a nicer person. I am more sensitive to what people say about their children, grandchildren. I am more sensitive to colors, light, and sounds. I didn't think I could be so angry—that really scared me. I didn't know I could be so jealous of other people who had children, grandchildren."

As was true for many of the mothers in the study, the support Cathy received from family and friends was starkly different. She said the few family members she did have had been "very unhelpful. They would only recently mention my daughter's name. I thought they forgot about her or did not care about my pain." Her friends, however, had been "very helpful. Friends have allowed me to talk about her. They have remembered her birthday, death day, other meaningful days."

Cathy felt she had survived her daughter's death: "I did not allow my anger to kill me. I know the difference between missing Sally (and all she has missed) and just plain feeling sorry for myself. I have channeled my anger and my disappointment into my work." She also felt participating in the study was helpful to her.

> I waited until the last minute to answer this survey. I wish I had written more, maybe another page or two to explain some of my answers. It's nice to be asked how I feel and what has happened to me. Maybe I can help anyone who has not experienced this pain to better understand. This survey has helped with my perception of myself. Actually, I am doing well. I am anxious to read the findings.

Reflecting on how her bereavement had evolved in the 11 years since Sally's death helped Cathy see the positive outcome of channeling her anger and disappointment into her work with other girls who need her. This work is meaningful and helps her honor and remain connected with Sally on a daily basis. Cathy also provides an example of another challenge that bereaved parents can face in helping others—the need to take positive action while living with coexisting, opposing feelings. Working with other children can remind parents of how much they miss their own child, how angry and/or jealous they are of other parents. Yet at the same time, making a difference in the lives of other children can invoke a meaningful connection to their deceased child and bring the renewed joy of being needed again.

Janet: "Volunteering Saved My Life and Gave Me a Purpose"

The death of her 15-year-old daughter Kelly in a car accident led Janet to The Compassionate Friends (TCF). "I made a choice after the first year of hell," she said. "I wanted to die day after day but I knew I wouldn't take my life. I made a choice to become very involved in TCF. My TCF friends and my faith (knowing God was by my side every moment) made the difference."

Janet said she hadn't volunteered to help others prior to her daughter's death. "Volunteering as a leader in TCF—this saved my life, gave me a purpose and a way to connect with other grieving parents to help others. I felt I had lost my purpose in life." Six years after Kelly's death, Janet started a task force to prevent child abuse and remained an active member of that community-service organization.

An elementary teacher and divorced mother since 12 years before her daughter's death, Janet continued to find teaching meaningful. "I love my job. I look forward to my work. I take a lot of workshops to continue growing and to stay motivated."

Janet said she found herself prioritizing her life differently since her daughter died. "I want to live each day, not wait to experience things but do what I want today or as it comes up. Lots of troubles or problems seem insignificant to me now. I worry less and get less upset by things that go wrong." She also said Kelly's death had made her faith in God stronger. "I believe Kelly's in heaven and that gives me great comfort and I'll be with her again one day."

Jane: "Using This Life Experience is Rewarding"

At the time that her 21-year-old son died in a motorcycle accident, Jane worked full-time for an accounting firm. "I decided I could not handle full-time employment since I needed to deal with my grief. I continued working for the firm part-time for 8 months. Then I started my own accounting practice. This gives me time to do volunteer work and also have time for myself."

Two years after her son's death, Jane began volunteering at a crisis pregnancy center one afternoon a week. "This involves talking to pregnant girls and assessing their needs, counseling, pregnancy tests, and helping needy women with children. I volunteer at TCF and at church. I was a single parent. I was 18 when my son was born. I feel I can relate my experiences to pregnant girls. I find using this life experience rewarding."

Contacted 5 years after her son's death, Jane said she had survived.

Although there is always that emptiness and a pain which will never totally go away, I have healed and I feel joy and happiness again. When my son died, I didn't think it would be possible to ever find an interest in things or to laugh and enjoy life. It was a long healing process, and I started to feel alive again approximately two years after his death.

Note that Jane's "feeling alive again" coincided with her beginning to volunteer at the crisis center.

Jane felt she had survived and not let her son's death make her "a bitter person." She added that participating in the study "has helped me get in touch with my feelings and reflect on the long road I have traveled during the grief process. I can see that I have come a long way. Healing has taken a long time. I can now talk about my son's life without it being too painful."

Barbara: "I Care More About People"

Barbara's 19-year-old son died 9 months after he was diagnosed with cancer. A year later, Barbara began working part-time as a caregiver for the terminally ill. "Sitting with the family of the sick helps me more by letting them know I've been there," she wrote. She also began volunteering 2 years after her son's death, "taking older people to the store or just sitting with a lonely person while the family goes out. [It's] meaningful because they need someone to talk to and I'll listen to them." Like Jane, it was Barbara's having been there that allowed her to help others facing terminal illness.

Her spiritual beliefs also played an important part in Barbara's survival. "I am still a mother. That didn't change; only my son is no longer here on Earth, as some mothers' children are. I know where he is. He is in heaven. That's why I can keep going on with my life. I have more to go to heaven for than I did before he died."

Barbara said she'd changed since her son died. "I care more about people that have a hard time in their life. When I see a need in a child's life that I can help, I do something about it. Like if they don't have the money to go on a trip or need shoes or clothes."

Edna: "I Think of Myself as a Mother-at-Large"

Edna's 15-year-old daughter Candy died suddenly from anaphylactic shock after an allergic reaction. Six months after her death, Edna began volunteering as a choir director. She had resolved a spiritual crisis and been changed as a result. "I have a deeper understanding of God's care and his faithfulness to me," she wrote. "I believe that God cares personally for me. He has experienced the same kind of pain and knows how I feel. Through the Holy Spirit, he comforts me and reassures me. He has given me the hope of eternity where there will be no death, no crying. My beliefs have given me strength and at times the reason for going on." She said volunteering as a choir director "gave purpose and direction to my life."

Edna had graduated from college the month before Candy died. A year later she began working as a part-time school teacher. She described her work as

> extremely meaningful—it gives me a chance to meet my nurturing, mothering needs as well as bring meaning to others as a facilitator of growth. It allows me to experience with them some of what I missed with Candy's death. I relate to my students in a rather motherly fashion when they need it and want it. I find this very fulfilling. I think of myself as a "mother-at-large" and they and I reap the benefit. There is almost always the real mother for them to turn to. I play a special friend–mother role that is different and often very needed. It makes me feel needed, special, useful, significant.

Edna wrote she had "doubled my conviction that things are not as important as people. I have a better understanding of myself and the pieces of my life." She also continued a relationship with other children: "Two young men, both my daughter's age, have chosen to call me mom and to relate on this level. It took some difficult and long-term processing to accept and participate in these relationships but they are very important to me. They both knew my daughter."

Edna felt she had "more than survived; I have become richer, deeper, more mature." She found participating in the study helpful. "Being able to share the experience to help someone, even a survey, brings more meaning to a senseless death. It is also kind of a chart of my progress and I like what I see! I've been through the worst and come a long way."

SUMMARY

The preceding examples from both groups of "Mothers Now Childless" illuminate the complexity involved in surviving the death of a child and becoming able to reinvest in life again. Their stories suggest that sometimes it is reaching out to help others that promotes healing but for others, reaching out may only be possible as a result of healing, and resolving specific issues. This is to say, there is no clear cause-and-effect relationship between helping others and healing the self. Rather, there appear to be two types of factors that can impact outreach. Some factors contribute to ongoing debilitating grief and make it very difficult to reach out to help others. These debilitating factors include the following:

Unresolved spiritual questions.
Inadequate support from others.
Additional and/or multiple losses.
Ongoing intense emotional and psychological pain.

On the other hand, there are healing factors that can be both cause and consequence of helping others. These include:

Restoring and/or strengthening spiritual beliefs.
Receiving adequate and appropriate support from others.
Remembering and maintaining a connection with the deceased child.
Forgiving self and/or others; feeling forgiven by the child and/or others.
Deciding to survive and reinvest in life in some personally meaningful way.
Feeling needed by others again.
Using what has been learned to help and nurture others.
Reflecting on how grief changes and evolves.
Experiencing increased self-awareness and self-esteem.

Dr. Rachel Remen (1993) helped clarify the reciprocal relationship between healing and being healed. She said, "It is our woundedness that allows us to trust each other. I can trust another person only if I can sense that they, too, have woundedness, have pain, have fear. Out of that trust we can begin to pay attention to our own wounds and to each other's wounds—and to heal and be healed." Thus it is important for bereaved parents to understand the reciprocal healing process and factors associated with it. A decision to help others can be a positive response to agonizing existential pain, the woundedness, which Bonnie so eloquently described as falling "free-fall; no past; no future."

Dr. Susan Trout, founder and executive director of the Institute for Attitudinal Studies, maintained that "the goal of all work, of all service, is simply to bring out what is already there, to unveil the soul. . . . Outside forces of painful experiences serve as catalyst for inner change and transformation. . . . Life is service. The purpose of life and thus of service is to awaken the knowledge of the soul" (Trout, 1997, p. 12). Fifty centers for attitudinal healing across the country help people resolve anger from the past and embrace a life of giving and receiving service (Trout, 1990).

Building on the work of Dr. Gerald Jampolsky (author of *Love Is Letting Go of Fear*), those who promote "attitudinal healing" believe that forgiveness is the key to happiness. Healing happens through a process of letting go of painful, fearful attitudes in order to choose peace rather than conflict and love rather than fear. As discussed in chapter 4, bereaved parents often struggle with the concept and process of forgiveness of others and/or themselves. Reaching out to help others can help with this process because it involves a commitment to care for others, recognition of inner strength as well as woundedness, conscious reflection on the motivations for serving others, and assuming personal responsibility for one's attitude and actions. As Trout pointed out (1997), it is what Carl Jung called "the law of synchronicity" that makes it possible for individuals to serve and be served with the "right amount," in the "right way," and in the "right time and place." In serving others, many bereaved parents experience this synchronicity and begin to feel an eternal connection to all humanity, both the living and the dead—what Jung called "the collective unconscious." As discussed in chapter 11, many of those who reach out to serve others grow beyond the role of bereaved parent in ways that profoundly impact their personal growth and identity.

Reinventing the Self:
Parents Ask, "Who Are We Now?"

> The losses in my life over the years had been many, each loss stripping me down to another layer, bringing me closer to the center of myself. But the loss of [my son] Carter had not stripped off another layer—it had exploded the core of what I had known myself to be, and a new self would have to be born if I were to survive. (Vanderbilt, 1996, p. 118)

Evidence of the self changing in response to loss is apparent not only in bereavement research but also in the psychological and human development literature (cf. Beebe & Lachmann, 1988; Healy, 1989; Honess & Yardley, 1987; Kegan, 1982; Miller, 1981; Valent, 1998; Weenolsen, 1988; Young-Eisendrath, 1996). This chapter discusses the types of changes, both negative and positive, that can impact the identity and personal development of bereaved parents.

THE IMPACT OF LOSS AND TRAUMA ON HUMAN DEVELOPMENT

In the course of a lifetime, everyone confronts inevitable losses, which are a necessary part of human development.

> For healthy growth involves being able to give up our need for approval when the price of that approval is our true self. It means being able to give up defensively splitting and to integrate our good with our bad self. It means being able to give up our grandiosity and make do with a human-proportioned self. It means that although we may, in the course of our life, be beset by emotional difficulties, we possess a reliable self, a sense of identity. (Viorst, 1986, p. 61)

But what happens to human development when one meets with tragedy and overwhelming trauma? How does one discover meaning in traumatic, non-normative experiences? Compelling examples have been given by Bettelheim (1952) and Frankl (1978) in their descriptions of how they and others survived the atrocities and mass killings of World War II concentration camps.

During his confinement in the camps of Dachau and Buchenwald, Bettelheim used his psychological training and knowledge to observe the process of surviving what he called "extreme situations" that strip people of their dignity and their defenses. He noted that some camp survivors achieved personal integration both by recognizing the severity of their trauma and by trying to salvage something positive from their experiences (Bettelheim, 1952, pp. 34–37).

> If an experience has made a deep impact on us, its integration will affect and be reflected in both our inner and outer lives, albeit in different manners and degrees. Such integration may require alterations in our attitudes and feelings about ourselves and our lives, and what we do about this makes up our external behavior. In fact, integration of a truly important experience requires both that we deal constructively *with what it did to us* as an inner experience, and also that *we do something about it* in our actions relating to it. (Bettelheim, 1952, p. 241)

There were those, too, who survived the camps physically yet "allowed their experience to destroy them" and others who "tried to deny it any lasting impact" (p. 28).

In his writings on existential psychology which followed his incarceration, Frankl viewed human development as finding the meaning of one's life (1955, 1963, 1969, 1975, 1978, 1997). He pointed out that although instinct is transmitted through the genes and values through traditions, meaning is truly personal— it must be discovered by each individual (Frankl, 1978, p. 38). And the meaning that is discovered must be reconciled against the individual's current spiritual beliefs and assumptions about the world. When we are confronted with a hopeless situation that we cannot change, we are challenged to change ourselves. Thus Frankl (1978) concluded, "Suffering can have meaning if it changes oneself for the better" (p. 39). It follows that a changed self can be seen as a very real representation of the meaning of individual experience.

Researchers have looked at the effects of emotional stress in other, more common life situations and tried to predict outcome. In her study of how stress influences health, Kobasa (1979) described some survivors of corporate downsizing as possessing "psychological hardiness." In a corporate climate of high stress due to changes in management, about half the employees developed a variety of physical ailments. The other half of the workforce who remained physically healthy had three factors in common: control, commitment, and challenge. These "psychologically hardy" employees felt in control of their lives, versus feeling hopeless or helpless. They were committed to lives in which they found meaning both at home and at work, and they felt challenged by events that others found threatening. Kobasa noted that these three qualities have also been identified in the exceptional patient who beats the odds and recovers from life-threatening illness, as well as in survivors of the concentration camps.

The results of a study of "resilient adults" who overcame extremely cruel childhoods (Higgins, 1994) are consistent with Kobasa's findings about psychological hardiness. This longitudinal study of 40 adults with a history of multiple, significant stressors during childhood and adolescence focused on the factors and processes that promoted psychological maturity and health in spite of extreme physical and psychological stress. Higgins found "two overarching themes" among the resilient in her study: "*faith in surmounting* and *faith in human relationships* as the wellspring of overcoming" (p. 171). Her participants demonstrated "fierce fidelity to an anchored and elaborate vision of a more humane life" (p. 175).

> First, the resilient are largely convinced that they can *choose* their own path. . . . There is ample evidence that they choose how to *see*, how to *be*, and how *not* to be. Second, my subjects' faith is largely sustained outside formal religious communities, although, ...these people are no less devout for their secularity. Third, they prize relationships and see them as integral to their own overcoming. Thus not only do they experience faith as inherently relational, but, in many respects, humane relationships *are* their faith. (Higgins, 1994, pp. 178–179)

The resilient in Higgins's study demonstrated a "capacity to recruit others' invested regard" during childhood (p. 73). It was just such "surrogate love" that provided the vision for a hopeful future and allowed the abused child to reject a victim mentality and "build an internalized model of self and other that allowed love, rather than hate, to predominate in their relationships" (p. 128). These resilient adults also were very committed to social and political activism, which Higgins termed "the *anchor* of their ongoing health. . . . In discussing resilient motifs . . . altruism holds great transformative potency among the resilient . . . it may even be *essential* to healing from horrific abuse. . . . Since the resilient derive intense pleasure and a sense of spiritual expansion from their altruism, they offer us insights into how a more balanced capacity to give well to the self *and* others both demonstrates and potentiates human overcoming" (pp. 227–228).

A child's death interrupts parents' personal development, and most parents see themselves split into a "before self" and an "after self." Psychologist Henya Kagan (Klein) (1998), herself a bereaved mother, described how this splitting can be a part of the re-definition of self.

> It is probable that many of the behaviors seen in bereaved parents are a result of their identification with their children. I think, judging from my own experience, that it is a necessary step inward in order to reconstruct an identity of self. This emerging identity will include aspects of the parent's old self and of the child. This may explain why I used to say that I had a sense that my old self died with [my daughter] Gili and that a new self had started to emerge. I was no active mother to a young child anymore, I was no wife, and I was no university professor. Family and friends left me. Who was I? But once I realized that what was happening was allowing me to incorporate some aspects of Gili's personality, and later [my husband] Norm's, into my own, then my confusion ended. I did not need the external world anymore to define myself by. I knew who I was. It was then that my views about life

and death started to expand. I started to define my life as "before" (Gili's death) and "after." (pp. 118–119)

Psychiatrist Gordon Livingston (1999) wrote eloquently of surviving the death of his two sons who died a year apart—Andrew by suicide at age 22, Lucas at age 6 from leukemia.

> Parents who have lost a child speak of the "zero point." Our lives are divided into the time before and the time after our children died. No event—no graduation, no marriage, no other death – so defines us. At one moment I was one person, then suddenly, I was someone else. The task we face is to create with our new selves something that, in some measure, redeems our suffering. We plant gardens, establish memorials, cherish our children's memories and help those who must struggle, as did we, with despair. We read stories of other parents bereft; sometimes we reach out to them with our experience of bearing the unbearable. (p. 232)

It seems, as in the preceding examples, that personal development can be empowered by (a) how we explain the events of our lives to ourselves and (b) how we use what we have learned about ourselves in relating to others. We can and do choose how we will perceive and react to our experiences. Such choices are governed by our attitude. When confronted with overwhelming trauma and loss, our agony often motivates us to change our attitude. It is when we begin to see things differently and reach out to help and serve others (Trout, 1990, 1997) that we begin to grow beyond our losses.

Schneider (1994) noted such healing and growth in his model of transformative grief, as did Prend (1997) in her model of transcending loss. A loss that is fully recognized and grieved, wrote Schneider (1994),

> liberates us. We are more than we were before, despite having less. . . . Bit by bit, piece by piece, we discover a new life, one that weaves loss into its fabric. . . . Transformations are restorations of the human spirit, the throwing off of the burden of fear and loneliness. It defies our understanding when we recognize forces beyond the individual ego. . . . When we grow from a loss, we begin to have hope that the energies determined to destroy the world through greed, envy, war, environmental destruction and disease can be transformed. If *we* can change, aren't other transformations possible? (pp. 267–268)

LOSS AS A CATALYST FOR CHANGE

Human development has been viewed as progression through various stages (cf. Erikson, 1982; Gilligan, 1982; Jung, 1960; Kohlberg, 1963; Piaget & Inhelder, 1969) or "cultures of embeddedness" (Kegan, 1982) toward the goals of self-actualization (Maslow, 1968) and self-transcendence (Trout, 1997; Weenolsen, 1988). It also can be viewed as a web of experiences woven together to produce a continually changing and frequently unpredictable tapestry of becoming. Regardless of the viewpoint, major loss is an important catalyst for self-development. In her book about transforming suffering into meaning and purpose, Polly Young-Eisendrath (1996) noted that "Pain, loss, and limitation awaken us to the problem of a separate self, how we feel cut off and alienated and cheated. These conditions, coupled with some experience of love (given or received), provide opportunities for us to improve ourselves if we're able to see things from a perspective beyond the separate self" (p. 184). The death of a child is a loss that separates parents from others in our society, especially the majority of other parents who, thankfully, will never experience this loss. But loss of the daily, physical parenting role does not take away the bereaved parent's inner definition of self as the deceased child's parent. For most, this self-construct is an essential part of who they know themselves to be. Changing the inner definition of self from parent to bereaved parent is a slow, cellular change process.

"All people have a tendency to create an image of an essential self and to defend and protect that image, even at their own peril," said Young-Eisendrath (1996, p. 116). "But the degree to which the individual self is regarded as boundaried or shared, private or public, unique or collective, changing or unchanging, is a matter of society and culture—and is an important difference between people" (p. 116). American and other Western societies, founded on rugged individualism, promote independence and self-development. Many people in American society define themselves by what they do and the various roles they serve, including that of parent, with success or failure often judged by what they produce and acquire. The birth of a child brings most parents great pride; they have produced a unique new being. Their work in raising that child has the potential to offer the world an improved version of themselves. When the child dies, parents not only grieve for and miss the child, but some also feel a sense of personal failure; their work is not complete—part of their evolving self has died along with the child.

"To transform the self, to let it die, and incorporate a whole new identity," said Young-Eisendrath (1996), "is to know and embrace a nonessential self—one that is willy-nilly metamorphizing over time. We suffer when we cling to a True Self or demand that life should meet us in a particular way. A crisis, great pain, or confrontation with physical death can shake us out of our habitual attitudes and demand that we change. In this way there is a paradoxical relationship between death and life: to engage wholly with life, we must die many times" (p. 137). She described the human pancreas as "a useful metaphor" for

> experiencing the self as a function, not as a discrete, knowable, permanent *thing.* . . . The pancreas changes all of its cells every twenty-four hours; every day we have a new pancreas. Yet every day the pancreas carries out roughly the same functions, although it is affected by what goes through it, by what it absorbs. Like the pancreas, the self is reconstituted every day as a new self, and yet its functions are the same: to help us integrate complexity into unity, to feel that we exist over time, and to provide us with the basic ego functions of willing, choosing, taking

initiative (p. 117). . . . Eventually we are persuaded by our experiences that there is no essential way to be, no *thing* that resides at the core of our being; there is only the ongoing function of engaging with others around us and the tasks at hand. (p. 118)

Bereaved parents experience their loss both in the internal personal world of psyche, soma, and soul and in the external world of cultural conventions and social interactions. Loss is a "psycho-social transition" (Parkes, 1988) requiring a revision of one's assumptions about how the world works. How bereaved parents, as "social animals" (Aronson, 1992), deal with the multiple aspects of their loss greatly influences their ability to incorporate these aspects into their sense of self and continue to function and grow within society. Doka (1993b) highlighted the interrelationship between social influence and the process of identity reconstruction during bereavement. New situations and experiences lead to continual modifications in the concept of self, he noted. But most of these changes are so gradual as to be barely perceived. The loss of a significant other, though, can lead to radical change in one's social world and thus to radical redefinitions of self. Doka noted that such identity reconstruction "will have to be validated by the parent's social group unless that parent is highly individualized. Further, it too is open to modification and reshaping either as new information becomes available or as the society itself changes" (Doka, 1993b, p. 11). As noted in chapter 9, not only do bereaved parents have to reconstitute their own identity, they also have to reconstruct the identity of the deceased child and decide how that child will be remembered.

This process of coming to know who they are now that their child has died is confusing, chaotic, and painful for bereaved parents and frequently is not understood by those around them. Society often places "inappropriate social expectations" on bereaved parents to "get over" their loss, and parents' normal grief is frequently misdiagnosed as pathological (Rando, 1986, p. 57). Integrating this loss is a lengthy process that requires not only learning new things but unlearning things that are already present—attitudes, values, beliefs, habits, processes, roles, coping responses, and so on—which may be well integrated into a parent's personality and social relationships. Expectations about life's goals and purposes also come into question, sometimes even in the early months of grief. Livingston (1999) described this in his journal while on a family cruise after the death of his second son Lucas.

The ship as a metaphor for life has been much used and the reason is apparent. I feel as though, in my rush toward an unknown port, I have lost overboard two children who were the most compelling reasons and rewards for the journey. Andrew chose to abandon ship, but fate took Lucas in spite of our attempts to rescue him. The life preserver I threw, my bone marrow, sank and took him down with it. The ship sails on, destination as uncertain as ever, but my heart feels buried at sea. . . . Lucas died one month ago today. (p. 103)

Emotional and psychological adaptation to loss imposes a "functional ego-centrism" (Healy, 1989, p. 127) in which there is a shift in the balance of power between the self and the environment. Parents can experience a reduced sense of power over life. They often take on a hypervigilant stance toward the outer world as their drastically altered life situation forces them to become "embedded in, hyper-aware of, and extremely reactive" to their new situation (Healy, 1989, pp. 115–127). The ease with which they adapt emotionally can be influenced by their self-schema—the ways in which they mentally organize, classify, and describe themselves to themselves. This conceptual framework influences an individual's perceptions, memories, and inferences (cognitive processes) as well as behavior (Lippa, 1990, p. 151). Savage (1989) suggested that "the mourning process in its entirety, including the period of time extending beyond the behaviors of overt mourning, is a cryptic analogue for the process of individuation—a process that otherwise unfolds throughout a lifetime" (p. 46).

Many bereaved parents eventually gain a stronger sense of self from their struggle to survive the death of their child. They know more about who they are than at any previous point in life and expect to know even more in the future. Most also know they are very different from who they were before their child died. Prior experiences and events are reevaluated from this different perspective of now being a bereaved parent.

Erik Erikson (1982) saw the dominant theme of later life as the conflict between integrity and despair and the risks of that conflict as physical, psychological, and social loss. He further believed that the compelling element that will resolve this conflict and produce wisdom versus disdain is faith and that this faith is the matured form of the hope of infancy. "Hope," said Erikson, "connotes the most basic quality of 'I'-ness, without which life could not begin or meaningfully end" (p. 62). The death of a child confronts parents with their personal inability to control life and reveals instead that they can only control their responses to life. This jolting realization exposes the natural self-centeredness of the ego and its vulnerability to despair following major loss. Often the human ego cannot contain the horribleness of loss when a child dies, and some response beyond ego must occur in order for parents to accept as real and make sense of their awful new reality.

As discussed in chapter 6, the ego eventually may give way to a new spiritual awareness, an expanded state of consciousness where thoughts and emotions reflect the realization of a universal connectness. When this happens, the loss has opened the door to transpersonal awareness (Levine, 1982; Zenoff, 1986) and personal transformation. Virtually all of the women in the "Mothers Now Childless" study perceived major changes in their identity and self-awareness as a result of their child's death. Some felt they had become better, wiser, more compassionate, more interdependent people who value the meaningful connections made with others since and because of their child's death.

IDENTITY CHANGES AMONG "MOTHERS NOW CHILDLESS"

There have been extensive studies of American motherhood since the end of World War II. The changing role of women in American society, as well as the changing economy, has greatly impacted the role of motherhood in the United States. Far from the stereotypical representation of mother as suburban housewife, there are many "different faces of motherhood":

> The greater social order not only affects theories and ideologies about motherhood, it affects how women experience their lives as mothers. In order to understand the experience of an individual mother or group of mothers, we need information about the economic, social, and psychological environment of mother and child. For example, the experiences, thoughts, feelings, and behavior of a 25-year-old, single, impoverished Appalachian mother of three will be very different from those of a 35-year-old college-educated, urban, married mother of a 4-year-old only child. Differences in prenatal and postnatal medical care, maternal education, housing, and marital status will all affect how mothers relate to their children. In addition, the historical forces operating in a society influence the contemporary social context, which in turn shapes mothers' lives. (Birns & Hay, 1988, p. 5)

All of the factors just identified act together as an amalgam that incorporates the individual experiences of motherhood. Just as motherhood has been considered an important institution critical to the perpetuation of American as well as other cultures, it also has been identified by feminist researchers as a "root cause of oppression for women" (Dixon, 1991). I did not categorize the experiences of the women in the "Mothers Now Childless" study in regard to the feminist vis-à-vis traditionalist arguments. Nor did I evaluate the experiences of these women from the various theoretical perspectives (psychoanalytic, ethological, and sociological) about motherhood (cf. Birns & Hay, 1988; Boulton, 1983; Ireland, 1993; Kaplan, 1992; Leifer, 1980).

There is no dispute among women that becoming a mother is a major, life-changing event and one that is not free of ambivalence (see, e.g., Boulton, 1983; Kaplan, 1992; Lerner, 1998; Newman, 1990). For virtually all of the women in the "Mothers Now Childless" study, becoming a mother and then losing that role greatly impacted their identity construct—the system of ways in which they interpret themselves in relation to the world and as different from others within the world (Kelly, 1963).

The participant questionnaire did not ask the 80 women to classify identity changes as either negative, positive, or both. Rather, question 22 was an open-ended, fill-in question. It asked "How have you changed as a result of your personal struggles in dealing with your child's death?" It is assumed participants did not include all of the changes they may have experienced but rather those that came to mind most readily as they were completing the questionnaire. Of the 80 participants, only one left this question blank and only one said she was unsure whether she had changed. Six others reported changes not related to identity, such as "I try to do more of what has personal value to me."

As shown in Table 11.1, over half (55.6%) of those in the group representing "perpetual bereavement" reported *negative* identity changes that they attributed to their child's death and this contrasted with nearly two-thirds (59.7%) of the group representing "survival," who reported *positive* changes. Ellen gave an example of negative changes:

> I feel that my whole personality has changed. I don't feel like the same person. I can't have what I wanted from life and I have no goals due to my loss. I find my temper flares when I least expect it.

Other comments reflecting *negative* changes in identity included being depressed, disorganized, withdrawn from others, or becoming "defensively emotional." Jill provided an example:

> I don't know how to put into words how I have changed as a result of dealing with my child's death. I am no longer that person: mother, complete person, happy, energetic, emotionally sound, full of hopes and plans for the future. . . . Now I know I will never feel that kind of complete happiness again in this life. So I guess I've

Table 11.1 Comparison of Responses to Participant Questionnaire by Discriminant Groups: Changes in Personal Identity

Response to Questionnaire	Perpetual Bereavement ($n = 18$) Frequency (%)	Survival ($n = 62$) Frequency (%)	χ^2 (80)
Believe survived child's death:			23.03**
No	9 (50.0)[a]	3 (4.8)	
Yes	7 (38.9)	53 (85.5)[a]	
Yes and no	2 (11.1)	6 (9.7)[a]	
Types of changes in personal identity:			12.17**
Negative identity changes	10 (55.6)[a]	12 (19.4)	
Both negative and positive changes	1 (5.6)	8 (12.9)	
Positive identity changes	4 (22.2)	37 (59.7)[a]	
No identity changes reported	3 (16.7)	5 (8.1)	
Reaches out to help others by volunteering or working in a helping profession:			8.66**
No	11 (61.1)[a]	15 (24.2)	
Yes	7 (38.9)	47 (75.8)[a]	

[a]As discussed, these results highlight and contrast statistically significant differences between responses from the two groups.
* $p < .05$. ** $p < .01$.

come to know this is a burden you carry the rest of your life. Never has a day gone by I don't think of my child and ask God, "Why, why, why me?" My precious husband asks me, "Why not us? Are we so holy to be spared all pain in this life?" That question has a way of humbling me and reminding me of the many who share the same heartache as we. I have learned to write my feelings as I find it difficult to talk and I am not a crier. I hope sometime in the future to pass this information on.

Nine of the 80 participants in the study reported both *negative* and *positive* identity changes. Some made comments about being more compassionate toward others and more mature but at the same time also being more anxious, depressed, prone to anger, or unable to feel real happiness. Sonya described a mixture of positive and negative changes in herself:

> I am not as impatient as before. I have more compassion for others. I'm not afraid of dying. I have a hard time making decisions. Nothing really matters or is very important. The only decision I've made is that life is too short to let any one person make you unhappy. If someone does not add to my life in a positive way, I don't need that person around me.

Sally felt she had changed in several positive ways but also realized there were negative changes as well:

> I reach out more; I'm more generous and outgoing. I am less worried about what people think; less likely to be bullied. I am freer in some ways—in my self-expression, in my willingness to take risks. I have always been very spiritual but now I'm more willing to follow that inner voice. Negatively, I get depressed much more easily; I dread holidays; I feel like an outsider at times; I still feel guilt at times.

Many of the *positive* identity changes reported by the women in the study were attributed to learning from their grief and from reaching out to help others. Irene was surprised by how she'd changed: "After Bobby's death I found compassion for other people that I did not know existed in my personality. I can walk in a room sometimes now and I can zero in on the one person in that room that is hurting terribly for whatever reason." Carol had learned to be more assertive:

> I'm totally a changed person: more assertive, more open. I'm less fearful of allowing others to see deep inside of me. I will never allow anyone to hurt me unnecessarily or purposely again—I've taken more control of what I allow. Before I would listen and not say anything and allow them their thinking. Now I just flat tell them this is unacceptable.

Others reported *positive* changes that included learning to take better care of themselves and reorder their priorities. Jane provides an example:

> I have become a more relaxed and less uptight person. Before my son's death I would worry and get upset and annoyed about minor things. I have learned to deal

with each day and not to worry about things over which I have no control. I appreciate those who I am close to since I know any day may be their last day. If I have a chance to go places or do things, I go—I can always cut the grass or clean at another time. I also try to focus on the positives in my life instead of what I don't have.

A summary of the types of changes reported by the 80 women in the "Mothers Now Childless" study is presented in Table 11.2.

Note that the positive changes shown in Table 11.2 are consistent with the qualities psychotherapist Joanne Jozefowski (1999) identified in individuals transformed by trauma and loss. She called them "Phoenix Grievers"—people "who have endured profound personal tragedies and have risen from the ashes of grief as stronger, wiser, and more compassionate human beings. . . . Their lives have forever been changed by the deaths of loved ones. They each have a life almost unrecognizable from that which they lived before their tragedies." Although the people she described as "Phoenix Grievers" experienced "the same depth of pain as others who grieve," she said "the difference is that these people have channeled their pain into something meaningful and constructive" (p. 4).

As we saw in chapter 10, self-transformation—rising from the ashes of grief—often happens as bereaved parents channel their anger and disappointment into worthy causes that honor their child and make meaningful use of what they have learned from suffering and surviving.

PERSONAL GROWTH AFTER THE DEATH OF A CHILD

Zenoff (1986) explored how mothers who had suffered the sudden and unexpected death of a child transformed their suffering into personal growth through reinterpretation and transformation of the meaning of the loss. She defined transformation as "a change in the consciousness of the mother from one based on an ego perspective focused on material (everyday) reality to a consciousness based on a transpersonal perspective focused on universal and spiritual truths" (p. 17). Thirty-two women who had lost an infant, young child, or teenage or adult son or daughter were interviewed. Three of the mothers had lost an only child. Fourteen had been bereaved from less than 1 year to 1½ years at the time of the study. Eight had been bereaved 2 to 4 years, and 10 had been bereaved between 5 and 20 years. The experiences of these three groups of bereaved mothers were analyzed separately. Zenoff found that the experiences of mothers in the "first year" group revolved around issues of survival.

> The main question is, can they survive, and for many mothers the question is, do they want to survive? The main task during the first year is trying to exist in spite of the feeling that they have irretrievably lost a crucial part of themselves. The physical pain associated with this loss, the feeling of being tormented physically and psychologically, is so intense it seems unbearable. (p. 180)
>
> First-year bereaved mothers change in so many ways . . . that they lose a sense of themselves as they were before the child's death. They feel overwhelmed and

Table 11.2 Personal Changes Experienced by "Mothers Now Childless" Participants

Negative changes (22 of 80 responses)

Incapacitated; unable to function normally
Depressed; cover up true feelings
No goals or future
Lonely; life is empty
Disorganized; no passion or interest in life
Withdraw from others; don't celebrate holidays
Self-pity; bitterness
Anxiety; anger
No longer happy, complete, energetic, emotionally sound
Hard to make decisions of any kind
More selfish, self-centered
Less optimistic; more cynical; disillusioned about life
Live very defensively emotionally
Less confident; always on guard around others
Less patient, tolerant of others' "petty" problems

Positive changes (41 of 80 responses)

Stronger; calmer; more relaxed; worry less
Increased spiritual faith
Better values; different priorities
More loving, accepting, patient, and understanding of others
More compassionate and concerned about others
More assertive; outspoken; passionate in beliefs; expressive of feelings
More appreciative of others; caring; kinder
Value life more; more involved in life
Reach out more to others; value and help children
More honest; increased self-respect
Increased self-awareness; take better care of self
No fear of dying

Both positive and negative changes (9 of 80 responses)

More mature and compassionate *but* more anxious, angry, depressed
Stronger *but* colder to others
Less tolerant of others' "petty" problems *but* can laugh at absurdities in life
Less naive, fearful, worried *but* less gregarious
Reach out more; less worried *but* become depressed more easily
More compassionate *but* no longer feel real happiness
More compassionate in some ways *but* less compassionate in other ways
More patient, compassionate *but* no interest in life; nothing matters
Very honest *but* colder to others' "petty" problems

No identity changes or unsure (8 of 80 responses)

helpless and victimized by fate. They become angry, bitter, and pessimistic where before they were able to control negative feelings. . . . Their children's deaths precipitated a crisis in these mothers' identities—they were no longer the women they were before. (p. 182)

As the first-year mothers are feeling the trauma of grief, they are relatively unlikely to function at a level of transpersonal awareness. Although several . . . were able to recognize changes in themselves that were beneficial such as greater self-confidence and empowerment, relatively few of these mothers expressed a higher level of conscious awareness. The empowerment was more a recognition that they could survive tragedy, rather than that they had been transformed to function at a more aware state. (p. 184)

There was a clear feeling of non-acceptance of their lives. Only a few first-year mothers surrendered their will to a Higher Awareness. Many but not all . . . felt a psychic or spiritual connection to their dead children. For some . . . at the same time they were discarding their belief in a benevolent and personal God, they were reaffirming or developing a strong belief in human spirit, specifically, their child's spirit and it's [sic] relationship to them. (pp. 186–187)

Zenoff (1986) classified the second group of mothers bereaved from 1½ to 5 years as transitional. These mothers' experiences varied considerably.

For some mothers, the pain of loss continued unabated, or even increased; for others, the intensity of the pain subsided. Most still felt that they had lost an irretrievable aspect of a crucial part of themselves. A few continued to feel angry and bitter. Most were resigned to their grief, anticipating that they would grieve forever. Most transitional mothers felt they had greater control over their emotional expression of sadness. (p. 188)

Some transitional mothers expressed some transpersonal awareness. A few . . . talked about a renewed appreciation of life and people and themselves. One . . . mentioned feeling universal harmony and a new appreciation for nature. Again, having confronted death, some transitional mothers no longer feared death. With the release of fear, they felt an enrichment of life—greater awareness, understanding, and love for others. Acknowledging life's fragility forced a new reverence for life. . . . Those transitional mothers who felt empowered as a result of their grief experience felt they had become, not just stronger, but better persons. (p. 191)

The 10 mothers bereaved from 5 to 20 years represented the "ongoing years."

As these mothers go about their own lives, they are continually reminded of the children's absence from events marking the mothers' and children's development such as anniversaries and birthdays. They continue to witness other children of their dead children's age grow up and do things the dead children would be doing if they had lived. So new grief emerges along the imagined course of development of the dead children. . . . The lingering pain associated with the loss of their children (shadow grief) is a continuing part of their personal experience. Most ongoing mothers mentioned that they would always miss their children and be aware of their loss forever. (pp. 193–194)

The ongoing mothers have now firmly made the decision to survive even though their children have died. They have chosen to live knowing that life will never be the same and that they will always miss their children. They have made a conscious choice. The ongoing mothers realize they have the choice and the power to live. To have choice is to experience power. They have, consciously or unconsciously, made a choice to live under difficult and painful circumstances. These mothers have "hit bottom and survived" and feel better able to deal with old wounds or insecurities. They have a renewed sense of priorities—more of a sense of what is important and what is not. . . . Most of the ongoing mothers expressed positive attitudes toward themselves and an optimistic view of their lives. Most felt that they had found a personal inner strength on which they could rely and which gave them a feeling of empowerment. Only one of the ten mothers felt that nothing positive had come from her experience of her child's death. (pp. 192–194)

Zenoff, a psychotherapist and grief counselor in private practice and a bereaved mother herself, acknowledged that the idea that there can be a positive outcome as a result of the death of their child when expressed by someone else is rejected by many bereaved mothers. Yet all but one of the mothers in her study mentioned something positive that had come as a result of their experience.

Some of these positive aspects pertained to the mother's personal experience such as a sense of inner strength—and a feeling of self-regard for having suffered through such a tragedy and survived. Other themes mentioned were more transpersonal in nature. Most of the ongoing mothers mentioned a willingness to "be there" for other grieving parents. Some felt compassion, a desire to help, greater sensitivity, and greater understanding. A few mentioned that the experience had increased their feeling of loving regard toward others. A rearrangement of priorities was a commonly mentioned experience of the ongoing mothers. Some of these mothers expressed a feeling of having found meaning in their children's deaths. One mother said that she believed the way parents get over grief is by finding meaning in their grief experience. (pp. 195–196)

These findings from Zenoff's phenomenological study suggest that many of the transformative changes reported from the "Mothers Now Childless" study are also experienced by bereaved mothers with surviving children as their grief process evolves beyond the early years. Bereaved fathers are also transformed by the death of a child. Again, psychiatrist and bereaved father Gordon Livingston (1999) offered a compelling example, written 18 months after his youngest son's death:

I was unable to protect my boys. All that I had and all that I stood for is in question. My work has been to help others comprehend and change their lives. As I try to face my own grief and confusion, I wonder about everything I have done and been. . . . A case can be made that we all see life through a different lens. It is this feeling—that my lens has been forever altered—that weighs on me now. Nothing has looked the same to me since Lucas's death. It is the reverse of the moment in *The Wizard of Oz* when everything changes from black and white to Technicolor. For me the transformation has been to shadows of gray in which I struggle to find moments of brightness. They exist, but only in brief contrast to the fog of sadness that envelops the remainder of my life. Herein lies my quandry: I have tried to live a life of the mind and, in my moment of greatest need, I discover that there is no refuge in reason. (p. 184).

When reason and logic fail to save, to explain, to compensate, redemption becomes even more important. Perhaps this is why Weiss (1989) found "a tendency of bereaved parents to use their loss as a new starting point in their life. It seems that the social circumstances related to the loss encourage the individual to examine his relations in various realms, and to seek fulfillment of opportunities perceived as previously blocked" (p. 270). As Livingston (1999) put this, "It becomes clear that I must somehow emerge from this experience a better person or I will not have fulfilled my obligation to Lucas's memory. This grief must give way to some emotion of more lasting meaning" (p. 95).

In their research on posttraumatic growth, Calhoun and Tedeschi (1989–1990, 1998, 1999) noted that such growth "can only be discovered by the client" and may not occur at all for some but when it does it tends to unfold within the framework of two general questions: Who am I, and what is my life story (1999, p. 21)? Rosenblatt (2000a) identified "domains" or topics within the narratives of bereaved parents that enable parents "to name and organize realities and experiences and to focus attention, thought, and the flow of words. Each domain includes an account of the parent dealing with problems that need resolving and questions that call for answers, and each offers stories about routes to solving problems and answering questions" (p. 2). Resolving problems and questions is part of the grief process of bereaved parents as they discover who they are now that their child has died. Parents who feel they are "stuck" in their grief often identify specific issues or questions that they cannot bear to face, cannot see beyond, and/or cannot integrate into their life story. This "stuckness" can signal a critical juncture where taking some positive action, however minor or tentative, can help parents move forward, even as they carry with them unanswered and often unanswerable questions.

As parents repeatedly tell the story of the significant events surrounding their child's death, the narrative process becomes a way of taking in what has happened and the loss becomes more real. When bereaved parents become able to look back and reflect not only on what happened but how they themselves have coped with what happened, they often become conscious of internal changes. As we have seen, they make comments like "a part of me died with my child " or "I'm not the same person I was before." These metaphors are signals that a process of self-transformation is underway.

SUMMARY

Living with the pain of a child's death requires both individual courage and the support of others. To integrate this loss into a reconstructed self is no small project.

Stoicism and silent suffering won't suffice. Parents must at some point focus their energy and attention on the relational work of mourning. They must enter into a painful dialogue with themselves and with others about what forever means. As Brice (1987) put it: "Mourning cannot be completed by the bereaved person alone. Truths can be arrived at, some stumbling blocks may be overcome while alone, but it seems that the bereaved person doesn't fully mourn unless, or until, he or she has articulated his or her grief, pain, sadness, or self discoveries to at least one other person" (pp. 521–522). When a child dies, mourning does not end, it evolves. Bereaved parents continue to need supportive others to witness and participate in their ongoing developmental process.

Sukie Miller (1999) pointed out how limited the English language is in providing words to describe the liminal process of self-transformation after the death of a child. She said "We need words that symbolize both suffering and healing, that evoke honor and suggest experience, new strength, and deeper vision—because all these are true after the death of a child" (p. 144). She proposed that the word *initiation*, as defined by anthropologist Mircea Eliade, most closely describes the transformation parents undergo after their child dies. "Initiation is the equivalent to a basic change in [the] existential condition; the novice emerges from his ordeal endowed with a totally different being from that which he possessed before his initiation; he has become *another*" (Eliade, 1958, p. x). Miller (1999) noted that "only after initiation are we fully human" and have access to our humanity, including the ability to "admit that we are *only* human" (pp. 145–146). When parents pass through this transforming initiation into the new persona of bereaved parent, they realize that no human can "pretend to be God." This realization can bring clarity and relief from the sense of guilt parents often have in not being able to prevent their child's death. And, as Miller pointed out, "this, finally, is what may allow us to return to God, though as in everything else after the death of our child, not in the same way as before" (p. 146).

Chapter 12

The Legacy of Loss

Do with your pain that which nurtures the soul and adversity will not diminish but magnify you. (Fountain, 1996, p. 198)

HEALING EVOLVES—IT IS NOT A DESTINATION

In the preceding chapters we have seen that bereaved parents' responses to the death of their child are diverse, idiosyncratic, fluctuating, and expected to evolve over their lifetimes. The "Mothers Now Childless" study provides a snapshot in time of the moving target we researchers call "the grief process." That snapshot demonstrates the qualitative difference between the lives of those women in the study who felt they had survived their loss and those who felt they hadn't survived.

The "Mothers Now Childless" who said they hadn't yet survived and who, as a group, represented chronic mourning had these things in common:

1 They continued to struggle with acute grief reactions and unresolved conflicts associated with the circumstances of their child's death.
2 They had experienced the loss of motherhood as identity disintegration; most felt they had changed in negative ways.
3 Their needs for understanding and support from others remained mostly unmet.
4 The majority had experienced a spiritual crisis brought about by their child's death that remained unresolved.
5 All had experienced additional significant losses since their child died.
6 Most viewed their life as purposeless and meaningless.
7 All were courageous in sharing their suffering by participating in the study in the hope of helping others.

These women leave us wondering where they are in their grief process now. How have they changed? What does their loss mean to them now? In what ways would their answers to the study questions be different today? What have they learned about themselves and their child in the ensuing years?

Those women in the "Mothers Now Childless" study who said they had survived their child's death and who, as a group, represented survival (reinvestment in life) had these things in common:

1 They had developed and were using a wide variety of coping strategies to confront their grief and get the support they needed from others.
2 They had experienced the loss of motherhood as an identity crisis that required integration into a new identity; most felt they had changed in positive ways.
3 Most had made a conscious decision to survive their child's death, realizing this did *not* mean they would ever forget or stop missing their child.
4 Many had developed significant relationships with other children.
5 Most had resolved any dissonance in their spiritual beliefs and found their faith comforting.
6 Most had used their bereavement experiences as a catalyst for building an on-going spiritual relationship with their deceased child and reaching out to help others.
7 Most had been able to find and/or create new meaning and purpose in life.

These commonalities can be considered as healing effects. But do parents ever completely heal after a child dies? I don't think so. I think of healing as a process, not a destination. To reiterate, *healing after the death of a child does not mean becoming totally pain-free. Healing means integrating and learning how to live with the ongoing loss. It means becoming able to love others and actively reinvest in life again. Healing often comes when bereaved parents decide they will not permit pain to be the only expression of their continuing love for their child. Helping others is one way that healing evolves as bereaved parents create living legacies that reflect their love and gratitude for the honor of parenting the child who died.*

Thus, I submit that grieving the death of a child does not end, but it does get different. The same could be said of parents' love for their children. Perhaps the most important finding from the "Mothers Now Childless" study is that the women who believed they had changed in *positive* ways since the death of their child had continued nurturing themselves and others as part of a more compassionate identity. Rather than "detaching" from their child, many found new ways to continue their relationship with their deceased child. They had developed the capacity to live with ambivalence, to create a peaceful place within themselves to hold opposing emotions—both the pain of parting and the joy of remembering. Many identified with certain aspects of their child's personality and introjected that child's personality with their own. Many also used what they had learned from loss to help others and contribute to the world in a variety of ways. Angela provides one striking example. She took art lessons and began painting 7 months after her daughter's death as part of her grief therapy. Eventually she began selling her art, signing it with a new name that combines both her own and her daughter's name. "My talent," she said, "is on loan from God and as long as I paint, part of T. will be wherever one of my pieces hang."

Bereaved parents must decide what the legacy of their unique loss will be. Many confront this fundamental question: In what ways can love be my child's most important legacy to the living? It takes tremendous courage for bereaved parents to reengage with the world despite the ongoing pain brought about by their child's death. Blank (1998) described the severe limitations that acute grief imposes on parents' ability to think rationally:

> Some of the psychological effects I suffered were themselves almost physical and immediately apparent in my awkward sense of confusion, an inability to find my equilibrium. I had a sense of terror, of dread, loss of control, of utter chaos which permeated my every waking moment. It is hard to explain this to non-grievers, who can logically point out that I had already experienced the most dreaded thing I could possibly experience. Why was I overwhelmed by a sense of dread? What worse thing could happen to me? Yet there it was, that frantic flailing about to regain control. (p. 90)

It is not surprising that bereaved parents are alarmed by the symptoms that typically accompany their grief. These include repetitive, intrusive thoughts; hypervigilance; mental confusion; extreme mood fluctuations; inability to control emotions or conversely to feel much of anything at all; and stress-induced physical illnesses accompanied by a compromised immune system and disrupted sleep pattern. Even when family and friends are very supportive, many bereaved parents seek professional help to regain control and manage their grief symptoms.

THE CLINICIAN'S ROLE

Clinicians can and often do play a critical role in helping bereaved parents understand grief and become able to bear their pain while taking some form of positive action. It is important for clinicians to assure parents that feeling crazy and overwhelmed by a variety of emotional, mental, spiritual and physical symptoms is common and normal for this loss. Clinicians can help parents manage their symptoms so that even in the midst of pain, confusion, and exhaustion they can begin to take some positive action. Some parents do not realize that talking, praying, meditating, writing, collage making, and rituals such as candle lighting, tree planting, and balloon releases are all positive, active approaches to regaining control while in the midst of turmoil. Such actions do not, of course, change the awful fact that their child has died. But taking action helps to ameliorate the awesome powerlessness and helplessness that can lead to hopelessness and clinical depression.

The therapeutic relationship is central to whether and how clinicians are able to assist bereaved parents (Kagan, 1998; Rando, 1984, 1986, 1993; Talbot, 1996). Clinicians need to be particularly sensitive to bereaved parents' search for understanding and support. Approaches that convey a willingness to understand and act as an empathic listener (cf. Nichols, 1995) should be given priority. To establish a relationship of trust and understanding, it is important to resist the temptation to give advice and focus instead on mirroring and mentoring: that is, acknowledging the pain and facilitating the learning process of the bereaved at their own pace. As a clinician who is also a bereaved parent, I let clients know that sharing the same type of loss does not mean I automatically understand what their loss is like for them. I offer to share some of my experiences as specific topics come up during sessions, but I also tell clients that no one will ever totally understand their grief. This can lead to a discussion of what is realistic to expect from others who support them. Similarly, when I offer resources to my clients, I urge them to take away from such resources only those things that resonate as true for them at the time. And when something they read or some other experience triggers a reaction, I encourage them to explore why. What might be important to discern from this particular trigger?[1] Is there some action they feel they need to take in response?

Sometimes bereaved parents are adversely impacted by a clinician's response to their grief, most often, I believe, when "detachment" from the deceased child and "acceptance" of the loss are included as goals for therapy. Some parents feel no one else can understand them except another bereaved parent. But there are competent and compassionate clinicians who convey a willingness to learn from and support each unique client in their grief. Such clinicians encourage parents to reconstruct, in depth, the multiple meanings of their relationship with their child, what the child's death means for their life, and what new connections can be established and maintained with the child. Thus, a realistic goal for therapy can be helping the parent achieve a new, more integrated identity that acknowledges the child's death but also preserves the child's memory and honors the parent's past life.

Activities that help to integrate the loss and strengthen the bereaved parent's self-concept promote healing and reinvestment in life. "Research suggests that people who have varied self-concepts are more resistant to depression than are people whose entire identities are linked to one relationship . . . or to one role. . . . Another way to help people deal with profound losses is to encourage new and varied ways of seeing themselves" (Lippa, 1990, p. 213). Clinicians can serve as resources for information and learning opportunities aimed at building self-awareness, self-esteem, and identity integration. For example, the use of the Myers–Briggs Personality Type Indicator (MBTI; Myers & Briggs, 1962) can help bereaved parents who have moved beyond acute grief to understand their preferred ways of being in the world. The MBTI also can help parents struggling with relationship issues (cf. Ginn, 1994; Harbaugh & Tagliaffere, 1990). Therapy,

---

[1]For excellent client resources on anger and guilt during bereavement, see Baugher, Hankins, & Hankins (2000) and Baugher (1996).

however, must match each client's unique needs. "Practitioners should never force clients to do anything other than what is consistent with their own coping methods that have worked in the past" (Figley, 1998, p. xix).

Eventually many, if not most, bereaved parents discover the paradox in healing—the knowledge that it is better to understand than to be understood. Perhaps this is the teaching imparted by all liminal journeys. Awareness of this paradox seems to come to bereaved parents after, and perhaps because of, receiving appropriate support from others. These supportive others serve as mirrors that parents use to reflect upon their unique loss and who they are becoming as a result of that loss.

Above all, it is important for clinicians and parents to remember there is no one best way to survive the death of a child. Ultimately, parents must choose their own pathways through the valley of grief and into the new world beyond—but they should not have to journey alone, without understanding companions and caregivers. Such understanding can have a considerable positive impact on parents' attitude toward life following the death of their child, as well as on parents' ability to adapt to living with their ongoing, evolving loss.

As we have seen, the pathways to healing and personal growth after a child dies are uniquely individual but there are some important commonalities: By confronting pain and working through existential and spiritual issues, it is possible to decide to survive a child's death. By identifying and incorporating a deceased child's best characteristics and building a new relationship with that child, it is possible to find ways to honor the past while building a future. By understanding what has been learned from trauma and loss, it is possible to reach out and help make the world a better place for self and others.

References

Allen, J. (1995). *Burden of a secret: A story of truth and mercy in the face of AIDS.* New York: Balantine Books.

American Psychiatric Association. (1994). *Diagnostic and statistical manual of mental disorders* (4th ed.). Washington, DC: APA.

Antonovsky, A. (1987). *Unraveling the mystery of health.* San Francisco: Jossey-Bass.

Attig, T. (1996). *How we grieve: Relearning the world.* New York: Oxford University Press.

Arnold, J. C. (1997). *Seventy times seven: The power of forgiveness,* Farmington, PA: Plough Publishing House.

Aronson, E. (1992). *The social animal* (6th ed.). New York: W. H. Freeman.

Ascher, B. (1993). *Landscape without gravity: A memoir of grief.* New York: Penguin Books.

Battista, J., & Almond, R. (1973). The development of meaning in life. *Psychiatry, 36,* 409–427.

Baugher, R. (1996). *A guide to understanding guilt during bereavement.* Newcastle, WA: Author.

Baugher, B., Hankins, C., & Hankins, G. (2000). *Understanding anger during bereavement.* Newcastle, WA: Author.

Beebe, B., & Lachmann, F. M. (1988). Mother–infant mutual influence and precursors of psychic structure. In A. Goldberg (Ed.), *Frontiers in self psychology: Progress in self psychology* (Vol. 3, pp. 3–25). Hillsdale, NJ: Analytic Press.

Beck, A. T. (1967). *Depression: Clinical, experimental, and theoretical aspects.* New York: Harper and Row.

Belenky M. F., Clinchy, B. M., Goldberger, N. R., & Tarule, J. M. (1986). *Women's ways of knowing: The development of self, voice, and mind.* New York: Basic Books.

Bennett, S. (1998). *New fields and other stones: On a child's death.* Santa Marin, CA: Archer Books.

Benoliel, J. Q. (1985). Loss and adaptation: Circumstances, contingencies, and consequences. *Death Studies, 9,* 217–233.

Bentz, V. M. (1989). *Becoming mature: Childhood ghosts and spirits in adult life.* New York: Aldine de Gruyter.

Berger, D. M. (1996, October). A mother's story of a family's death and also a reinvestment in life again. *Alive Alone Newsletter, 8*(5), 12–13.

Bernstein, J. R. (1997). *When the bough breaks: Forever after the death of a son or daughter.* Kansas City, MO: Andrews McMeel.

Bertman, S. L. (1997, June). *The healing power of hope and grief.* Address to the Association for Death Education and Counseling annual conference, Washington, DC.

Bettelheim, B. (1952). *Surviving and other essays.* New York: Knopf.

Bevington, K. (1993). *Alive alone.* Van Wert, OH: Alive Alone, Inc.

Binswanger, L. (1957). *Sigmund Freud: Reminscences of a friendship.* New York: Grune & Stratton.

Birns, B., & Hay, D. F. (Eds.). (1988). *The different faces of motherhood.* New York: Plenum Press.

Blank, J. W. (1998). *The death of an adult child: A book for and about bereaved parents.* Amityville, NY: Baywood.

Boulton, M. G. (1983). *On being a mother: A study of women with pre-school children.* New York: Tavistock.

Bowlby, J. (1961). Processes of mourning. *International Journal of Psycho-Analysis, 42,* 317–340.

Bowlby, J. (1969). *Attachment and loss, Vol. I: Attachment.* New York: Basic Books.

Bowlby, J. (1980). *Attachment and loss, Vol. III: Loss.* New York: Basic Books.

Bramblett, J. (1991). *When goodbye is forever: Learning to live again after the loss of a child.* New York: Ballantine Books.

Braun, M. J., & Berg, D. H. (1994). Meaning reconstruction in the experience of parental bereavement. *Death Studies, 18,* 105–129.

Brice, C. W. (1987). What forever means: An empirical existential-phonomenological investigation of the maternal mourning of a child's death. *Dissertation Abstracts International, 49/01-B,* 0234. (University Microfilms No. 88-05348)

Brice, C. W. (1991). What forever means: An empirical existential-phonomenological investigation of maternal mourning. *Journal of Phenomenological Psychology, 22,* 16–38.

Calhoun, L. G., & Tedeschi, R. G. (1989–1990). Positive aspects of critical life problems: Recollection of grief. *Omega, 20*(4), 265–272.

Calhoun, L. G., & Tedeschi, R. T. (1998). Beyond recovery from trauma: Implications for clinical practice and research. *Journal of Social Issues, 54*(2), 357–371.

Calhoun, L. G., & Tedeschi, R. T. (1999). *Facilitating posttraumatic growth: A clinician's guide.* Mahwah, NJ: Erlbaum.

Callahan, R. J., & Callahan, J. (1997). Thought field therapy: Aiding the bereavement process. In C. R. Figley, B. E. Bride, & N. Mazza (Eds.), *Death and trauma: The traumatology of grieving* (pp. 249–267). Washington, DC: Taylor & Francis.

Casarjian, R. (1992). *Forgiveness: A bold choice for a peaceful heart.* New York: Bantam Books.

Clayton, P. J. (1980). Bereavement and its management. In E. S. Paykel (Ed.), *Handbook of affective disorders.* Edinburgh: Churchill Livingstone.

Clayton, P. J., Desmarais, L., & Winokur, G. (1968). A study of normal bereavement. *American Journal of Psychiatry, 125,* 64–74.

Cleiren, M. (1993). *Bereavement and adaptation: A comparative study of the aftermath of death.* Washington, DC: Hemisphere.

Cook, J. A., & Wimberley, D. W. (1983). If I should die before I wake: Religious commitment and adjustment to the death of a child. *Journal of Scientific Study of Religion, 22*(3), 222–238.

Craig, Y. (1977). The bereavement of parents and their search for meaning. *British Journal of Social Work, 7*(1), 41–54.

Crowne, D. P., & Marlowe, D. (1964). *The approval motive.* New York: Wiley.

Crumbaugh, J. C. (1977). The seeking of noetic goals test (SONG): A complementary scale to the Purpose-in-Life test (PIL). *Journal of Clinical Psychology, 33,* 900–907.

Crumbaugh, J. C., & Maholick, L. T. (1981). *Manual of instruction for the Purpose-in-Life test.* Munster, IN: Psychometric Affiliates. (Original work published in 1969.)

Currier, C. C. (1982). A pastoral theology of a child's death as developed through ministry to selected bereaved parents. *Dissertation Abstracts International, 43/04-A,* 1200. (University Microfilms No. 82-19951)

Dean, D. G. (1961). Alienation: Its meaning and measurement. *American Sociological Review, 26,* 753–758.

Deford, F. (1983). *Alex: The life of a child.* New York: Viking Press.

Detmer, C. M., & Lamberti, J. (1994, May). *Gender issues in grief: Death and divorce.* Association for Death Education and Counseling annual conference, Portland, OR.

Devers, E. (1997). *Goodbye again: Experiences with departed loved ones.* Kansas City, MO: Andrews & McMeel.

Dixon, P. (1991). *Mothers and mothering: An annotated feminist bibliography.* New York: Garland.

Doka, K. J. (1993a, April). *The many roads of resolution: Rethinking the experience of grief.* Association for Death Education and Counseling annual conference, Memphis, TN.

Doka, K. J. (1993b, January/February). Mind, self and mourning: Toward a sociology of grief. *The Forum: Association for Death Education and Counseling, 19*(1), 10–11/

Dyregrov, A., & Matthiesen, S. B. (1987). Similarities and differences in mothers' and fathers' grief following the death of an infant. *Scandinavian Journal of Psychology, 28*(1), 1–15.

Ebaugh, H. R. F. (1988). *Becoming an ex: The process of role exit.* Chicago: University of Chicago Press.

Edelstein, L. (1984). *Maternal bereavement: Coping with the unexpected death of a child.* New York: Praeger.

Edler, R. (1996). *Into the valley and out again: The story of a father's grief.* Torrence, CA: Merryweather.

Edwards, J. (1998). *One last time: A psychic medium speaks to those we have loved and lost.* New York: Berkley Books.

Eliade, M. (1958). *Rites and symbols of initiation: The mysteries of birth and rebirth.* New York: Harper.

Erikson, E. H. (1982). *The life cycle completed.* New York: Norton.

Ewing, C. P. (1997). *Fatal families: The dynaic of intrafamilial homicide.* Thousand Oaks, CA: Sage.

Ferch, S. R. (1998). Intentional forgiving as a counseling intervention. *Journal of Counseling & Development, 76,* 261–270.

Festinger, L. (1957). *A theory of cognitive dissonance.* Evanston, IL: Row, Peterson.

Figley, C. R. (Ed.). (1998). *Traumatology of grieving: Conceptual, theoretical, and treatment foundations.* Philadelphia: Brunner/Mazel.

Figley, C. R., Bride, B. E., & Mazza, N. (Eds.). (1997). *Death and trauma: The traumatology of grieving.* Washington, DC: Taylor & Francis.

Finkbeiner, A. K. (1996). *After the death of a child: Living with loss through the years.* New York: Free Press.

Fischer, W. (1974). On the phenomenological mode of researching being anxious. *Journal of Phenomenological Psychology, 4,* 405–523.

Fish, W. C. (1986). Differences in grief intensity in bereaved parents. In T. A. Rando (Ed.), *Parental loss of a child* (pp. 415–428). Champaign, IL: Research Press.

Fish, W. C., & Whitty, S. M. (1983). Challenging conventional wisdom about parental bereavement. *Forum: Association for Death Education and Counseling, 6*(8), 4.

Ford, L. (1985). *Sandy: A heart for God.* Downers Grove, IL: Intervarsity Press.

Fox, S. (2001). *I have no intention of saying goodbye: Parents share their stories of hope and healing after a child's death.* Lincoln, NE: Writers Club Press.

Fountain, J. (1996). *Nothing bad happens, ever.* San Francisco: Gold Leaf Press.

Frankl, V. E. (1955). *The doctor and the soul: An introduction to logotherapy.* New York: Knopf.

Frankl, V. E. (1963). *Man's search for meaning.* New York: Pocket Books.

Frankl, V. E. (1969). *The will to meaning: Foundations and applications of logotherapy.* New York: World.

Frankl, V. E. (1975). *The unconscious god: Psychotherapy and theology.* New York: Simon & Schuster.

Frankl, V. E. (1978). *The unheard cry for meaning: Psychotherapy and humanism.* New York: Simon & Schuster.

Frankl, V. E. (1997). *Man's search for ultimate meaning.* New York: Plenum.

Freud, S. (1957). Mourning and melancholia. In J. Strachey (Ed.), *The standard edition of the complete psychological works of Sigmund Freud, Vol. XIV* (pp. 243–258). London: Hogarth Press. (Original work published 1917.)

Gayton, R. R. (1995). *The forgiving place: Choosing peace after violent trauma.* Waco, TX: WRS.

Gibran, K. (1923). *The prophet*. New York: Knopf.

Gilbert, K. R. (1997). Couple coping with the death of a child. In C. R. Figley, B. E. Bride, & N. Mazza (Eds.), *Death and trauma: The traumatology of grieving* (pp. 101–121). Washington, DC: Taylor & Francis.

Gilbert, R. B. (1996). *Heartpeace: Healing help for grieving folks*. St. Meinard, IN: Abbey Press.

Gilligan, C. (1982). *In a different voice: Psychological theory and women's development*. Cambridge, MA: Harvard University Press.

Gillis, E. (1986). A single parent confronting the loss of an only child. In T. A. Rando (Ed.), *Parental loss of a child* (pp. 315–319). Champaign, IL: Research Press.

Ginn, C. W. (1994). *Voices of loss*. Gainsville, FL: Center for Applications of Psychological Type.

Giorgi, A. (1975). An application of phenomenological method in psychology. In A. Giorgi, W. Fischer, & E. Murray (Eds.), *Duquesne studies in phenomenological psychology* (Vol. 2, pp. 82–103). Pittsburgh, PA: Duquesne University Press.

Groopman, J. (1997). *The measure of our days: New beginnings at life's end*. New York: Viking.

Guggenheim, B., & Guggenheim, J. (1996). *Hello from heaven*. New York: Bantam.

Gunther, J. (1949). *Death be not proud*. New York: Harper & Row.

Hackett, D. (1986). *Saying Olin to Say Goodbye*. Plymouth, MA: Old Cedar Publications.

Harbaugh, G. L., & Tagliaferre, L. (1990). *Recovery from loss: A personalized guide to the grieving process*. Deerfield Beach, FL: Health Communications.

Healy, J. M., Jr. (1989). Emotional adaptation to life transitions: Early impact on integrative cognitive processes. In D. M. Buss & N. Cantor (Eds.), *Personality psychology: Recent trends and emerging directions* (pp. 115–127). New York: Springer-Verlag.

Higgins, G. O. (1994). *Resilient adults: Overcoming a cruel past*. San Francisco: Jossey-Bass.

Holtkamp, S. C. (1995). *Grieving with hope*. Chattanooga, TN: Franklin-McKinsey.

Honess, T., & Yardley, K. (Eds.). (1987). *Self and identity: Perspectives across the lifespan*. London: Routledge & Kegan Paul.

Horowitz, M. J. (2001). *Stress response syndromes: Personality styles and interventions* (4th ed.). Northvale, NJ: Aronson.

Hycner, R. H. (1985). Some guidelines for the phenomenological analysis of interview data. *Human Studies, 8*(3), 279–303.

Ireland, M. S. (1993). *Reconceiving women: Separating motherhood from female identity*. New York: Guilford.

Jacobs, S., Mazure, C., & Prigerson, H. (2000). Diagnostic criteria for traumatic grief. *Death Studies, 24*, 185–199.

Jampolsky, G. (1979). *Love is letting go of fear*. Berkeley, CA: Celestial Arts.

Jeffers, S. (1987). *Feel the fear and do it anyway*. New York: Fawcett Columbine.

Johnson, S. E. (1987). *After a child dies: Counseling bereaved families*. New York: Springer.

Jozefowski, J. T. (1999). *The phoenix phenomenon: Rising from the ashes of grief*. Northvale, NJ: Aronson.

Jung, C. G. (1960). The stages of life. In H. Read, M. Fordham, & G. Adler (Eds.), *The collected works of Carl Jung* (Vol. 8, pp. 749–795). Princeton, NJ: Princeton University Press.

Kagen (Klien), H. (1998). *Gili's book: A journey into bereavement for parents and counselors*. New York: Teachers College Press.

Kaplan, M. M. (1992). *Mothers' images of motherhood: Case studies of twelve mothers*. New York: Routledge.

Kegan, R. (1982). *The evolving self*. Cambridge, MA: Harvard University Press.

Kelly, G. A. (1963). *A theory of personality: The psychology of personal constructs*. New York: Norton. (Original work published 1955)

Kerlinger, F. N. (1979). *Behavioral research: A conceptual approach*. Chicago: Holt, Rinehart & Winston.

Klass, D. (1988). *Parental grief: Solace and resolution*. New York: Springer.

Klass, D. (1991). Religious aspects in the resolution of parental grief: Solace and social support. *Prevention in Human Services, 10*(1), 187–209.

Klass, D. (1993). The inner representation of the dead child and the worldviews of bereaved parents. *Omega–Journal of Death and Dying, 26*(4), 255–272.

Klass, D. (1996). The deceased child in the psychic and social worlds of bereaved parents during the resolution of grief. In D. Klass, P. R. Silverman, & S. L. Nickman (Eds.), *Continuing bonds: New understandings of grief* (pp. 199–215). Washington, DC: Taylor & Francis.

Klass, D. (1999). *The spiritual lives of bereaved parents.* Philadelphia: Brunner/Mazel.

Klass, D., Silverman, P. R., & Nickman, S. L. (Eds.). (1996). *Continuing bonds: New understandings of grief.* Washington, DC: Taylor & Francis.

Knapp, R. J. (1986). *Beyond endurance: When a child dies.* New York: Schocken.

Kobasa, S. C. (1979). Stressful life events, personality, and health: An inquiry into hardiness. *Journal of Personality and Social Psychology, 37,* 1–11.

Kohlberg, L. (1963). The development of children's orientations toward a moral order: A sequence in the development of moral thought. *Vita Humana, 6,* 11–33.

Koppelman, K. L. (1994). *The death of a sparrow: Of death and dreams and healing.* Amityville: NY: Baywood.

Koppelman, K. L. (1998). The circle of grief. In E. Levang (Ed.), *When men grieve: Why men grieve differently and how you can help* (pp. 155–158). Minneapolis, MN: Fairview Press.

Kübler-Ross, E. (1969). *On death and dying.* New York: Macmillan

Kushner, H. (1987). *When bad things happen to good people.* New York: Random House.

Lawson, L. (2000). *Visitations from the afterlife: True stories of love and healing.* New York: Harper-Collins.

Lefcourt, H. M. (1982). *Locus of control: Current trends in theory and research* (2nd ed.). Hillsdale, NJ: Earlbaum.

Leifer, M. (1980). *Psychological effects of motherhood: A study of first pregnancy.* New York: Praeger.

Lerner, H. (1998). *The mother dance: How children change your life.* New York: HarperCollins.

LeShan, L. (1990). *The dilemma of psychology: A psychologist looks at his troubled profession.* New York: Penguin.

Levang, E. (Ed.). (1998). *When men grieve: Why men grieve differently and how you can help.* Minneapolis, MN: Fairview.

Levav, I. (1982). Mortality and psychopathology following the death of an adult child: An epidemiological review. *Journal of Psychiatry and Related Sciences, 19*(1), 23–38.

Levine, S. (1982). *Who dies? An investigation of conscious living and conscious dying.* Garden City, NY: Anchor.

Lindemann, E. (1965). Symptomatology and management of acute grief. In R. Fulton (Ed.), *Death and identity* (pp. 186–201). New York: Wiley. (Original work published 1944)

Lippa, R. A. (1990). *Introduction to social psychology.* Belmont, CA: Wadsworth.

Littlefield, C., & Rushton, J. P. (1986). When a child dies: The sociobiology of bereavement. *Journal of Personality and Social Psychology, 51*(4), 797–802.

Livingston, G. (1999). *Only spring: On mourning the death of my son.* New York: Marlow. (Original work published 1995)

Lodzinski, A. (1979). *The Academic Goals Inventory (AGI).* Unpublished manual: Trent University.

Lowe, W., Gormanous, G., & Hubbard, J. (1979, October). The Death Perspective Scale (DPS): A multidimensional instrument for assessing attitudes towards death. Paper presented at the meeting of the Canadian Psychological Association, Quebec City, Quebec, Canada.

Martin, J., & Romanowski, P. (1994). *Our children forever: George Anderson's messages from children on the other side.* New York: Berkley.

Martin, T., & Doka, K. (2000). *Men don't cry... women do: Transcending gender stereotypes of grief.* Philadelphia: Brunner/Mazel.

Martinson, I. M., Davies, B., & McClowry, S. (1991). Parental depression following the death of a child. *Death Studies, 15*(3), 259–267.

Maslow, A. H. (1968). *Toward a psychology of being* (2nd ed.). New York: Van Nostrand Reinhold.

McCann, I. L., & Pearlman, L. A. (1990). Vicarious traumatization: A framework for understanding the psychological effects of working with victims. *Journal of Traumatic Stress, 3*(1), 131–149.

McCracken, A., & Semel, M. (1998). *A broken heart still beats.* City Center, MN: Hazelden.

McGovern, G. (1996). *Terry: My daughter's life-and-death struggle with alcoholism.* New York: Villard.

Mehren, E. (1997). *After the darkest hour the sun will shine again: A parent's guide to coping with the death of a child.* New York: Simon & Schuster.

Miles, M. S. (1979). *The grief of parents: A model for assessment and intervention.* Paper presented at the Association for Death Education and Counseling annual conference, Orlando, FL.

Miles, M. S., & Crandall, E. K. B. (1986). The search for meaning and its potential for affecting growth in bereaved parents. In R. H. Moos (Ed.), *Coping with life crises: An integrated approach* (pp. 235–243). New York: Plenum Press. (Original work published 1983)

Miller, A. (1981). *The drama of the gifted child: The search for the true self.* New York: Basic Books.

Miller, S. (1999). *Finding hope when a child dies: What other cultures can teach us.* New York: Simon & Schuster.

Mindess, H. (1988). *Makers of psychology: The personal factor.* New York: Human Studies Press.

Morrell, D. (1988). *Fireflies: A father's classic tale of love and loss.* New York: Warner Books.

Moustakas, C. (1994). *Existential psychotherapy and the interpretation of dreams.* Northvale, NJ: Aronson.

Murphy, S. A. (2000). The use of research findings in bereavement programs: A case study. *Death Studies, 24,* 585–602.

Murphy, S. A., Braun, T., Tillery, L., Cain, K. C., Johnson, L. C., & Beaton, R. D. (1999). PTSD among bereaved parents following the violent deaths of their 12 to 28-year old children: A longitudinal prospective analysis. *Journal of Traumatic Stress, 12,* 273–291.

Murphy, S. A., Lohan, J., Dimond, M., & Fan, J. J. (1998). Network and mutual support for parents bereaved following the violent deaths of their 12 to 28-year old children: A longitudinal prospective analysis. *Journal of Personal and Interpersonal Loss, 3,* 303–333.

Myers, I. B., & Briggs, K. C. (1962). *The Myers–Briggs Personality Type Indicator (MBTI).* Palo Alto, CA: Consulting Psychologist Press.

Nadeau, J. W. (1998). *Families making sense of death.* Thousand Oaks, CA: Sage.

Neimeyer, R. A. (Ed.). (1995). *Constructivism in psychotherapy.* Washington, DC: American Psychological Association.

Neimeyer, R. A. (1998). *Lessons of loss: A guide to coping.* New York: McGraw-Hill.

Neimeyer, R. A. (2000). *Trauma, therapy, and the quest for meaning: Research that matters for the practicing grief counselor.* Paper presented at the Association for Death Education and Counseling annual conference, Charlotte, NC.

Neimeyer, R. A., & Raskin, J. P. (Eds.). (2000). *Constructions of disorder: Meaning-making frameworks for psychotherapy.* Washington, DC: American Psychological Association.

Neumann, E. (1970). *The origins and history of consciousness.* Princeton, NJ: Princeton University Press.

Newman, S. (1990). *Parenting an only child.* New York: Doubleday.

Nichols, M. P. (1995). *The lost art of listening: How learning to listen can improve relationships.* New York: Guilford.

Oliver, K. (1990). The lives of mothers following the death of a child: Toward an understanding of maternal bereavment. *Dissertation Abstracts International, 51/11-A,* 3677. (University Microfilms No. 91-10200)

Osterweis, M., Solomon, F., & Green, M. (Eds.). (1984). B*ereavement: Reactions, consequences, and care.* Committe for the Study of Health Consequences of the Stress of Bereavement, Institute of Medicine. Washington, DC: National Academy Press.

Paget, M. A. (1983). Experience and knowledge. *Human Studies, 6,* 67–90.

Parkes, C. M. (1988). Bereavement as a psychosocial transition: Processes of adaptation to change. *Journal of Social Issues, 44*(3), 53–65.

Parkes, C. M., & Weiss, R. M. (1983). *Recovery from bereavement.* New York: Basic.

Peppers, L. G., & Knapp, R. J. (1980). *Motherhood and mourning: Perinatal deaths.* New York: Praeger.

Piaget, J., & Inhelder, B. (1969). *The psychology of the child.* New York: Basic Books.

Pollock, G. H. (1961). Mourning and adaptation. *International Journal of Psycho-Analysis, 42,* 341–361.

Prend, A. D. (1997). *Transcending loss: Understanding the lifelong impact of grief and how to make it meaningful.* New York: Berkley.

Quezada, A. (1985). *Goodbye my son, hello.* St. Meinrad, IN: Abbey Press.

Ramsey, J., & Ramsey, P. (2000). *The death of innocence: The untold story of JonBenet's murder and how its exploitation compromised the pursuit of truth.* Nashville, TN: Thomas Nelson.

Rando, T. A. (1983). An investigation of grief and adaptation in parents whose children have died from cancer. *Journal of Pediatric Psychology, 8*(1), 3–20.

Rando, T. A. (1984). *Grief, dying, and death: Clinical interventions for caregivers.* Champaign, IL: Research Press.

Rando, T. A. (1986). Parental bereavement: An exception to the general conceptualizations of mourning. In T. A. Rando (Ed.), *Parental loss of a child* (pp. 45–58). Champaign, IL: Research Press.

Rando, T. A. (1993). *Treatment of complicated mourning.* Champaign, IL: Research Press.

Rando, T. A. (1994). Complications in mourning traumatic death. In I. Corless, B. Gemino, & M. Pittman (Eds.), *Death, dying and bereavement: Theorietical perspectives and other ways of knowing* (pp. 253–271). Boston: Jones and Bartlett.

Raskin, J. D., & Lewandowski, A. M. (2000). The construction of disorder as human enterprise. In R. A. Neimeyer & J. P. Raskin (Eds.), *Constructions of disorder: Meaning-making frameworks for psychotherapy* (pp. 15–40). Washington, DC: American Psychological Association.

Raskin, V. D. (1997). *When words are not enough: The women's prescription for depression and anxiety.* New York: Broadway Books.

Redmond, L. M. (1989). *Surviving when someone you love was murdered: A professional's guide to group grief therapy for families and friends of murder victims.* Clearwater, FL: Psychological Consultation and Education Services, Inc.

Reid, D. W., & Ware, E. E. (1974). Multidimensionality of internal versus external control: Addition of a third dimension and non-distinction of self versus others. *Canadian Journal of Behavioural Science, 6,* 131–142.

Reker, G. T. (1992). *Manual for the Life Attitude Profile–Revised.* Peterborough, Ontario, Canada: Student Psychologists Press.

Reker, G. T. (1992). *The commitment survey.* Unpublished manuscript, Trent University, Peterborough, Ontario, Canada.

Reker, G. T. (1992). *The psychometric properties of the Ladder of Life Index (LOLI).* Peterborough, Ontario, Canada: Student Psychologists Press.

Reker, G. T. (1992). *The psychometric properties of the Locus of Evaluation Scale (LES).* Unpublished manuscript, Trent University, Peterborough, Ontario, Canada.

Reker, G. T. (1995). *Reliability and validity of the Perceived Well-Being Scale–Revised (PWB-R).* Peterborough, Ontario, Canada.: Student Psychologists Press.

Reker, G. T., & Peacock, E. J. (1981). The Life Attitude Profile (LAP): A multidimensional instrument for assessing attitudes toward life. *Canadian Journal of Behavioral Science, 13,* 264–273.

Reker, G. T., & Wong, T. P. (1984). Psychological and physical well-being in the elderly: The Perceived Well-Being Scale (PWB). *Canadian Journal on Aging, 3*(1), 23–32.

Remen, R. N. (1993). Wholeness. In B. Moyers (Ed.), *Healing and the mind* (pp. 343–363). New York: Doubleday.

Rinpoche, S. (1992). *The Tibetan book of living and dying.* San Francisco: HarperCollins.

Riordan, R. J. (2001, Winter). Scriptotherapy: The way it works. *Maddvocate: A magazine for victims and their advocates.* Irving, TX: Mothers Against Drunk Driving.

Ripple, P. (1986). *Growing strong at broken places.* Notre Dame, IN: Ave Maria Press.

Robinson, R. O. (1998). Follow the wind: Songs for stained souls. In E. Levang (Ed.), *When men grieve: Why men grieve differently and how you can help* (pp. 5–9). Minneapolis, MN: Fairview.

Rosenblatt, P. C. (1996). Grief that does not end. In D. Klass, P. R. Silverman, & S. L. Nickman (Eds.), *Continuing bonds: New understandings of grief* (pp. 45–58). Washington, DC: Taylor & Francis.

Rosenblatt, P. C. (2000a). *Parent grief: Narratives of loss.* Philadelphia: Brunner/Mazel.

Rosenblatt, P. C. (2000b). *Help your marriage survive the death of a child.* Philadelphia: Temple University Press.

Rosof, B. D. (1994). *The worst loss: How families heal from the death of a child.* New York: Henry Holt.

Rothschild, B. (2001). *The body remembers: The psychophysiology of trauma and trauma treatment.* New York: W. W. Norton.

Rouner, L. S. (1989). *The long way home.* South Bend, IN: Langbord.

Rubin, S. (1984). Maternal attachment and child death: On adjustment, relationship, and resolution. *Omega–Journal of Death and Dying, 15*(4), 347–352.

Rubin, S. (1992). Adult child loss and the two-track model of bereavement. *Omega, 24*(3), 183–202.

Rubin, S. (1993). The death of a child is forever: The life course impact of child loss. In M. Stroebe, W. Stroebe, & R. O. Hansson (Eds.), *Handbook of bereavement* (pp. 285–299). Cambridge, UK: Cambridge University Press.

Rubin, S. (1996). The wounded family: Bereaved parents and the impact of adult child loss. In D. Klass, P. R. Silverman, & S. L. Nickman (Eds.), *Continuing bonds: New understandings of grief* (pp. 217–232). Washington, DC: Taylor & Francis.

Ryff, C. D. (1989). Happiness is everything, or is it? Explorations on the meaning of psychological well-being. *Journal of Personality and Social Psychology, 57,* 1069–1081.

Ryff, C. D., & Heincke, S. G. (1983). Subjective organization of personality in adulthood and aging. *Journal of Personality and Social Psychology, 44,* 807–816.

Sanders, C. M. (1979–1980). A comparison of adult bereavement in the death of a spouse, child, and parent. *Omega, 10,* 303–322.

Sanders, C. M. (1992). *How to survive the death of a child: Filling the emptiness and rebuilding your life.* Rocklin, CA: Prima.

Sanders, C. M. (1999). *Grief: The mourning after—Dealing with adult bereavement* (2nd ed.). New York: Wiley.

Sanders, C. M., Mauger, P. A., & Strong, P. N. (1977). *A manual for the Grief Experience Inventory.* Palo Alto, CA: Consulting Psychologist Press.

Savage, J. (1989). *Mourning unlived lives: A psychological study of childbearing loss.* Wilmette, IL: Chiron.

Scheier, M. F. & Carver, C. S. (1985). Optimism, coping, and health: Assessment and implications of generalized outcome expectancies. *Health Psychology, 4,* 219–247.

Schneider, J. M. (1994). *Finding my way: Healing and transformation through loss and grief.* Colfax, WI: Seasons Press.

Schutz, A. (1966). *Collected papers III: Studies in phenomenological philosophy.* The Hague: Martinus Nijhoff.

Schwab, R. (1990). Parental and maternal coping with the death of a child. *Death Studies, 14,* 407–422.

Schwab, J. J., Chalmers, J. M., Conroy, S. J., Farris, P. B., & Markush, R. E. (1975). Studies in grief: A preliminary report. In B. Schoenberg, I. Gerber, A. Wiener, A. H. Kutscher, D. Peretz, & A. C. Carr (Eds.), *Bereavement: Its psychosocial aspects.* New York: Columbia University Press.

Shanfield, S. B., & Swain, B. J. (1984). Death of adult children in traffic accidents. *Journal of Nervous and Mental Disease, 172,* 533–538.

Shapiro, F., & Forrest, M. S. (1997). *EMDR: The breakthrough therapy for overcoming anxiety, stress, and trauma.* New York: Basic Books.

Shneidman, E. S. (1996). *The suicidal mind.* New York: Oxford University Press.

Shostrom, E. L. (1962). *The Personal Orientation Inventory (POI): An inventory for the measurement of self actualization.* San Diego, CA: Educational and Industrial Testing Service.

Silverman, P. R., & Nickman, S. L. (1996). Setting the stage. In D. Klass, P. R. Silverman, & S. L. Nickman (Eds.), *Continuing bonds: New understandings of grief* (pp. 29–30). Washington, DC: Taylor & Francis.

Singh, B., & Raphael, B. (1981). Postdisaster morbidity of the bereaved: A possible role for preventive psychiatry? *Journal of Nervous and Mental Disease, 169*(4), 203–212.

Sittser, G. L. (1996). *A grace disguised: How the soul grows through loss.* Grand Rapids, MI: Zondervan.

Slodov, L. K. (1992). A personal collage of survival: A journey of healing through art. *Dissertation Abstracts International, 30/04,* 1489. (University Microfilms No. 13-47862)

Spungen, D. (1983). *And I don't want to live this life.* New York: Ballantine.

Spungen, D. (1997). *Homicide: The hidden victims—A guide for professionals.* Thousand Oaks, CA: Sage.

Staudacher, C. (1991). *Men and grief.* Oakland, CA: New Harbinger.

Stroebe, M. S. (1997, June). *Coping with bereavement: The sense and nonsense of science.* Keynote address, Association for Death Education and Counseling annual conference, Washington, DC.

Strommen, M. P., & Strommen, A. I. (1993). *Five cries of grief: One family's journey to healing after the tragic death of a son.* New York: HarperCollins.

Talbot, K. (1996). Transcending a devastating loss: The life attitude of mothers who have experienced the death of their only child. In D. L. Infeld & N. R. Penner (Eds.), *Bereavement: Client adaptation and hospice services* (pp. 67–82). New York: Haworth.

Talbot, K. (1996–1997). Mothers now childless: Survival after the death of an only child. *Omega– Journal of Death and Dying, 34,* 177–189.

Talbot, K. (1997–1998). Mothers now childless: Structures of the life-world. *Omega–Journal of Death and Dying, 36,* 45–62.

Talbot, K. (1998–1999). Mothers now childless: Personal transformation after the death of an only child. *Omega–Journal of Death and Dying, 38,* 167–186.

Talbot, K. (1999, March/April). The gift of forgiveness. *Bereavement Magazine,* 24–26.

Talbot, K. (2000a). What everyone should know about the first year of grief. *CareNote #21377.* St. Meinrad, IN: Abbey Press.

Talbot, K. (2000b). Where is God when bad things happen? In R. P. Etienne (Ed.), *God at work in times of loss* (pp. 9–19). St. Meinrad, IN: Abbey Press.

Talbot, K. (2001, August). *The Gift of Forgiveness.* Keynote address, In Loving Memory Conference for Bereaved Parents with No Surviving Children, Alexandria, VA.

Tedeschi, R. G., & Hamilton, K. (1991). Support group experiences of bereaved fathers. *Thanatos, 16,* 25–28.

The Compassionate Friends, Inc. (1999, June). *When a child dies: A survey of bereaved parents* (conducted by NFO Research, Inc. on behalf of The Compassionate Friends, Inc.). Oakbrook, IL.

Trout, S. S. (1990). *To see differently: Personal growth and being of service through attitudinal healing.* Washington, DC: Three Roses Press.

Trout, S. S. (1997). *Born to serve: The evolution of the soul through service.* Alexandria, VA: Three Roses Press.

Valent, P. (1998). *From survival to fulfillment: A framework for the life-trauma dialectic.* Philadelphia: Brunner/Mazel.

Vanderbilt, G. (1996). *A mother's story.* New York: Knopf.

VanPraagh, J. (2000). *Healing grief: Reclaiming life after any loss.* New York: Dutton Penguin.

Videka-Sherman, L. (1982). Coping with the death of a child: A study over time. *American Journal of Orthopsychiatry, 52*(4), 688–698.

Viorst, J. (1986). *Necessary losses: The loves, illusions, dependencies, and impossible expectations that all of us have to give up in order to grow.* New York: Ballantine.

Volkan, V. D. (1981). *Linking objects and linking phenomenon: A study of the forms, metapsychology, and therapy of complicated mourning.* New York: International University Press.

Wagner, H. R. (1983). *Phenomenology of consciousness and sociology of the life-world.* Edmonton, Albert, Canada: University of Alberta Press.

Walsh, J. (1997). *Tears of rage: From grieving father to crusader for justice—The untold story of the Adam Walsh case.* New York: Pocket Books.

Walter, T. (1996). A new model of grief: Bereavement and biography. *Mortality, 1,* 7–25.

Weenolsen, P. (1988). *Transcendence of loss over the life span.* New York: Hemisphere.

Weiss, M. (1989). The bereaved parent's position: Aspects of life review and self-fulfillment. *Current Perspectives on Aging and the Life Cycle, 3,* 269–279.

Wheeler, I. P. (1990). The role of meaning and purpose in life in parental bereavement. *Dissertation Abstracts International, 52/04-B,* 2319. (University Microfilms No. 91-17334)

Wheeler, I. P. (1998–1999). The role of linking objects in parental bereavement. *Omega–Journal of Death and Dying, 38*(4), 289–296.

Williams, S. L. (1986). *Physical grief.* Louisville, KY: Accord Aftercare Services.

Wiitala, G. C. (1996). *Heather's return.* Virginia Beach, VA: A.R.E. Press.

Wolfelt, A. D. (1997). *The journey through grief.* Ft. Collins, CO: Companion Press.

Wolterstorff, N. (1987). *Lament for a son.* Grand Rapids, MI: Eerdmans.

Wong, P. T. P., Reker, G. T., & Gesser, G. (1992). The Death Attitude Profile–Revised (DAP–R): A multidimensional measure of attitudes towards death. In R. A. Neimeyer (Ed.), *Death anxiety handbook: Research, instrumentation, and application* (pp. 121–148). Washington, DC: Taylor & Francis.

Wood, V., Wylie, M. L., & Sheafor, B. (1969). An analysis of a short self-report measure of life satisfaction: Correlation with rater judgments. *Journal of Gerontology, 24,* 465–469.

Worden, J. W. (1991). *Grief counseling and grief therapy: A handbook for the mental health practitioner.* New York: Springer.

Yalom, I. D. (1980). *Existential psychotherapy.* New York: Basic Books.

Young-Eisendrath, P. (1996). *The resilient spirit: Transforming suffering into meaning and purpose.* Reading, MA: Perseus.

Zenoff, N. R. (1986). *The mother's experience after the sudden death of a child: Personal and transpersonal perspectives.* Doctoral dissertation, Institute of Transpersonal Psychology, Menlo Park, CA. (University Microfilms No. LD01052)

Zunin, L. M., & Zunin, H. S. (1991). *The art of condolence: What to write, what to say, what to do at a time of loss.* New York: HarperCollins.

Resources

Abbey Press Publications
One Caring Place
St. Meinrad, IN 47577
www.abbeypress.com
Catalog of grief and loss resources

Alive Alone, Inc.
11115 Dull Robinson Road
Van Wert, Ohio 45891
www.alivealone.org
Quarterly newsletter and support for bereaved parents with no surviving children

American Suicide Foundation
120 Wall Street
22nd Floor
New York, NY 10005
1-800-531-4477
Resources for suicide prevention and suvivors of suicide

Aquarius Health Care Videos
PO Box 1159
Sherborn, MA 01770
www.aquariusproductions.com
Catalog of videos addressing grief and loss issues

Association for Death Education and Counseling
342 N. Main Street
West Hartford, CT 06117-2507
www.adec.org
Referral source for grief counselors and therapists

Bereaved Parents of the U.S.A.
PO Box 95
Park Forest, IL 60466-0095
www.bereavedparentsusa.org
Nationwide support organization for bereaved parents.
Quarterly newsletter: *A Journey Together*

Center for Loss and Life Transition
3735 Broken Bow Road
Fort Collins, CO 80526
National workshops
Companion Press Resource Catalog

Centering Corporation
PO Box 4600
1531 N. Saddle Creek Road
Omaha, NE 68104
www.centering.org
Catalog of selected grief and loss resources

Compassion Books
477 Hannah Branch Road
Burnsville, NC 28714
www.compassionbooks.com
Catalog of selected grief and loss resources

The Compassionate Friends, Inc.
PO Box 3696
Oak Brook, IL 60522-3696
www.compassionatefriends.org
Contact information for local chapters and resource catalog
Annual national and international conferences
Quarterly publication: *We Need Not Walk Alone*

In Loving Memory Conference
PO Box 3527
Reston, VA 20195
www.inlovingmemoryonline.org
National conference for parents now childless

Mental Health Resources
346 West Saugerties Roadd
Saugerties, NY 12477
Mhr@ulster.net
Books on loss, trauma, grief, mental health issues

Mothers Against Drunk Driving
511 E. John Carpenter Freeway, #700
Irving, TX 75062
www.madd.org
Bi-annual magazine, chapter information, and literature

National Hospice Organization
1901 North Moore Street, Suite 901
Arlington, VA 22209
www.nho.org
Referrals to programs, service, support groups

The National Organization of Parents of Murdered Children
100 E. Eighth Street, B-41
Cincinnati, OH 45202
www.pomc.com
National conference, chapter contact information, education and training, murder
    response teams, and speaker's bureau

SHARE Pregnancy and Infant Loss Support
National Office
St. Joseph Health Center
300 First Capitol Drive
St. Charles, MO 63301
Support resources for families bereaved by miscarriage, stillbirth, or neonatal death

SIDS Educational Services
PO Box 2426
Hyattsville, MD 20784-0426
www.sidsalliance.org
The SIDS Survival Guide and other resources for families bereaved by sudden
   infant death syndrome

The NAMES Project Foundation
310 Townsend Street
Suite 310
San Francisco, CA 94107
AIDS support group that sponsors "The Quilt" memorial for families bereaved by
   acquired immunodeficiency syndrome
CDC National AIDS Hotline: 1-800-342-2437
National AIDS Clearinghouse: 1-800-358-9295

Appendixes

Life Attitude Profile–Revised (LAP–R)

© Gary T. Reker*

This questionnaire contains a number of statements related to opinions and feelings about yourself and life in general. Read each statement carefully, then indicate the extent to which you agree or disagree by *circling* one of the alternative categories provided. For example, if you STRONGLY AGREE, circle SA following the statement. If you MODERATELY DISAGREE, circle MD. If you are UNDECIDED, circle U. Try to use the undecided category sparingly.

SA	A	MA	U	MD	D	SD
STRONGLY AGREE	AGREE	MODERATELY AGREE	UNDECIDED	MODERATELY DISAGREE	DISAGREE	STRONGLY DISAGREE

1. My past achievements have given my life meaning and purpose.   SA A MA U MD D SD

2. In my life I have very clear goals and aims.   SA A MA U MD D SD

3. I regard the opportunity to direct my life as very important.   SA A MA U MD D SD

4. I seem to change my *main* objectives in life.   SA A MA U MD D SD

5. I have discovered a satisfying life purpose.   SA A MA U MD D SD

6. I feel that some element which I can't quite define is missing from my life.   SA A MA U MD D SD

7. The meaning of life is evident in the world around us.   SA A MA U MD D SD

8. I think I am generally much less concerned about death than those around me.   SA A MA U MD D SD

9. I feel the lack of and a need to find a real meaning and purpose in my life.   SA A MA U MD D SD

* Used with permission.

SA	A	MA	U	MD	D	SD
STRONGLY AGREE	AGREE	MODERATELY AGREE	UNDECIDED	MODERATELY DISAGREE	DISAGREE	STRONGLY DISAGREE

10. New and different things appeal to me.   SA   A   MA   U   MD   D   SD

11. My accomplishments in life are largely   SA   A   MA   U   MD   D   SD
determined by my own efforts.

12. I have been aware of an all powerful and   SA   A   MA   U   MD   D   SD
consuming purpose towards which my life
has been directed.

13. I try new activities or areas of interest and   SA   A   MA   U   MD   D   SD
then these soon lose their attractiveness.

14. I would enjoy breaking loose from the   SA   A   MA   U   MD   D   SD
routine of life.

15. Death makes little difference to me one   SA   A   MA   U   MD   D   SD
way or another.

16. I have a philosophy of life that gives my   SA   A   MA   U   MD   D   SD
existence significance.

17. I determine what happens in my life.   SA   A   MA   U   MD   D   SD

18. Basically, I am living the kind of life I   SA   A   MA   U   MD   D   SD
want to live.

19. Concerning my freedom to make my   SA   A   MA   U   MD   D   SD
choice, I believe I am absolutely free to
make all life choices.

20. I have experienced the feeling that while I   SA   A   MA   U   MD   D   SD
am destined to accomplish something
important, I cannot put my finger on just
what it is.

21. I am restless.   SA   A   MA   U   MD   D   SD

22. Even though death awaits me, I am not   SA   A   MA   U   MD   D   SD
concerned about it.

23. It is possible for me to live my life in   SA   A   MA   U   MD   D   SD
terms of what I want to do.

24. I feel the need for adventure and "new   SA   A   MA   U   MD   D   SD
worlds to conquer."

25. I would neither fear death nor welcome it.   SA   A   MA   U   MD   D   SD

26. I know where my life is going in the future.   SA   A   MA   U   MD   D   SD

27. In thinking of my life, I see a reason for   SA   A   MA   U   MD   D   SD
my being here.

28. Since death is a natural aspect of life,   SA   A   MA   U   MD   D   SD
there is no sense worrying about it.

29. I have a framework that allows me to   SA   A   MA   U   MD   D   SD
understand or make sense of my life.

SA	A	MA	U	MD	D	SD
STRONGLY AGREE	AGREE	MODERATELY AGREE	UNDECIDED	MODERATELY DISAGREE	DISAGREE	STRONGLY DISAGREE

30. My life is in my hands and I am in control of it.   SA   A   MA   U   MD   D   SD

31. In achieving life's goals, I have felt completely fulfilled.   SA   A   MA   U   MD   D   SD

32. Some people are very frightened of death, but I am not.   SA   A   MA   U   MD   D   SD

33. I daydream of finding a new place for my life and a new identity.   SA   A   MA   U   MD   D   SD

34. A new challenge in my life would appeal to me now.   SA   A   MA   U   MD   D   SD

35. I have the sense that parts of my life fit together into a unified pattern.   SA   A   MA   U   MD   D   SD

36. I hope for something exciting in the future.   SA   A   MA   U   MD   D   SD

37. I have a mission in life that gives me a sense of direction.   SA   A   MA   U   MD   D   SD

38. I have a clear understanding of the ultimate meaning of life.   SA   A   MA   U   MD   D   SD

39. When it comes to important life matters, I make my own decisions.   SA   A   MA   U   MD   D   SD

40. I find myself withdrawing from life with an "I don't care" attitude.   SA   A   MA   U   MD   D   SD

41. I am eager to get more out of life than I have so far.   SA   A   MA   U   MD   D   SD

42. Life to me seems boring and uneventful.   SA   A   MA   U   MD   D   SD

43. I am determined to achieve new goals in the future.   SA   A   MA   U   MD   D   SD

44. The thought of death seldom enters my mind.   SA   A   MA   U   MD   D   SD

45. I accept personal responsibility for the choices I have made in my life.   SA   A   MA   U   MD   D   SD

46. My personal existence is orderly and coherent.   SA   A   MA   U   MD   D   SD

47. I accept death as another life experience.   SA   A   MA   U   MD   D   SD

48. My life is running over with exciting good things.   SA   A   MA   U   MD   D   SD

HISTORY OF THE LAP–R

The LAP–R is a revised version of the Life Attitude Profile originally developed and validated by Gary Reker and Edward Peacock (1981). The original instrument was refined following use in a number of studies to improve its psychometric properties.

Based on Viktor Frankl's (1969, 1978) theory of each person's "will to meaning," the LAP–R in its present form is a multidimensional measure of discovered meaning and purpose in life and the motivation to find meaning and purpose in life (Reker, 1992).

The Life Attitude Profile has been used to study a broad range of populations (undergraduate psychology students, guidance counselors, the elderly) and in wide-ranging research contexts. For example, it has been used to measure:

1 Life attitude change after near-death and out-of-body experiences.
2 Life attitude change following bereavement stress in older widows.
3 Life attitude change following a structured reminiscence program for institutionalized elderly.
4 Life attitudes as predictors of the frequency and pleasantness of reminiscence activity in older adults.
5 Life attitudes as predictors of health promotion activities in adult employed women.
6 Life attitudes as predictors of coping.

The Life Attitude Profile–Revised includes items from existing scales, including Crumbaugh and Maholick's (1969/1981) Purpose in Life Test, Crumbaugh's (1977) Seeking of Noetic Goals Test, Shostrom's (1962) Personal Orientation Inventory, and Lowe, Gormanous and Hubbard's (1979) Death Perspective Scale, as well as original items.

LAP–R VALIDITY AND RELIABILITY

The LAP–R has been found to have internal consistency, stability, and validity.

INTERNAL CONSISTENCY

Alpha coefficients were computed to assess internal consistency. "The coefficients are highly satisfactory, ranging from .77 to .91, and remain consistently high across age groups and gender" (Reker, 1992, pp. 22–23).

STABILITY

"Test–retest stability coefficients were computed on a subsample of participants ($n = 200$) retested at a 4–6 week interval. Stability estimates . . . range from .77 to .90" (Reker, 1992, p. 23).

VALIDITY

Factor analysis provided an empirical test of the internal structure of the LAP–R.

There is an extremely good fit between the six LAP–R dimensions and the empirically derived factor structure. . . . The construct validity of developmental scales, such as the LAP–R, is enhanced when it can be demonstrated that the factor structure remains invariant across different age groups and between men and women. . . . The normative sample was divided into three age groups: young adults (17–24 years), middle-aged adults (25–40 years), and older adults (41–89 years) and on the basis of gender. Principal components factor analyses with varimax rotation to simple structure were conducted separately for the young ($N = 348$), middle-aged ($N = 212$), and older ($N = 190$) adults and for men ($N = 259$) and women ($N = 491$). In each case the number of factors to be extracted and rotated was set at 5. (Reker, 1992, p. 29)

Results revealed a "striking similarity in the factor structure across the three age groups and between men and women, providing strong support for factorial invariance of the LAP–R" (Reker, 1992, p. 32).

According to Frankl (1963), an ultimate meaning and purpose already exists in the world, but it must be personally discovered. . . . Frankl theorized that the ultimate meaning in life could only be attained when one moves beyond the self toward a self-transcendent state. . . . This implies that meaning and purpose in life may be age-related. Older adults are predicted to have a higher sense of meaning and purpose in life and greater death acceptance compared to middle-aged and younger adults. There should also be a corresponding decrease in existential vacuum and goal seeking. Thus, support for these predictions would provide evidence for the construct validity of the LAP–R. Accordingly, the normative sample was divided into four age groups: Group 1 (17–24 years), Group 2 (25–44 years), Group 3 (45–59 years), and Group 4 (60–89 years). One-way analysis of variance was conducted on the LAP–R scores, followed by Tukey HSD post-hoc tests. . . . The findings clearly support the predictions, thus attesting to the construct validity of the LAP–R. (Reker, 1992, pp. 32–35)

The concurrent validity of the LAP–R was assessed in a series of studies involving the following criteria:

Purpose in Life Test (PIL; Crumbaugh & Maholick, 1969/1981)
Life Regard Index–Framework (LRI–F; Battista & Almond, 1973)
Ryff's Purpose in Life (RYFPIL; Ryff, 1989)
Academic Goals Inventory (AGI; Lodzinski, 1979)
Ladder of Life Index (LOLI; Reker, 1992)
Sense of Coherence (SOC; Antonovsky, 1987)
Dean's Alienation Scale (POQ; Dean, 1961)
Commitment (COMMIT; Reker, 1992)
Locus of Evaluation (LES; Reker, 1992)

Internal-External Local of Control (I-E; Reid & Ware, 1974)
Death Attitude Profile-Revised (DAP-R; Wong et al., 1992)
Life Orientation Test (LOT; Scheier & Carver, 1985)
Ryff's Integrity (RYFINT; Ryff & Heincke, 1983)
Beck Depression Inventory (BDI; Beck, 1967)
Perceived Well-Being Scale–Revised (PWB–R; Reker & Wong, 1984)
Life Satisfaction Index–Z (LSI–Z; Wood et al., 1969)
Physical Health (PHYHEA; Reker, unpublished)
Social Desirability (SOCDES; Crowne & Marlowe, 1964)

Correlations from these studies are shown in Fig. A.1 (Reker, 1992, pp. 40–41).

DEATH ATTITUDE PROFILE–REVISED

LAP–R	COMMIT	LES	I – E	NEUTRA	FEAR	AVOIDA	APPROA	ESCAPE
PU	.39*	.38**	–.31*	.11	–.14	.17	.03	–.04
CO	.41**	.40**	–.43**	.17	–.17	.08	.13	–.06
LC	.21	.62**	–.46**	.38*	–.46**	.01	–.08	–.02
DA	.14	.14	–.27	.59**	–.60**	–.03	.08	.11
EV	–.08	–.39**	.18	–.19	.22	–.19	–.11	.18
GS	.11	.10	–.25	–.11	–.19	–.35*	–.19	–.21
PMI	.45**	.42**	–.40**	.15	–.17	.14	.09	–.05
LABI	.30	.50**	–.40**	.41**	–.38*	.18	.11	.00
MEAN	12.68	92.88	15.62	5.66	3.52	3.21	4.22	3.43
SD	1.40	14.91	5.92	0.67	1.29	1.24	1.50	1.49
N	42	81	47	42	42	42	42	42

PWB–R

LAP–R	LOT	RYFINT	BECK	PSY	PHY	LSI–Z	PHYHEA	SOCDES
PU	.23	.55**	–.39**	.72**	.53**	.60**	.24**	.34**
CO	.28	.49**	–.38**	.67**	.32**	.50**	.21**	.34**
LC	.19	.37**	–.11	.48**	.45**	.36**	.18**	.19
DA	.03	.13	–.01	.00	.05	.08	.00	.27*
EV	–.52**	–.60**	.43**	–.78**	–.59**	–.47**	–.24**	–.30**
GS	–.15	–.33**	.21*	–.39**	–.22	–.19*	–.10*	–.16
PMI	.29	.54**	–.40**	.74**	.45**	.58**	.24**	.36**
LABI	.40**	.62**	–.43**	.78**	.55**	.57**	.25**	.42**
MEAN	28.98	67.64	3.04	49.04	45.66	19.22	3.78	15.04
SD	5.75	12.62	3.34	6.58	6.61	5.51	0.89	6.08
N	42	171	96	47	47	119	570	78

* $p < .05$ ** $p < .01$ (two tailed)

Figure A.1   Concurrent Validity of the LAP–R—Sheet 1 of 2. From Reker (1992, pp. 40–41), with permission.

LAP–R SCORING

LAP–R	PIL	LRI–F	RYFPIL	AGI	LADDER OF LIFE INDEX (LOLI)			
					PAST	NOW	FUTURE	LOLI
PU	.75**	.77**	.51**	.71**	.20	.78**	.72**	.61**
CO	.77**	.78**	.42**	.55**	.21	.57**	.60**	.49**
LC	.67**	.40**	.15	.67**	.23	.56**	.55**	.49**
DA	.16	.20*	.29	−.04	−.04	−.17	−.02	−.13
EV	−.66**	−.67**	−.55**	−.67**	−.20	−.66**	−.55**	−.51**
GS	−.11	−.18*	−.04	−.22	−.06	−.25	−.06	−.11
PMI	.82**	.81**	.50**	.65**	.22	.72**	.71**	.59**
LABI	.81**	.78**	.55**	.70**	.22	.68**	.66**	.55**
MEAN	108.60	53.32	66.69	99.14	6.45	8.42	9.28	24.09
SD	15.14	8.71	9.93	18.88	2.37	1.51	1.00	3.88
N	72	161	42	36	47	47	47	47

LAP–R	SENSE OF COHERENCE				DEAN'S ALIENATION (POO)			
	COMPRE	MANAGE	MEANIN	SOC	POWERL	NORMLE	SOCISO	POO
PU	.30**	.36**	.57**	.50**	−.26	−.22	−.42**	−.41**
CO	.21	.39**	.48**	.43**	−.33*	−.36*	−.44**	−.50**
LC	.24	.16	.23	.27	−.36*	−.33	−.26	−.40**
DA	−.09	.00	.04	−.03	.03	.20	−.04	.06
EV	−.50**	−.56**	−.53**	−.65**	.40**	.14	.33*	.38*
GS	−.36**	−.28**	−.07	−.30*	.20	−.11	.16	.12
PMI	.28*	.40**	.56**	.50**	−.30	−.30	−.44**	−.46**
LABI	.36**	.44**	.49**	.52**	−.42**	−.22	−.47**	−.49**
MEAN	23.42	18.94	20.92	63.29	16.26	11.81	18.33	46.41
SD	5.19	3.88	4.18	10.76	3.30	3.11	4.50	8.44
N	52	52	52	52	42	42	42	42

* $p < .05$ ** $p < .01$ (two tailed)

Figure A.1 Concurrent Validity of the LAP–R—Sheet 2 of 2. From Reker (1992, pp. 40–41), with permission.

The correlations of LAP–R dimensions with the criterion variables . . . reveal excellent convergence for all LAP–R scales with the respective criterion measures. . . . Of particular note is the excellent discriminant validity of the Death Acceptance dimension of the LAP–R. . . . The LAP–R is a valid measure of current and future meaning and purpose in life. Moreover, the LAP–R is predictive of a large number of outcome variables including psychological and physical well-being, physical health, integrity, life satisfaction, and the absence of feelings of depression and alienation. The findings lend support to the notion that the LAP–R is a valid generalized measure of quality of life. (Reker, 1992, pp. 36–39, 43)

LAP–R SCORING

Point scoring for each of the 48 questions on the LAP–R is the same, as follows:

Strongly agree = 7 points (H = highest)
Agree = 6 points
Moderately agree = 5 points
Undecided = 4 points
Moderately disagree = 3 points
Disagree = 2 points
Strongly disagree = 1 point (L = lowest)

Each of the six dimensions (scales) of the LAP–R is scored by summing the response to the related questions, which are:

Dimension	Corresponding LAP–R Question Numbers
Purpose (PU)	1, 2, 5, 18, 26, 31, 37, 48
Coherence (CO)	7, 12, 16, 27, 29, 35, 38, 46
Life Control (LC)	3, 11, 17, 19, 23, 30, 39, 45
Death Acceptance (DA)	8, 15, 22, 25, 28, 32, 44, 47
Existential Vacuum (EV)	4, 6, 9, 13, 20, 33, 40, 42
Goal Seeking (GS)	10, 14, 21, 24, 34, 36, 41, 43

The scoring formula shown next was used to calculate a Life Attitude Balance Index (LABI) score for each participant who completed the LAP–R:

Life Attitude Balance Index = (PU) + (CO) + (LC) + (DA) – (EV) – (GS)

The EV and GS terms in this equation are approached as follows: For the *normative sample* (N = 750; 491 women and 259 men), the Existential Vacuum (EV) scale correlated negatively with the Purpose (PU) [–.60], Coherence (CO) [–.48], and Life Control (LC) [–.27] scales. Correlations for women and men were very comparable (Reker, 1992, p. 25). For the *normative sample*, the Goal Seeking (GS) scale correlated negatively with the Purpose (PU) [–.18], Coherence (CO) [–.17], and Death Acceptance (DA) [–.03] scales. Correlations for women and men were very comparable (Reker, 1992, p. 25).

Perceived Well-Being Scale–Revised

© Gary T. Reker*

This questionnaire contains a number of statements related to your mental and physical well-being. Read each statement carefully, then indicate the extent to which you agree or disagree by *circling* one of the alternative categories provided. For example, if you STRONGLY AGREE, circle SA following the statement. If you MODERATELY DISAGREE, circle MD. If you are UNDECIDED, circle U. Try to use the undecided category sparingly.

SA	A	MA	U	MD	D	SD
STRONGLY AGREE	AGREE	MODERATELY AGREE	UNDECIDED	MODERATELY DISAGREE	DISAGREE	STRONGLY DISAGREE

1.	I have many physical complaints.	SA A MA U MD D SD
2.	No one really cares whether I am dead or alive.	SA A MA U MD D SD
3.	I think that I have a heart condition.	SA A MA U MD D SD
4.	I have plenty of physical energy.	SA A MA U MD D SD
5.	I am often bored.	SA A MA U MD D SD
6.	I have aches and pains.	SA A MA U MD D SD
7.	It is exciting to be alive.	SA A MA U MD D SD
8.	Sometimes I wish that I never wake up.	SA A MA U MD D SD
9.	I am in good shape physically.	SA A MA U MD D SD
10.	I feel that life is worth living.	SA A MA U MD D SD
11.	I think my health is deteriorating.	SA A MA U MD D SD
12.	I don't seem to care about what happens to me.	SA A MA U MD D SD

* Used with permission.

SA	A	MA	U	MD	D	SD
STRONGLY AGREE	AGREE	MODERATELY AGREE	UNDECIDED	MODERATELY DISAGREE	DISAGREE	STRONGLY DISAGREE

13. I don't get tired very easily.   SA   A   MA   U   MD   D   SD
14. I can stand a fair amount of physical strain.   SA   A   MA   U   MD   D   SD
15. I have peace of mind.   SA   A   MA   U   MD   D   SD
16. I am afraid of many things.   SA   A   MA   U   MD   D   SD

HISTORY OF THE PWB–R

The Perceived Well-Being Scale–Revised (PWB–R) is a 16-item measure of psychological, physical, and general well-being. Eight items measure psychological well-being and eight items measure physical well-being. Reker and Wong (1984) defined psychological well-being as "the presence of positive emotions such as happiness, contentment, joy, and peace of mind and the absence of negative emotions such as fear, anxiety, and depression." Physical well-being is defined as "self-rated physical health and vitality coupled with perceived absence of physical discomforts." General well-being is defined as "the composite of psychological and physical well-being" (p. 24). The PWB–R requires about 5 to 10 minutes to complete.

PWB–R VALIDITY AND RELIABILITY

Factor analysis (principal components, varimax rotation based on a sample $n = 703$) was conducted to validate the PWB–R internal structure with eight questions predicting psychological well-being and eight questions predicting physical well-being. Alpha coefficients were computed to assess internal consistency of the PWB–R. The coefficients were highly satisfactory, ranging from .74 to .86, and remaining consistently high across age groups (Reker, 1995).

PWB–R SCORING

Psychological Well-Being (Questions 2, 5, 7, 8, 10, 12, 15, and 16)

For questions 2, 5, 8, 12, and 16:

Strongly agree = 1 point
Strongly disagree = 7 points

For questions 7, 10, and 15:

> *Strongly agree* = 7 points
> *Strongly disagree* = 1 point

Lowest possible score = 8 and highest possible score = 56.

Physical Well-Being (Questions 1, 3, 4, 6, 9, 11,13, and 14)

For questions 1, 3, 6, and 11:

> *Strongly agree* = 1 point
> *Strongly disagree* = 7 points

For questions 4, 9, 13, and 14:

> *Strongly agree* = 7 points
> *Strongly disagree* = 1 point

Lowest possible score = 8; highest possible score = 56.

Total PWB–R Score = sum of psychological and physical well-being

Lowest possible PWB–R score = 16; highest possible PWB–R score = 112.

"Mothers Now Childless" Study— Participant Questionnaire

ID #_____

Please answer the following questions about your life and your experience of losing your only child. If necessary, use additional paper for your responses.

1. Your child's age at time of death: ____ sex: ____ date of death: ____

2. Cause of death:

____ disease or illness (please name)

____ accident (please describe)

3. How much time was there between when your child's illness was diagnosed or your child's accident occurred and your child's actual death?

no warning ____ # of days: ____ # of months: ____
# of hours: ____ # of weeks: ____ # of years: ____

4. How much time between when you first realized your child might die and the actual death?

no warning ____ # of days: ____ # of months: ____
# of hours: ____ # of weeks: ____ # of years: ____

5. Your religious affiliation:

____ Protestant ____ Catholic ____ Jewish
____ Other (please identify) _____
____ None

6. How important is your religious affiliation in your life?

_____ not very important _____ somewhat important _____ important

_____ very important

Please comment about what makes your religion meaningful to you:

_____

_____

7. Has your religious affiliation changed since your child's death?

_____ no

_____ yes (please describe how and why)

8. What is your total family income per year?

_____ less than $10,000   _____ $25,000–$49,999

_____ $10,000–$24,999   _____ $50,000–$99,999

                                         _____ $100,000 and above

9. What is your ethnic or cultural background?

_____ Anglo/White   _____ Black/African American

_____ Hispanic   _____ Asian

_____ American Indian   _____ Other: _____

10. What is your educational level?

_____ less than twelfth grade   _____ college graduate

_____ high school graduate   _____ advanced degree(s)

11. Are you currently employed outside your home?

_____ no

_____ yes (full-time _____; part-time _____)

Please describe the type of paid work you do:

Did you begin doing this work before or after your child's death?

_____ before (please indicate approximately how long before: _____)

_____ after (please indicate approximately how long after: _____)

Do you find this work meaningful, rewarding, etc? Please comment:

____ No: _____

____ Yes: _____

12. Do you volunteer your services to community or church groups?

____ no ____yes (occasionally ____; regularly ____)

Please describe the type of volunteer work you do:

Did you begin doing this work before or after your child's death?

____ before (please indicate approximately how long before: _____)

____ after (please indicate approximately how long after: _____)

Do you find this volunteer work meaningful, rewarding, etc? Please comment:

____ No: _____

____ Yes: _____

13. Have you attended meetings of The Compassionate Friends support group or other bereavement groups at some time since your child died?

____ never ____ once or twice ____ occasionally ____ regularly

Please identify which group(s) you have attended:

_____ (attend now? ____ yes ____ no)

_____ (attend now? ____ yes ____ no)

_____ (attend now? ____ yes ____ no)

14. Have you sought professional grief therapy or counseling since your child's death?

____ never ____ once or twice ____ occasionally ____ regularly

15. *Prior to* your child's death had you experienced the death of a person significant to you and/or other significant losses (for example: divorce, major illness, physical impairment, job loss)?

____ no

____ yes (please describe each loss and when each loss occurred—how long before your child died):

_____

16. *Since* your child's death have you experienced the death of another person significant to you and/or other significant losses (for example: divorce, major illness, physical impairment, job loss)?

    _____ no

    _____ yes (please describe each loss and when each loss occurred—how long
    after your child died):

    _____

17. Had you experienced a significant change in your life (that was not associated with your child's illness or another's death) during the <u>two years BEFORE</u> your child's death?

    _____ no

    _____ yes (please describe change(s))

    _____

18. Please check the statement below that best describes the role of grief in your life today:

    _____ Grief dominates my life today.

    _____ I feel grief on a daily basis but it no longer dominates my life.

    _____ At times I don't feel grief for several days but it's unusual for a week or two to go by without feeling some grief.

    _____ Grief surfaces only occasionally now.

    _____ I no longer grieve.

19. Do you discuss your grief with friends and/or relatives in your life today?

    _____ no

    _____ yes   _____ rarely   _____ occasionally   _____ often

20. Please indicate to what degree you feel your family and friends have been helpful to you during your bereavement?

    _____ very unhelpful   _____ unhelpful   _____ somewhat helpful

    _____ very helpful

    Please give some examples of ways they have been helpful and/or unhelpful:

21. Please give examples of the kinds of decisions you have made about your life since your child's death:

    _____

    _____

22. How have you changed as a result of your personal struggles in dealing with your child's death?

    _____

    _____

23. Have your spiritual/religious beliefs been helpful to you in dealing with your child's death?

    ____ no (please describe what has not been helpful)

    ____ yes (please describe what has been helpful)

24. Have you found ways in which to memorialize your child (for example, by writing and publishing poetry, making contributions to a memorial fund or charity, planting a tree, etc.)?

    ____ no
    ____ yes (please describe)

25. Are you aware of having learned from your experience of being a mother?

    ____ no
    ____ yes (please describe your most important learnings)

    _____

    _____

26. Do relationships with other children play a significant part in your life today?

    ____ no
    ____ yes (please describe these relationships and how they are important to you)

    _____

27. Do you believe you have survived the experience of losing your only child?

    ____ no
    ____ yes (please describe the ways in which you have survived)

    _____

28. Are you currently:

    ____ married (to father of child)
    ____ married (but not to father of child)
    ____ single—divorced
    ____ single—never married

29. Has participating in this study been helpful to you?

_____ no (please describe what has *not* been helpful)

_____

__ yes (please describe what has been helpful)

_____

30. Would you like to receive a summary of the findings of this study?

_____ no
_____ yes

Thank you so much for taking the time and effort to complete the questionnaires and participate in this study. Your willingness to share your experience will be of great help to those working with other mothers who lose an only child.

Please mail the completed questionnaires in the envelope provided.

Date completed: _____

Interview Guide

Prior to starting the interview, participants were encouraged to ask any questions they might have about the study or about my background. I explained that our interview would be more like a conversation than a question-and-answer session, and that we could decide to take breaks at any time. I stated that the purpose of our discussion was for us to recreate her story of surviving the death of her only child and that when she felt we had sufficiently achieved this goal, the interview would be complete. I then reviewed the Informed Consent Form and asked her to sign both copies and keep the second one.

1   What do I need to know in order to understand what it has been like for you to survive your child's death?

     Probes:

           Just tell me your story in your own way.

           Perhaps you have photos or momentos that would help me understand?

           Tell me more about ____?

           How were you feeling at the time?

           Do you remember being consciously aware of ____?

           How did you go about deciding to ____?

           Was that feeling/event/etc. unexpected? Why did it surprise you?

           Can you say more about what that means to you?

           Have you changed your thinking or how you feel about that now? If so, how did that change occur?

           Do you think you made a conscious decision to survive? What was that process like?

2   What does your child's death mean to you today?

Probes:

When you think about ____'s death today, what do you tell your self?

How has ____'s death affected your relationship with God and with your church?

Would you say you have come to resolution about why ____ died?

How has that resolution happened? If not, what is still bothering you?

When you tell others about ____'s death, what do you say?

3   What has it been like for you to lose the role of mother?

Probes:

Do you have a relationship with today? What is that like?

Do you expect to be reunited with ____ again?

What did being ____'s mother mean to you?

Are you able to use some of your mothering skills today? In what ways?

What do you say when someone asks you how many children you have?

4   Do you see yourself as different from bereaved mothers with surviving children? In what ways?

5   What would you like to tell other bereaved mothers about how to survive and what it means to survive?

Index